Speaking Up

Besides his work for *The Times* and the *Observer*, Bernard Levin has also been theatre critic for the *Sunday Times*, television critic for the *Guardian*, Parliamentary and political correspondent for the *Spectator* under the pseudonym of Taper, theatre critic for the *Daily Express* and the *Daily Mail*. He is the author of an account of the 1960s entitled *The Pendulum Years* and a first collection of his journalism, *Taking Sides* (both also published by Pan).

Bernard Levin

Speaking Up

Pan Books London and Sydney

The author and publishers are grateful to the National Trust
and Eyre Methuen Ltd for permission to quote from the poem
'Russia to the Pacifists' by Rudyard Kipling on pp. 258–62.

First published 1982 by Jonathan Cape Ltd
This edition published 1983 by Pan Books Ltd,
Cavaye Place, London SW10 9PG
© Bernard Levin 1982
ISBN 0 330 28120 8
Printed in Great Britain by ·
Hunt Barnard Printing Ltd, Aylesbury, Bucks

Contents

Introduction

IN THE INTRODUCTION to *Taking Sides*,* a first selection of my journalism, I said that there would be a second volume. With this book I am therefore carrying out my stated intention.

I calculate that both volumes together represent some 2 per cent of my total journalistic output; well, it is an ephemeral trade. And none the worse for that, considering the nature of so much of the subject matter; the journalist's words may wrap the cinders before dinner-time, but those of the politician are exceptional if they get as far as tea. Nor is this state of affairs without real significance; has there ever been a time in our history when our leaders – political, legal, spiritual, business – said so little of interest in such abominable English? Take a sheet of paper; think of the seven Prime Ministers from Eden to Thatcher; write down anything you remember them having said. I do not believe that the following list can be far extended. Eden: 'a property-owning democracy' (whatever, incidentally, he meant by that). Macmillan: 'Most of our people have never had it so good' and 'the wind of change' (though the latter was not his own). Home: nothing. Wilson: 'the pound in your pocket'. Heath: 'the unpleasant and unacceptable face of capitalism'. Callaghan: nothing. Thatcher: 'There is no alternative'.

Of course, the coining of memorable phrases is not the principal function of a politician. But a man who never says

* Jonathan Cape, 1979. Pan Books, 1980.

anything interesting or original is unlikely ever to think anything interesting or original either. And there is more to it than that. The Great Battle of the Pekes and the Pollicles now seems more important and more fascinating than the strife of party in Britain in the 1970s (the period mostly covered by both this book and *Taking Sides*, neither of which is chronological in its selection); but this is not the familiar and fallacious complaint that politicians spend all their time pretending to hate one another while in truth pursuing much the same ends, for the political struggle of the past decade was unusually rich in matters of political substance, and this became more emphatically true as the decade wore on.

The trouble was not that nothing important was going on in politics, nor that the politicians had nothing to say about what *was* important. It was that the proposals of politics, like the language thereof, seemed (and seem) to be rooted only in illusion and fantasy.

It used to be said of British foreign policy that it consisted of taking powders in Asia for headaches in Europe, and the same inconsequentiality ruled the arguments over the struggle for control of the Labour Party, the cause, effects and cure of inflation, Britain's role in, and relations with, the E.E.C. and NATO, and the efficacy of monetarism as an economic policy. 'The hungry sheep look up, and are not fed'; while the same failed remedies were applied to the same ills, the profound dissatisfaction and unease felt by ever-increasing numbers, a distress in no way caused by the price of fresh vegetables or the deteriorating condition of British Rail's rolling-stock, was hardly discussed at all, and never by those in authority. A friend has related that among the group of people with whom he was talking when the news that the Pope had been shot came through, one immediately responded with the words 'Oh, good'; the extent to which disintegration is taking place in a society that can contain such an instinctive expression of a nihilistic approval of evil (it is typical – it would not be worth mentioning if it were not – of a great deal that is happening today) is obviously considerable, and no less obviously in urgent need of examination. Not since General Millan Astray went into battle for Franco, in the Spanish Civil War, under the slogan '*Viva la muerte!*' has the Western world so clearly proclaimed its wish for self-destruction as it does daily and hourly at the present time.

Item: a group of youths begin to insult a young girl, not known to them, who is standing quietly, in the company of her parents, at a bus-stop; the girl's father remonstrates, verbally, with them, so they knock him down and kick him in the head; he dies.

Item: a youth, disturbed by the seventy-nine-year-old woman tenant of a house he has broken into, knocks her down and, before making his escape, pauses to stamp on her face; when she is found, his boot-print is clearly visible there.

Item: a criminal, serving a long sentence for a series of particularly revolting and brutal crimes, including torture, escapes; while on the run he writes a long letter to *The Times* couched entirely in jargon taken over from the modern, debased form of sociology; the purpose of the letter is not to protest his innocence of the crimes for which he was convicted, but to argue that it is not his fault, but society's, that he became and remained such a criminal. The view commands widespread sympathy.

Item: in Cambodia, the Khmer Rouge rulers organize and carry out the destruction of roughly one-seventh of the entire population; in Britain, there are voices raised in condonation of this action.

Item: a widely respected financial journalist is hideously injured, along with his wife, in a motor-car accident; a satirical magazine, the editorial policy of which he has once mildly criticized, finds this funny, and his ensuing death even funnier.

Item: a football-match having been arranged between teams representing Scotland and England at Wembley Stadium, precautions are taken which include the complete closure of three lines of the London Underground and the banning of all alcohol from all trains between Scotland and England for four days before the match is to take place and three after, these measures being deemed necessary in view of the violence and destruction that followed the same match in the previous year.

Horror-films abound, vying with each other in the variety and intensity with which agonized and terror-filled death or mutilation is visited upon the victims, victims no longer (as in earlier forms of such entertainment) of prehistoric, extra-terrestrial or similar monsters, but of other human beings. In Brixton, racial violence erupts in a night of arson, buildings being burnt out on a scale not seen in England since the Blitz. The preservation of the Welsh language being by some considered desirable, it is thought helpful for this end to be pursued by the destruction of houses in rural Wales belonging to Englishmen. In pursuit of a dubious cause, young men in prison in Northern Ireland commit suicide by the slowest and possibly most painful means ever devised: voluntary starvation.

Hate had found respectable motives and had ceased to be a personal idiosyncrasy, indulged in secret . . . The sight of evil kindles evil in the soul – there is no getting away from this fact. The victim is not the only sufferer; everybody in the vicinity of the crime, including the murderer, suffers with him. Something of the abysmal darkness of the world has broken in on us, poisoning the very air we breathe and befouling the pure water with the stale, nauseating taste of blood. True, we are innocent, we are the victims, robbed, betrayed, outraged; and yet for all that, or precisely because of it, the flame of evil glowers in our moral indignation . . . Nevertheless it should be clear to everyone that such a state of degradation can come about only under certain conditions. The most important of these is the accumulation of urban, industrialized masses – of people torn from the soil, engaged in one-sided employment, and lacking every healthy instinct, even that of self-preservation . . . It means that the whole nation is in a fair way to becoming a herd of sheep, constantly relying on a shepherd to drive them into good pastures. The shepherd's staff soon becomes a rod of iron, and the shepherds turn into wolves.

The words are Jung's, and he is describing Germany's descent into Nazi barbarism; I am not of the apocalyptic school of political pessimists, and even if I were I would not envisage Britain going that way, but the passage seems to me more important psychologically than politically, as indeed it was obviously intended to seem by Jung. Faced with evidence of such danger, our political leaders meet it with unrelenting somnambulism; is it any wonder that a commentator who must perforce attend day by day to contemporary political affairs can see no point in preserving mayfly comments on mayfly matters?

Nothing could better illustrate what I mean when I refer to the somnambulism of our political leaders than the extraordinary phenomenon of the Social Democratic Party. The phenomenon, of course, is not the rise of such an organization; in democratic societies such as ours political parties grow in response to a political need not otherwise being met, and when the Labour Party ceased to meet not only the need that had originally called it into being (the directly political representation of the industrial working-class) but any discernible purpose whatever, it was inevitable that it would be replaced by something related, however remotely, to the real political interests of a substantial part of the nation. As I write, it is impossible to predict the future course of the new party and of its alliance with the Liberals, but in this matter I am in the business neither of prophecy nor even of psephology, for the point I am making is that it matters very little indeed *what* happens, electorally speaking, to the new grouping. No doubt a Government drawn from the combined ranks of the alliance would arrange in a manner different from that proposed by

other parties such grave matters as Britain's relations with the
E.E.C., the proper allocation of resources between private and
municipal house-building, the desirable limits of the Public
Sector Borrowing Requirement and the introduction of a
form of proportional representation for Parliamentary elections. In all these areas, and many more, I would expect
moderate and generally sensible policies to emerge from such a
Government, and even those who would expect nothing of
the sort will hardly deny that matters in our political and
economic national life could not well be made worse by a
Government of that stripe than they have hitherto been made
by Governments of a more traditional character.

But that is not what I mean when I call the rise of the S.D.P.
an extraordinary phenomenon. What I am referring to is the
evidence it provides of the increasing desperation of an elec-
torate which can apparently face anything except the truth –
the truth being that if a Government composed of Social
Democrats and Liberals, or for that matter one composed
entirely of Archangels, were to take office and thereupon
proceed, within a fortnight, to bring about economic prosperity, political stability, harmonious industrial relations, an
international accord that markedly diminished or even elimin-
ated the danger of conflict between the super-powers, and
the institution of perpetual fine weather, its achievements,
however praiseworthy and welcome, would have done nothing at all to touch the state of affairs implied by my catalogue
of modern horrors, above, and Jung's summation of what lies
behind such frightfulness.

For the point is that these things do not arise from political
conditions, and they are not susceptible to political remedies.
Yet it certainly seems obvious to me that the public response
to the new political groupings reflects partly an unconscious
realization of this truth (whence the widespread disposition to
treat the Social Democrats as in some way not really politicians
at all, but beings in a different category altogether) and partly a
fear of allowing that truth to rise into the light of full under-

standing. On the one hand, a longing to seek and find a plane on which the deepest ills of our society may be diagnosed and treated; on the other, an almost hysterical insistence that the old medicine, provided only that it comes in a new bottle, will be enough.

But before the Social Democrats had appeared and such thoughts had presented themselves to me I had already begun to deduce similar conclusions from my reluctance to include my political comments in the journalism I was willing to preserve. And there was something else, even more important, that was making me think along these lines.

When, on November 30th, 1978, Times Newspapers suspended publication of all its papers, pending the resolution of the company's industrial relations problems, few people inside or outside the organization could have guessed that the papers would remain silent for almost exactly a year. Certainly I did not, even though in the matter of the duration of the conflict I was of the pessimistic school, which – to the disbelief of the optimists – held that hostilities might last as long as three months. Now for those outside the curious trade of journalism, I must explain that for anyone in it there is no possible substitute for seeing in print in the morning words written the night before. An out-of-work bricklayer can occupy himself productively in building an extension to his house; an unemployed accountant can keep himself busy and even happy on a study of the financial system of the Roman Empire; a redundant actor can learn the role of Hamlet and recite it to his bathroom mirror (which will applaud). But a journalist deprived of publication, no matter that (as was the case with the *Times* stoppage) he is still receiving his full income, can do nothing but despair, and the effect of the shut-down on those who wrote full-time for the papers was exactly the same as what happens to the gods in *Das Rheingold* when the supply of Freia's golden apples is abruptly withdrawn; they began to wither and fade. For many months after the end of the Great Siege, I was repeatedly asked, 'What did you all do while it was going on?' and my standard reply – 'We went mad' – was not very far from the literal truth.

But the heart hath its methods, which method knows not of. As there was gradually borne in upon us the realization that Troy would not fall quickly, so I began, no less gradually, to realize and face the truth about the life I was leading. 'Workaholism', which began as a joke coinage, is now widely recognized as a genuine disease, and a dangerous one. Moreover, the greatest danger is not the physical kind, in the form of the coronary, nor even the mental, in the form of the breakdown; it lies in the fact that the workaholic comes to believe that, because work takes so enormous a proportion of his time and energy, it is also the most important thing in his life.

I was a workaholic, and I had the malady in a particularly acute and chronic form. I was writing three columns a week in *The Times*, and I was also the theatre critic of the *Sunday Times*, seeing an average of at least four plays a week and therefore writing a fourth article. And when, overnight, this came to an end, I experienced, along with my colleagues, the withdrawal symptoms characteristic of the addict abruptly deprived of the stuff of his addiction. But the metaphor provides the clue to what happened next, which was that I realized that for many years I had, because I enjoyed my work, been drugged into believing that I had found an acceptable, even an admirable, way to live. And what happened after *that* was that I began to face, slowly and painfully, a threefold truth. First, there must be more to life than even the most satisfying and absorbing work. Second, there came upon me the grim realization that for many years I had not, except for brief periods, thought seriously about anything but my work. Third was the discovery I made, when the Great Siege came to an end and my professional life returned to normal, that my work was no longer satisfying to me.

It took me more than a year to act on the newly-acquired understanding. Obviously, I could not leave my job then and there; when the mothball fleet is at last putting out to sea again, it is no time for one of the officers to resign his commission. But much stronger even than this feeling, I regret to say, was the colossal weight of inertia and apprehensiveness that between them half persuaded me to believe that these feelings were mistaken, no more than a spasm of regret that the *dolce far niente* was coming to an end. As the months went by, however, I found it more and more difficult to go on pretending to believe such obvious nonsense, and eventually I took the inevitable course of action that my feelings had indicated: I resigned from both newspapers at once, determined to follow the beckoning light wherever it might lead, having given myself the freedom to do so by getting rid, for the time being, of my subservience to regular newspaper deadlines, and moreover without setting a definite term to my period at large.

In the Introduction to *Taking Sides*, I described myself as

> a liberal increasingly aware of the inadequacies of liberalism and a rationalist who finds himself less and less able to rely on rationalism; a man at ease with the art of the eighteenth century but distrustful of the basis of the Enlightenment's optimism; above all one who, day by day, finds himself more and more convinced of the importance of the inexplicable.

I have often been amazed – indeed, I have often expressed such amazement in print and out – at the terror that overcomes many intelligent and thoughtful people at the suggestion that there might be some principle, force or cause in the universe that is too big for them to comprehend, and too different to be examined by any or all of the five senses. When we consider that *nothing* of real significance in the lives of human beings – love, belief, fear, thought, laughter, pain, infinity, sleep – has yet been explained by science (that is not altogether surprising – the scientists have not yet discovered what causes hiccups, never mind cancer, so the really complex mysteries are hardly likely to have yielded to their enquiries), the natural inclination, it seems to me, is to be excited and stirred by wonder in the face of such enduring riddles. We do not have to go so far as Lorenzo:

> . . . look, how the floor of heaven
> Is thick inlaid with patines of bright gold:
> There's not the smallest orb which thou behold'st
> But in his motion like an angel sings,
> Still quiring to the young-eyed cherubims;
> Such harmony is in immortal souls;
> But whilst this muddy vesture of decay
> Doth grossly close it in, we cannot hear it.

But dull would he be of soul (and indeed he is, the evidence being all around us) who feels, or, worse, feels obliged to persuade himself to feel, or even – worst of all – to proclaim publicly and untruthfully that he does feel, *nothing* of awe or wonder at all the echoing and unsolved mysteries, from the innermost secrets of the atom to the outermost secrets of space, that fill the universe.

It begins to appear to me that until 'the importance of the inexplicable' is more widely recognized, the psychic split from which we suffer (and which has led to the kind of psychic anarchy some of the fruits of which I have representatively listed above) will remain unhealed, with all the frightful consequences inevitably attendant upon any permanently suppurating wound. And it also seems to me, and this, too, I have frequently pointed out, that there has never been a time when so many people have been seized more or less consciously with an inexplicable dissatisfaction despite the fact that they are provided with ample quantities of all those things that our world insists are both essential and sufficient for satisfaction. More important, there has never been a time when so many people were seeking an explanation of this curious condition; of course, many of the avenues they explore in their seeking lead to spurious or nonsensical conclusions, but I have said more than once that just as it is possible to deduce, *a posteriori*, from dustbins full of bones and bottles, that someone has been feasting, so we may infer, from dustbins full of ephemeral nostrums, that someone has been seeking fare even more nourishing than the physical kind. And on this search I, too, am engaged.

Meanwhile, here is my second (and final) selection of the journalism I have written so far, and a word about the text is perhaps necessary. All the pieces appeared in *The Times*, the *Sunday Times* or the *Observer*, and I am grateful and happy to acknowledge these newspapers as the original sources, as I am to acknowledge most warmly the compilation of the index by Oula Jones of the Society of Indexers, and the reading of the proofs by Brian Inglis. A few of the pieces have been slightly amended since their first appearance, none significantly; I have corrected a few factual or typographical errors (I was once misprinted as writing, in a *Times* column not included here, of Bach's 'Bass in B minor', which moved a correspondent to suggest that I should now turn my attention to 'Handel's Lager'), together with a few lapses of style or grammar. The passage of time has inevitably rendered unintelligible a few references; I have solved this problem sometimes by an explanatory footnote and sometimes by a small excision. In no article have I altered my expression of the views I held when I wrote it, though obviously I have modified various views over the decade that this book spans.

I have no doubt that I shall modify more as time goes by. I do not know which I care for less; the man who never changes his mind, or the one who, having changed it, insists that he hasn't. But not only do I dislike both categories; I find both baffling. Are there really people who think that growth stops merely because the milk-teeth are shed, and are content that that should be so? Evidently there are; they are all around us. But for my part I have welcomed the evidence I have found in sifting and selecting the material for this volume – evidence that I am not the man I was in 1970, nor any of the men I have been year by year since. And I look forward to shedding more skins as more time passes. I would not go quite so far as Logan Pearsall-Smith:

> That I should permit a misquotation like this to pass made me doubt my own identity. Or, it occurred to me, my personality might be changing; was I undergoing, perhaps, like an insect in the silence of its cocoon, some curious metamorphosis? I waited to see what I might be turning into – a Low Church Curate? A Major with a big moustache? or a Licensed Victualler, perhaps?

My fears and hopes do not run that way (though I, too, should certainly be disturbed to find that I could let pass a misquotation). But Stevenson said more than he intended when he observed that 'to travel hopefully is a better thing than to arrive', and so, in his famous metaphor, did Michael Oakeshott, when he said of political activity that

> men sail a boundless and bottomless sea; there is neither harbour for shelter nor floor for anchorage, neither starting-place nor appointed destination. The enterprise is to keep afloat on an even keel; the sea is both friend and enemy; and the seamanship consists in using the resources of a traditional manner of behaviour in order to make a friend of every inimical occasion.

We do not know the answers to any question that matters. But if we conclude from that truth that it is a waste of time to seek the answers, then we err most grievously, and would still be in the wrong even if we had conclusive proof that we should never find the answers however long and hard we sought them. The truth is that Shelley's 'spells by which to re-assume An empire o'er the disentangled doom' are no less potent in their magic merely because they do *not* enable us to conquer the disentangled doom.

Journalism, as I remarked in the Introduction to *Taking Sides*, is a very odd profession. I have since realized that it is even odder than I then supposed, for I never imagined that its grip on its bonded servants could be prised loose, yet I have demonstrated, at any rate to my own satisfaction and for the moment, that it can; powerful testimony to the lure of the rainbow. I do not regret the 98 per cent wastage-rate among what I have written; journalism, like Hope in Turandot's first riddle, is born each night to die next day, and he would be a foolish baker who grumbled because as fast as he made a batch of loaves the public bought and ate them. Besides, if I know anything at all with certainty it is that vain regrets are the most foolish objects a human being can spend time on. I have written many millions of words and seen them in print; most of them have long since vanished into a profound oblivion. But we have it on good authority that the same is true, or eventually will be, of the cloud-capped towers, the gorgeous palaces, the solemn temples and the great globe itself, so I can hardly complain. 'It is something', says the judge in one of A. P. Herbert's Misleading Cases, 'to dot an i in perpetuity', and indeed it is. Here, therefore, are a few thoughts which I have felt were worth preserving for a moment longer than their fellows. No reader is obliged to agree.

March 1982   B.L.

Holy loathing and the Professor

AMID ALL THE questions being asked about *l'affaire* Blunt ('Did they tell the Queen?', 'Why didn't they tell Lord Home, or has he simply forgotten that they did?', 'Did anybody ever bother to tell Henry Brooke anything?', 'Are you surprised?') the most important of all, it seems to me, concerns not Professor Blunt and the security services, or even the constitutional implications. It is about *us*, and the pretty pass we have come to.

The prettiness of the pass may be gauged from two letters in this newspaper last Saturday in which some of Professor Blunt's former students sprang to his defence; their wish to praise their former teacher for his kindness and the quality of his teaching does them nothing but credit.

But it is in the other comments in the two letters that matter for wonder and terror resides. One of them expresses the writer's 'indignation'; the news of Professor Blunt's treachery is only 'material for sensational journalism', and rightly considered, is only 'a minor and ultimately irrelevant aspect of his life'.

Can you really not hear passing-bells in those words? *Is* the revelation of Professor Blunt's treason only 'material for sensational journalism', or is it not rather material for anger at a man who, trusted and respected by the highest in the land, betrayed his free country in the interests of one of the most terrible tyrannies the world has ever seen? And *is* Professor Blunt's treachery 'a minor and ultimately irrelevant aspect of his life'? It is certainly irrelevant to the fact that he knows more about Poussin than anybody else alive, but is it really also less important?

But if we can hear knells in the first letter, we should surely hear, in the letter signed by three other former students of Professor Blunt's, the clods of earth raining down upon this nation's coffin. For them, his unmasking as a servingman of death and evil, though it may have some effect 'on his reputation *with the press*' (my italics), has none on his reputation with them; it 'in no way diminishes him in our esteem'.

In *no* way? You really do not think *any* less highly of a man when you discover that he has betrayed his country, which is also your country, in the interests of slave-masters, and tried (quite hard, it seems) to make the rest of us their slaves as well?

To my question, then. How did we reach a time and place in which educated, gifted and distinguished men and women, not themselves traitors or potential ones, do not seem to mind a bit when another educated, gifted and distinguished man turned out to be thus tainted? What is there in the sulphurous air of our time that – for this is what it amounts to – erases for so many the distinction between right and wrong?

Note first that although I describe as 'so many' the victims of this moral blindness, they are in fact a very tiny minority, and they are almost all to be found among those who are better educated than the majority. Orwell said of some pestilent rubbish being propagated in his time (rubbish very similar, incidentally, to the views I am examining) that, 'You have to be an intellectual to believe that – no ordinary man could be so stupid', and in that remark there lies an enormously important clue.

Once upon a time, *nobody* would have had any difficulty in feeling disgust at the revelation of Professor Blunt's treachery. But there are those who live by an enervated reason that owns no master in the soul, and who can find arguments that enable them to claim that the atrophy of the moral sense from which they suffer is in fact a form of rational judgment. To pity Professor Blunt is one thing, and a thing I hope we all do; but to claim that what he was and did is of no significance, and that it provides no reason for holding him in diminished esteem – no, this suggests that somebody has not read the story of Faust lately, and would be wise to do so.

There are people who call their confusion relativism, and assure us that you can't have an omelette without breaking eggs. Some of them say that what animated Professor Blunt was idealism, or at least *misplaced* idealism. They are often to be found occupying what I have called the tin thrones of public comment; the B.B.C., for instance, is full of them. (So, for that matter, is the Church of England.) They tend to begin sentences 'You must admit'; if somebody mentions God in their presence they make a face, and if someone says 'patriotism' they giggle. They think the most significant thing about the I.R.A. is its opposition to Northern Ireland's discriminatory policies in the fields of housing and education. They invented the word 'counter-productive', to spare themselves the embarrassment of using the already existing word 'wrong', and then they forgot that it *did* exist. They say 'but' when they should say 'so'. They do not read Dostoevsky. Much of the time they feel bored. If they saw a ghost, they would pretend they hadn't.

And they do it all in the name of reason, which only needs a 't' in front of it to bring us back to where we started. Rebecca West, in that haunting study of murder most foul, *Mr Setty and Mr Hume*, describes thus the discovery of the body:

> They sat in the punt together and looked at the great thing held up above the grey waters by the stake, and the constable said to Mr Tiffen, 'There's something wrong here,' and Mr Tiffen answered him, 'Yes, I think there's something wrong here.' Then the constable said, 'It's my opinion this is a murdered body,' and Mr Tiffen said, 'Yes, I do think it is a murdered body.'

These comments on a torso which had been found wrapped in felt and tied up with rope might seem comically obvious; but they were said for a purpose. The constable and Mr Tiffen saw the remains of a human being who had been dispatched without mercy, and they had neither of them ever seen such a thing before, and they knew that if too many of such things happened it would be the doom of their kind . . . murder is so rare an event that there is no widely known formula for expressing the feeling it arouses, and so they had to do what they could for themselves. They did it well enough, for as Mr Tiffen solemnly repeated what they said, their holy loathing of murder was manifest, and as we listened we were moved back several stages nearer the first and appropriate shock caused by Cain.

The trouble with the people I have been describing, and whose domination of this country's intellectual life has led the four signatories of those letters into the moral morass that engulfs them, is a lack of feeling of 'the first and appropriate shock caused by Cain', while a 'holy loathing of murder' is a concept unknown to them; they do not condone murder, of course, any more than treason, but they think it is something to be weighed, like pounds of butter, and to keep calm about, and to think of 'objectively'. But he who thinks of murder objectively is himself dead in the most important part of him.

Professor Blunt sold his soul to the Devil; for every one who does so, there are a hundred who only lend theirs to His Satanic Majesty, and boast of their foresight in drawing up the contract to include a clause allowing them to claim it back at a day's notice. But a day is a long time in Hell, as well as in politics, and anyway, as Chesterton said, 'The devil is a gentleman, and never keeps his word.' Chesterton also said something else:

They twisted even decent sin to shapes not to be named;
Men were ashamed of honour; but we were not ashamed.

But who now are the 'we', who are not ashamed of honour? Well, there is Mr Tiffen and the constable, who never read

New Society in their lives, and who knew that if you call black white and white black you will have done something rather worse than causing confusion when you want to buy paint. Mr Tiffen and the constable should not be forgotten, if only because they may one day save us all. But once upon a time almost all the men and women in positions of authority and influence took the same view, and 'knew that if too many of such things happened it would be the doom of their kind'. They have been largely replaced by the kind of men and women who are now gathering to say that treason was a minor and ultimately irrelevant aspect of Professor Blunt's life, or that although the revelation of his treason may lower his reputation with the press, it in no way diminishes their esteem for him.

'O, my fortunes have corrupted honest men!' cries Antony. It occurs to me that the line would make a most fitting epitaph for our world. If some people have their way, it will be needed quite soon.

The Times November 20th, 1979

Free speech, Camden style

There is a man with a beard in Holborn who really does believe in free speech, and since – this being the way of today's world – he is being penalized for such *outré* convictions, I thought I might break a lance for him today.

His name is Peter Cadogan, and he is a kind of Philosophical Anarchist in the sense meant by those words in the days when they both had meanings. He has been in and out of various political movements, including C.N.D. and its unruly offspring, the Committee of 100, but he is far too honest and open-minded a man ever to give his entire allegiance to any ideology, let alone to any political party. He is probably mad, but if so there are an awful lot of people I wish he would bite, starting with most of the members of Camden council. But Camden council's relevance comes later; I shall begin at the beginning.

Mr Cadogan is the general secretary of the South Place Ethical Society, whose base of operations is the Conway Hall, where I heard much fine chamber music of a Sunday evening in my youth, and some less harmonious strains only the other day when the London Freelance Branch of the N.U.J. held its annual general meeting there. It is an austere hall, in which frivolity would die on the lips of the frivolous; over the proscenium arch is inscribed the stern motto of Polonius: TO THINE OWN SELF BE TRUE.

That invocation, however, Mr Cadogan and the society take seriously. The South Place Ethical Society has a fascinating history; it used to be a Unitarian chapel, but then turned

itself into what it called 'a free religious society', the members
of which recognized – as they still recognize – only one philosophical and moral obligation: to seek the truth wherever it
may be found, to bar no road at all to the seekers, and to hear in
courtesy and in a spirit of enquiry any seeker who claims to
have returned from the quest bearing a fragment of the
treasure. *Felix qui potuit rerum cognoscere causas.*

Mr Cadogan says of the society that its Faith 'is in the
possibilities of human experience', its Inspiration 'stems from
prophets and artists and our response to them', its Belief is
'that if we seek we shall find', its Philosophy 'the way we
integrate our understanding of religion, art, science and history', and its Vision 'that we can live differently'. This catalogue of ideals sums up the South Place Ethical Society very
well, and it is not surprising that it has always enjoyed
charitable status as a religious foundation.

Or rather, it has done so until recently. Following a legal
decision in another matter to the effect that to be classed as a
religious body a group must believe in a 'Supreme Being', the
society, which could not maintain its members collectively
believed in any such principle, if only because its members do
not *collectively* believe in anything, was unable to convince the
Charity Commissioners that it was nevertheless a religious
body if the phrase means anything at all, and thus lost its
charitable status.

Philosophically, that did not matter; financially it did. As a
charitable body it could claim a rebate of roughly half the
£8,000 rates it pays on Conway Hall; without that standing it
cannot, and the £4,000 difference is simply not to be made up
out of its slender income. Since the decision (while the society
awaits the outcome of a ten-year legal battle to make the
Charity Commissioners change their minds), the society's
reserves have been used to close the gap; now these are almost
exhausted, and other means must be found.

Mr Cadogan and his colleagues approached the Borough of
Camden (in whose territory Conway Hall stands) for a grant

of a sum roughly equivalent to what the council would have allowed by way of rate rebate – i.e., £4,000 a year. At first, the officials and councillors they spoke to were sympathetic, but then came the horrid revelation I referred to in my opening sentence: Mr Cadogan, and the South Place Ethical Society, believe in free speech.

I must explain that, in addition to the programme of lectures, meetings, discussions and other activities that the society itself operates, Conway Hall itself is always available for any organization wishing to use it for a gathering, at a reasonable fee. The only stipulations made are that the users of the hall shall do and say nothing against the law of the land, and that they shall not advocate or employ violence in the furtherance of their ends.

Within that ample room for manoeuvre, every imaginable kind of group, together with many which are quite impossible to imagine, have hired the Conway Hall to inform, declare, persuade, insist, denounce, assert, deny, declaim and even discuss, everything that can be thought by the human mind.

Many of these groups are non-political, proclaiming their belief in the flatness of the earth, the dangers of fluoride or the benefits of vegetarianism. Many, of course, are religious. But many, too, are partly or wholly political and, subject to the conditions I have mentioned, all are welcome. And it is not only democratic political bodies that have held the stage at Conway Hall: virtually all the totalitarian groups in our society have held meetings there, including the Socialist Workers Party, the Communist Party, the International Marxist Group – and the National Front.

And that, of course, is where the shoe pinches. After discovering that Mr Cadogan's philosophical integrity and commitment to free speech within the law really are absolute, so that the National Front, vile though it is, was entitled to make its voice heard at Conway Hall just as much as the S.W.P. or the C.P., vile though *they* are, Camden council, after much thought and the meeting of more than one committee, refused the appeal for a grant. Provided that the only totalitarian groups permitted at Conway Hall were of the left, the money would be forthcoming; if their mirror-image of the right was permitted a similar freedom, it would not.

It is not as though Camden council has ever shown any sign of being careful with its ratepayers' money. Only last week it published a report which strongly deplored the council's 'poor public image', which, it complained, was 'one of profligacy', and it was perhaps unfortunate that the report in question simultaneously revealed that the council's public relations department has a budget for the present year of £144,620, with a staff of *nine*; but at any rate that figure suggests that a grant of £4,000 to the Conway Hall would not exactly bring down the wrath of the district auditor, or for that matter the tormented ratepayers. No, the test is purely political; it is proper to use the Conway Hall for furthering the aims of every variety of communist tyranny, but not for furthering those of one variety of fascist tyranny.

Now as it happens, one of the principal elements in the lawsuit the South Place Ethical Society is bringing in order to regain its charitable status is that it has a commitment to *all* forms of philosophical, religious or political enquiry, and that its allegiance is to thought in general. It could not, therefore, ban the expression of any particular attitude and maintain its case. But I must make clear that even if no such question arose, Mr Cadogan and the society would still maintain unswervingly that free speech means free speech for *all*, not just for those of whom the members of Camden council approve.

Mr Cadogan, of course, thinks the National Front is every bit as vile as it actually is. Whenever it has broken the terms on which the hall is let, he has refused its bookings for a specified period thereafter, in punishment for a specified offence. But he maintains that while and when it remains within the law, the freedom of thought and assembly and speech by which the society lives shall be available to it, just as these are available to the S.W.P. or the C.P. while and when *they* remain within the law.

'In a constitutionally governed society,' says Mr Cadogan, 'rotten values, mistaken ideas and ignorance wither in an atmosphere of freedom. The truth is ultimately more powerful than coercion.' That, of course, is what I believe, too, and the electoral showing in Britain of totalitarians of both left and right is powerful evidence in support of the view. Camden council, or at any rate a majority of its members, seem to think otherwise (this, of course, is to say nothing of those members who are themselves actually sympathetic to totalitarian ideas of the left), and the South Place Ethical Society may be compelled to close its premises in consequence.

I always knew that a commitment to free speech could be dangerous; now, it seems, it can also be expensive. But Mr Cadogan, if the worst happens, will be entitled to comfort himself, as he locks the doors of Conway Hall for the last time, with a last proud look at the words over the stage, and reflect that he has indeed to his own self been true.

The Times February 20th, 1980

Of rats and mice and men

I AM, AS MUST be tolerably well known, a deeply sceptical man, the basis of whose philosophical belief is that there is no limit, actual or theoretical, to human folly. But not even I could have imagined the latest wheeze for proving me right.

In the 1950s, a new type of rat-poison was developed, and sold in this country under the name of Warfarin. Its unprecedentedly lethal action was delayed, so that the furry vermin failed to twig the connection between eating it and dropping dead: but one sniff of the Warfarin-impregnated bait and the beast's whiskers lost their lustre, its tail drooped and its doom was sealed.

Now the rats and mice, understandably, did not much care for this caper; who would? A. E. Housman had a word for it:

> There was a king reigned in the East:
> There, when kings will sit to feast,
> They get their fill before they think
> With poisoned meat and poisoned drink.

There was no known antidote to Warfarin, or at any rate none available to the rats and mice. So the rats and mice developed a biological immunity to Warfarin. Constant ingestion of the stuff meant that those rats and mice which survived it – either by having stronger constitutions or by absorbing non-lethal doses – developed a higher tolerance to it, and bred descendants which followed, in this respect, in their parents' pawsteps. The consequence was that within only five years there were types of rats and mice on which Warfarin had no effect, and – by the processes of natural selection – these strains flourished more and more.

> He gathered all that spring to birth
> From the many-venomed earth;
> First a little, thence to more,
> He sampled all her killing store;
> And easy, smiling, seasoned sound,
> Sate the king when healths went round.

That, of course, is exactly what happened in the case of the antibiotics; the micro-organisms against which they were directed developed immunity. The scientists responded to the appearance of micro-organisms immune to existing antibiotics by developing more powerful antibiotics. They thus ensured that the micro-organisms became immune to those, too, whereat the scientists (where on earth did science get its reputation for drawing conclusions from observations?) devised more powerful antibiotics still, whereupon . . . well, whereupon we have today antibiotics that will kill any micro-organism you care to mention, but which also kill the patient.

As with germs, so with rats and mice. At the weekend, the men in the white coats unveiled a new poison, called Sorexa CR. Sorexa CR, it seems, is to Warfarin as is the hydrogen bomb to the javelin, the jet aeroplane to the canoe, or Sir William Blackstone to Sir Peter Rawlinson. In field trials on farms, rats and mice immune to Warfarin were each offered a dose of Sorexa CR: before you could say squeak, there was another cat out of a job. The scientists described the results as 'highly encouraging'. They would.

The date today is December 4th, 1973. On December 4th, 1983 (please synchronize your watches) we shall meet on this very spot and discuss the recent spate of reports that rats and mice immune to Sorexa CR have been found throughout the country; we shall then adjourn until December 4th, 1993, when we shall once again foregather here and drink a toast to the scientists who, ever-mindful of our interests, have developed a rat-poison as far superior to Sorexa CR as is colour television to the epidiascope, the typewriter to the scribe, or Sir Edward Coke to thingummy. Or, for that matter, as Sorexa CR to Warfarin.

> They put arsenic in his meat
> And stared aghast to watch him eat;
> They poured strychnine in his cup
> And shook to see him drink it up:

Now sooner or later, *all* the micro-organisms against which the antibiotics are still effective will have developed immunity to any agent other than those so powerful that they are also toxic to the patient. Similarly, we shall eventually breed rats and mice against which no poison at all will work, other than one which will contaminate every living thing for miles around, including the crops and the earth they grow in.

> They shook, they stared as white's their shirt:
> Them it was their poison hurt.

The fact of the matter is that, as St Paul remarked to the Galatians (who took no notice), whatsoever a man soweth, that also shall he reap. If you feel depressed, as which of us does not, and go to a doctor like the scientists who tested Sorexa CR, he will provide you with a prescription for tranquillizers. If you take the stipulated dose, you may feel less depressed, and resolve to take the tablets every time you feel depressed again. After a bit, however, a puzzling effect will become apparent; the pills will begin to seem less efficacious. Returning to the doctor you will point this out, and he will recommend a slight increase in the dose. You will be much relieved to find that the increased dose is as effective at dealing with the depression as the old, lesser dose was. But after a bit, a puzzling effect will become apparent . . .

Now that, as a matter of fact, is how Roche Products made a high proportion of all the money that was getting everybody so indignant not long ago. But the argument concerned the price they charged for Valium and Librium and similar products; the Government alleged that they charged too much, and the company replied that they did not. What nobody bothered to ask was whether there would be the slightest point in anybody ever taking the pills even if they were given away free. Expensive public relations officers will doubtless insist that there is every point in taking such things, and declare that huge numbers of people have gained rapid and astonishing relief by their use. I have no doubt they have; Warfarin killed vast numbers of rats and mice, and Sorexa CR will kill even more. But in the end, the rats beat Warfarin and the mice will beat Sorexa CR, just as the micro-organisms beat the antibiotics and the depressions beat the antidepressants. If we are ever to break into any of these circles, we shall have to begin by recognizing that if you go far enough round the world you end up where you started.

> I tell the tale that I heard told
> – Mithridates, he died old.

The Times December 4th, 1973

The vertical man

A CAR-DEALER IN Frankfurt, a Herr Jaromir Wagner (no relation), has announced an ambition to be the first man to cross the Atlantic while standing on top of an aeroplane. My immediate duty, therefore, is to offer him an assurance for which, I am sure, he has been anxiously waiting: his ambition is in no danger from me. I hereby formally renounce all intention of crossing the Atlantic while standing on top of an aeroplane, and if Herr Wagner thinks that my word alone is insufficient to ensure my abstinence from competition with him, I am perfectly prepared to set his mind at rest by posting a large sum of money with a trustworthy stake-holder, to be paid to him in the event of my breaking my promise and of his living long enough to collect.

That said, however, I return, as so often, to my old mum's observation that there's more out than in. It is true that nobody has hitherto crossed the Atlantic standing on an aeroplane (at least, I assume that if it had already happened we would have heard about it), and Herr Wagner can argue that man is entitled, indeed obliged, to continue pushing out the frontiers of knowledge and experience if he is to be true to his destiny. Some years ago, I read of a man who jumped out of an aeroplane without a parachute, having arranged to collect one from a passing friend on the way down; that had certainly not been done before, and I daresay has never been done since, either. But if it comes to that, Beachcomber once published an account of a thrilling race, between Iron-Nostril Balzarotti and Evans the Hearse, to be the first man to push a pea up

Snowdon with his nose, and what I want to know is: what's the difference?

Of course, I could go and discuss the matter calmly with the upright aviator. ('Herr Wagner, why do you want to cross the Atlantic standing on top of an aeroplane?' 'To get to the other side. Ha-ha-ha. Ho.' 'No, but seriously, Herr Wagner.' 'Because it's there.' 'The aeroplane or the Atlantic?' 'Both, *du blöder Trottel.*') But the truth, apart from the fact that I am in any case much too lazy, is that I do not really want to know why a German car-dealer wants to cross the Atlantic in a manner even more informal than that offered at such a handsome reduction by Sir Freddie Laker's Skytrain; I merely wish to observe that the farthest limits of human oddness have not yet been reached, and are most unlikely ever to be.

It has been aptly remarked that the incomprehensibility of the mathematical concept of infinity is well demonstrated by the fact that however large a number we can think of, we have only to say 'Plus one' to demonstrate that neither it nor any other can ever be the largest. And much the same, it seems to me, can be said of Herr Wagner and his project. As soon as he has achieved his ambition, he will, I warn him, discover that a rival is about to cross the Atlantic standing on top of an aeroplane *on his head*, and after that another will do it blindfolded and on one leg, and then it will be while riding a bicycle up and down the outside of the fuselage. Juggling cups . . . balancing a billiard-cue on the nose . . . playing the violin . . . reciting the Rubaiyat . . . reciting the Rubaiyat backwards blindfolded while riding a bicycle *and* balancing a billiard-cue on the nose *and* playing the violin . . . is there no end to it?

Indeed, no; no end at all. For ('plus one') as soon as it is impossible to play any more variations on Herr Wagner's theme, someone will fly the Atlantic hanging on to a piece of string tied to the wheels, and someone else will then do so hanging on to it by his teeth, and so on. Beachcomber's Charlie Suet (I apologize for bringing in Beachcomber twice in a morning, but since the real world is now almost indistinguishable from the one he invented it is not altogether surprising that he should spring so readily to mind) rang up the Ministry of Supply (this was during the war, when there were constant appeals to the public to save and collect waste paper) and said that he had 20,000 punch-holes, cut out of the pages of loose-leaf files. The puzzled official said that if they were holes, there was presumably no paper involved, whereupon Suet replied 'that it had been necessary, when cutting them out, to leave a narrow rim of paper round the hole'; he added that if that was not considered sufficient he was willing to paste small circular pieces of paper over the holes. (The official, remarked Beachcomber, 'screamed twice and fell to the floor with a sickening thud.')

'Men are unwise, and curiously planned,' sang the poet (my headmaster's brother, incidentally, and the black sheep of the family). For all I know, there is a man in Wapping carrying out Suet's trick with the holes at this very moment; I have myself seen a scale-model of the Queen Mary, some eight feet long, made out of butter; and the really extraordinary thing about the famous claim by Miss Joyce McKinney that she would, for love, 'have skied down Mount Everest in the nude with a carnation up my nose' is that no lovestruck young lady immediately suited her own action to Miss McKinney's words.

From the report of Herr Wagner's project (it came from the Reykjavik Correspondent of the *Daily Telegraph*, which itself suggests that Beachcomber is alive and well and living in Peterborough Court), it is not absolutely clear who is actually driving the aeroplane on which the intrepid birdman is to make his perilous flight, and on one reading of the words it would be possible to conclude that he is doing so himself. No aviator I, but unless he is proposing to nip below from time to time to adjust the controls and have a word with the automatic pilot, I can't quite see how he would manage it unless, I suppose, he has built an entire set of controls on the roof. You may say that for a man to build an entire set of controls on the roof of an aeroplane would be a pretty strange thing to do, but ten minutes ago you would have said the same about a suggestion that a Frankfurt car-dealer called Wagner was planning to fly the Atlantic standing on the roof in question, controls or no controls.

There is a story, too long to tell today (and to tell the truth not funny enough, either) which ends, 'Good God, man, there's a dead horse in your bathroom' – 'I know.' It would be tragic if Herr Wagner were to arrive in New York only to find that nobody was impressed by his feat, but he must realize that it is getting harder and harder to astonish the by-standers these days, and the first person he stops in order to boast may well reply, 'Look, bud, a common slave – you know him well by sight – held up his left hand, which did flame and burn like twenty torches joined, and yet his hand, not sensible of fire, remained unscorched', only to be capped by another passer-by saying, 'That's nothing, Mac – against the Capitol I met a lion, who glared upon me and went surly by, without annoying me, and there were drawn upon a heap a hundred ghastly women, including in particular Gloria Steinem and Susan Sontag, transformed with their fear, who swore they saw men all in fire walk up and down the streets, and yesterday the bird of night did sit, even at noon-day, upon the market-place, hooting and shrieking', beside which Herr Wagner will surely find that his own achievement ranks so low by the standards his hearers are accustomed to that he can interest nobody at all in it.

When Lindbergh made the first solo aeroplane crossing of the Atlantic and arrived in Paris, there was a colossal demonstration of public acclaim back home. Headlines a foot deep, speeches, bands, parades, nation-wide preparations to give him a hero's welcome on his return – the whole country was convulsed by the courage of his attempt and its successful accomplishment. When the uproar had continued unabated for days on end, Robert Benchley cabled a friend in Paris: ANY

NEWS LINDBERGH YET? LEFT HERE WEEK AGO AM WORRIED — BENCHLEY. I promised Herr Wagner that I would not fly the Atlantic standing on top of an aeroplane; nor shall I, for I am a man of my word. But I said nothing about not jeering at him, and reserve the right to do so when he arrives. Laugh that off, Jaromir.

The Times October 1st, 1980

The odds is gone

Fᴿᴼᴹ ᴘᴇᴛᴇʀ ʙʀᴏᴏᴋ's first Shakespearian production in this country since 1970 (and that was his reading of *A Midsummer Night's Dream*, which still warms the lives of those who saw it), much was inevitably expected. Mr Brook, however, like Eliot's Fourth Tempter, precedes expectation; it is never any use looking for him where he was last seen, for he will always have moved on.

What he has moved on to now is a version of *Antony and Cleopatra* which breaks decisively with the voluptuous tradition that reached its apogee in the Byam Shaw–Ashcroft–Redgrave performances of 1953. But Mr Brook is not in the business of breaking with tradition simply *pour épater les bourgeois*; he has something to say about the play, and deserves an attentive hearing when he says it.

The scene is set in a plastic shell. Inside is a world of relationships; outside, battle. Twice, the 'real' world makes its presence felt; once when the enemy outside pelts the walls of the shell with great gobbets of blood, and again when the Parthian war scene (usually cut) erupts through the gaps in the screen to defile the sanctuary itself. Mr Brook has said of the mature Shakespeare that he 'did nothing by accident', and the same is certainly true of him, for in the text of this scene Pacorus is already dead; Mr Brook has him butchered before our eyes, just when we have been feasting with the quatuorvirs on Pompey's galley. The rout there becomes a true Bacchanal, Brook at his magical, balletic best, and the abruptness of the transition makes the point with shocking violence. Besides,

the wall around the scene is translucent, but not fully transparent; the figures outside are shadows, as unreal to us as to
those who play out the rituals of love and death in the
innermost arena of all, which is the human heart.

There are more clues. The stage, for instance, is almost bare;
a few low, severe benches, rarely moved; a few cushions;
matting; a couple of gilded stools; a plain red hanging that
suggests Cleopatra's monument and, having suggested it, is
lowered to the floor. Scenes overlap, Rome and Alexandria
constantly appearing before the other has gone, and the two
High Commands on the eve of battle sharing the stage, back to
back, to make their dispositions. Cleopatra hasn't even a chair,
let alone a throne to die on; the lighting is of the utmost
simplicity, scarcely more, it seems, than a straightforward
increase or diminution in the wattage, with an almost complete darkening when the battle's lost and won; for the sea-
fight we hear only the rise and fall of a mighty wave, and see
only the solitary figure of Enobarbus, silhouetted with his
back to us outside the magic circle, looking out on desolation;
Antony sits cross-legged, hands folded, for the fatal sword-
stroke that never comes, and commits his own hara-kiri in a no
less ritually stylized manner; even the programme, stripped of
the Royal Shakespeare Company's usual esoteric drivel, contains nothing but facts.

Then are these only bare ruined choirs where late the sweet
birds sang? Not quite; it is Mr Brook who is in charge,
remember, not Mr Brecht. And what he has crammed within
this perspex O is a pair of narcissists three-quarters in love
with easeful death because they cannot take life seriously –
because, presumably, they cannot believe that it is real. Glenda
Jackson's edgéd, disembodied voice delivers even the catalogue of her forthcoming humiliations as Caesar's captive in
tones of amused indifference; Alan Howard makes 'Oh my
fortunes have corrupted honest men' wry, not heartbroken,
speaks 'All is lost' with a broad smile on his face, turns his
single-combat challenge to Octavius into a wild, self-

consciously absurd boast, and swings from his rage at the messenger who dares to kiss Cleopatra's hand to a forced euphoria at the prospect of her birthday party. Even in their embraces, they seem moved less by lust than by what history will say; though they roll together on the floor, I cannot help feeling that they are only playing 'Last one up's a cissy'. (Compare this coolness to the heat with which Tutin and Finney pursue their vain quest for oblivion through the hunger of their embraces in the National Theatre *Macbeth*.)

'These strong Egyptian fetters I must break,' says Antony, 'or lose myself in dotage'; anon, 'I must from this enchanting Queen break off.' But Mr Howard is not only unable to keep his word; he clearly has no serious intention of doing so, any more than Miss Jackson really believes that there is nothing left remarkable beneath the visiting moon merely because Antony is dead. Is not Cleopatra still alive?

The conception of Miss Jackson's Cleopatra, indeed, takes the analogy with the Sphinx to an almost literal conclusion; there are hieratic arm and hand movements, and poses, as formal as the inscription on a stele, and at one point she enters in a robe and headdress clearly modelled upon the great riddle itself.

What is most striking about the production is that this solipsism does not extend to the other characters; Jonathan Pryce's Octavius, for instance, is far more vulnerable than the usual icy killer, constantly looking to his allies for re-assurance at the peace conference; David Suchet's Pompey, even more unusually, is tentative and ingratiating; Patrick Stewart's Enobarbus has his master's cynicism, but a heart to break as well; the infallible Richard Griffiths makes the asp-bearing clown a true clown, red nose and all, with even a hint of Harlequin about his costume – I have rarely seen a better demonstration of the truth that there is no such thing as an insignificant character in Shakespeare, provided that there is a director in charge who understands how the hum-blest figure becomes a comment on the action and even

('I wish you joy o' the worm') on the very meaning.

This 'pair so famous' go to their deaths in Mr Brook's production as blindly as they have lived, never suspecting that death can be a triumph, and without even believing whole-heartedly in the consolation of a world well lost for love. 'We have kissed away kingdoms' indeed; including the greatest kingdom of all.

You will have noticed that I have said nothing about my emotions at this performance, only my thoughts. But I think that is inevitable, given such detachment on the stage. The production is consistently interesting, and is valuable as clearing away the accretions of false romanticism that have gathered upon the play. Yes, but there is true romanticism, too, and verse as magnificent as any ever written, and it is the racing of the blood that these provide that is largely lacking amid the irony here. This is an *Antony and Cleopatra* for collectors and connoisseurs, rather than those who feel, and anyone taking to it a guest who has never seen or read the play will, I think, sense disappointment at his elbow.

Sunday Times October 15th, 1978

Generalissimos die in bed

THE REPEATEDLY POSTPONED death of Tito has inevitably prompted thoughts of a political nature: my own principal reflection, however, has nothing to do with his career, the position of Yugoslavia in relation to the Soviet Union, or even dictatorship. It is to the effect of a resolution that, should I have the misfortune to become fatally ill, I shall endeavour not to do so in Yugoslavia, or for that matter Spain.

Modern history offers few scenes as macabre and repulsive as the deathbeds of Tito and Franco, so alike in their brutal lives and characters, and now, by a dark irony, in their dying as well. The doctors, of course, have acted within well-recognized political constraints; in each case, the repercussions that might follow the patient's death were unpredictable, and fraught with national (in the case of Tito also international) danger. Every day Franco stayed alive increased the chances of an orderly transfer of power into new hands; every day that Tito's passing could be staved off made it less likely that the Soviet Union would strike and that the Yugoslav armed forces would be ready if she did. All the same, Arthur Hugh Clough would have had to amend his *New Decalogue* to encompass a principle that not even his cynicism could imagine when he wrote it. Today he would have to say:

> Thou shall not kill; but needs must strive
> Officiously to keep alive.

But it is only the spotlit nature of the deaths of the two dictators that makes their cases exemplary, for the same sort of thing has happened more quietly to more ordinary men and women:

> When beggars die, there are no comets seen;
> The heavens themselves blaze forth the death of princes.

And what is the principle at the heart of such prolonged death agony? It is this: of all the rights, real or ridiculous, that the modern world claims, one of the most fundamental is daily being eroded, and that is the right to a decent death.

To speak of a *right* to death must sound odd: we shall all die sooner or later, and that which must inevitably happen hardly needs guaranteeing in a Bill of Rights. But death hath a thousand doors to let out life, and the one opened so slowly for Franco and Tito was perhaps the worst of all. And more and more people today are going that way. It is, of course, a doctor's duty to save life, and to prolong it when it is fatally stricken. Nor is it easy to lay down any general guidance to doctors to help them decide at what point they should cease to keep literally alive one who is in all other meanings dead. This difficulty has been much increased by the modern fashion for organ transplants, which I long ago pointed out has become a sporting contest; I don't know which is in greater danger: the 'donor' (an inappropriate word if ever there was one) whose spare parts are wanted, or the recipient on whose behalf they are solicited.

The fashion, like fashions in hemlines, will be forgotten and replaced by some other fashion; the history of medicine is bestrewn with brief enthusiasms of no ultimate value to anybody except the doctors. But meanwhile we face a growing tendency towards the kind of raree-show seen first in Madrid and now in Belgrade, and the fact that for most of its victims it is done without the limelight makes it worse, not better.

Since we have to die, and since, indeed, that is the *only* fact of our lives that is known with certainty on the day we are born, the least we can ask is that we be allowed to die with dignity; is there any more terrible and haunting image in all the horror-strewn course of our century than that of the bulldozers shovelling those emaciated corpses into the common graves of liberated Belsen? But why is that picture so unforgettable, and so deeply stained with shame? Not only – I believe not even mainly – because of the foul way they were done to death, but because there was no way in which their poor bodies could be disposed of, in order to avoid the risk of hideous epidemics among the survivors, other than in this collective anonymity. And is there a man or woman of any sensibility anywhere who did not feel an extra stab of shame and sorrow at the news that the American dead were left behind after last week's disaster in Iran,* and a feeling of profound revulsion at the foulness with which their bodies were treated? Surely not; and surely those feelings represent something very old and very deep in the human psyche, for which the body is far more than a mere container.

Timor vitae conturbat me; a view that by now must have acquired a good deal of popularity, though it is not yet universal. Do you remember the outcry when it was learnt that the letters N.T.B.R. on the progress charts of terminally ill hospital patients stood for 'Not to be resuscitated'? Certainly, many wish to cling to life, however meaningless life may be, till the last possible moment. At any rate, that is their attitude before the point is reached; do we know what dreams may come when we have shuffled off all but the last inch of this mortal coil, and if we did know would we be quite so eager to remain in irreversible coma as long as the machine was keeping our hearts beating?

There is an essay by Chesterton in which he describes his boarding, at a country halt, of a train that is apparently empty, and in darkness throughout, after being advised by the guard to wait for the next one. When he asks why, the guard tells him it is because there is a dead man on the train, and Chesterton,

* The attempt to rescue hostages held by the Iranians.

by then inside his carriage but standing at the window for this exchange, did something that, as he says, was entirely instinctive and only thought about after it was done: 'I threw away my cigar.' He did so under the influence of that same deep understanding of reverence for death that, if we have the smallest spark of imagination, we must all feel.

But those who prolong empty life seem to lack that imagination altogether, as indeed do many of those in the transplant business who are quite unable to understand why there is something deeply, and by no means irrationally, repulsive about the entire business.

Stewart Alsop, the American columnist (brother of Joseph Alsop), died not long ago of a form of leukaemia. It was an odd form, puzzling to the doctors; for a long time it was not clear that it would kill him at all. While he was waiting for this interesting question to be resolved, he wrote a book about the experience, called *Stay of Execution*, in which he analysed his feelings, his fears and his hopes, and came to the dignified and surely admirable conclusion that 'Sooner or later there comes a time when a dying man has to die, as a sleepy man has to sleep.' And so there does; may we all remember that when our time comes, and may we be spared the agony of a Franco or a Tito, and of all those whose doctors deny the proposition by their actions. Charles the Second apologized for being 'an unconscionable time a-dying', and of George the Fifth the last bulletin on his condition said simply, 'The King's life is moving peacefully towards its close.' These seem to me, like Stewart Alsop's words, to provide a better guide for the dying than the well-meant endeavours of those who have persuaded themselves that life on any terms whatever is preferable to death, and who have forgotten that

> . . . all that lives must die,
> Passing through nature to eternity.

The Times April 29th, 1980

Smoke signals

I KNOW WHAT I want to find in my stocking tomorrow; nor do I begrudge the extra cost the present will involve me in, which is the price of a large handkerchief, the purpose of which will be to mop up the tears of nostalgia that the thing will provoke.

A firm called Foster-Callear, in Hatfield, has had the idea of buying a large collection of sets of cigarette-cards, framing them, and selling the result (each set split between two frames) as pictures to hang on the wall. The illustration in the advertisement looked charming, but to tell you the truth I don't really want them framed at all; the backs of the cards are, to me, quite as important as the fronts, and anyway, I want to handle them.

I suppose I had better pause here and explain to my younger readers what I am talking about, as they will certainly have no means of knowing if I don't. In the 1930s, cigarette manufacturers, to promote their brands, included in each packet of their product a card, measuring some 2½ inches by 1¼. On the *recto*, there was a picture; on the *verso*, a text concerning the illustration. There was also a number from one to fifty; and therein lies the heart of the matter.

For the cards were not designed with random interest in mind; each set of fifty had a theme of its own, and the idea from the cigarette manufacturer's point of view was that the collector would want to complete the set and would therefore have to go on buying cigarettes until he had done so. And this might be quite a long time, because although (as far as I know) the number of copies of each card of a set was the same, there was nothing on the outside of the packet to indicate which card was inside.

In practice, I suppose, most of the collecting was done not by the smokers but by the smokers' children. The only smoker in my home was my grandfather (though he was a fifty-a-day man, he lived to be eighty-four, and used his very last breath not to speak memorable words but to take a puff on a cigarette); his preferred brand was Kensitas, which I seem to remember went in for somewhat classier cards than the other manufacturers, including one spectacular set not of cards but of leaves of silk, on which were reproduced the flags of the nations. But if one's smoking relations stuck to a single brand, the scope for card-collecting in the family circle was limited, and there was only one solution. We used to hang about the doorways of tobacconists, and accost emerging purchasers with a cry of 'Got any cigarette-cards, mister?'

This, no doubt, conjures up for you a picture so startling that you find it difficult to believe. Reckless Jack Levin, the man of many scoops, you are familiar with; Levin the gourmet and bibber of fine wines you likewise know; Levin the wit and man-about-town, the glass of fashion and the mould of form, the observed of all observers, is no less a byword among you. Levin the Bisto Kid, however, is another matter. Well, *tempora mutantur*; my rough youth is behind me, and unlikely to return. Nor do I propose to elaborate; suffice it that I collected cigarette-cards in my youth, and gathered my manna where it was to be found.

The range of subjects covered by the cards was astonishing; the advertisement that set me off on this *recherche du temps perdu* listed twenty sets, half each from Wills and Players. Footballers, Film Stars and Motor Cars are obvious enough, though I cannot recall ever having been sufficiently interested to collect any of these. But even in this list, which represents what must have been a total of many hundreds (remember that the manufacturers regularly and frequently phased out one set and introduced a new one), there are such less obviously appealing subjects as Household Hints, Air Raid Precautions (if my younger readers will come back next week, I will tell them what an Air Raid was, and what Precautions you took against it), Military Uniforms, Wild Flowers, Butterflies and Old Bicycles.

And also Railway Equipment. This is one of the sets I remember collecting myself, and what is more, completing; many a set, inevitably, was left unfinished, but for this one I bagged the lot (a brisk trade in 'swaps' went on all the time of course, and one's surplus copies of those cards acquired in duplicate or triplicate might be exchanged for the missing ones in another set), as I did with a set of Coronation Regalia, and one of Schoolboy Howlers, from which I learned, among other items of information I have never succeeded in forgetting, that Julius Caesar must have been a very strong man because he threw a bridge across the Rhine, that a myth is a female moth and an epistle the wife of an apostle, and that when Wellington died it took eight men to carry the beer.

Of the ones I remember, only Railway Equipment is included in the present offer; I think I could recite the details of many of the cards in it to this day, though how I ever became interested in the Westinghouse Brake System I cannot imagine. The point is, however, that the cards were, for the most part, not rubbish and were prepared with considerable care. The text on the back was correct and genuinely informative, and some of the fronts extremely attractive. I remember, for instance, a very swish set (probably by Kensitas) which consisted of real photographs, of scenery in Britain; I wish I had kept that one. (Indeed, I wish I had kept them all – complete sets of the rarer ones change hands today at substantial prices.)

From time to time, one of the tobacco companies thinks of starting the issue of cards again (they disappeared with paper rationing at the beginning of the war), but the industry as a whole is against the idea, no doubt because of the cost involved, and since it would almost certainly have to be all manufacturers or none, it seems that we shall never see them again. The cost, incidentally, must have been considerable; in addition to the preparation and manufacture of the cards, there were, as I recall, albums to hold them, and I think you got one of these free, at any rate from some manufacturers, when you completed a set.

My memories of collecting cigarette-cards include some of the most notable misunderstandings of my youth. There was a series on sportsmen, for instance, which gave you a biography of the player illustrated, ending with a question to which the answer would be found on a different card. There was a woman golfer on one of the set, and the question was: 'Has she holed in one?' Having no knowledge of the game of golf, I was quite unable to understand the question, and puzzled over it in vain for a long time. (I cannot now recall whether I ever got the card with the answer, but presumably it said only 'Yes' or 'No', which would not have got me much further.)

Another such crux came in the series of Howlers, in the form of a dialogue: 'How high is Mont Blanc?' – 'It depends on the mould.' This, a feeble enough pun anyway, was only intelligible to those who had heard of blancmange; I never had, for that unspeakable substance was unknown in my home, and it took me approximately seventeen years to see the joke, which may well be a record. But worst of all from this point of view was a set called Famous Minors. My spelling in those days was by no means what it has since become, and I assumed that Minors were people who worked underground hewing coal. Even at that age, I could not quite see Lady Jane Grey and the poet Chatterton at the coalface, but there they were in the set, and I assumed, in the trusting way of child-hood, that they must have done a stint at the hewing business before settling down to their brief life's work.

I suppose somebody has written, or is writing, an immense scholarly study of the cigarette-card. Somebody else, no doubt, is at work on an analysis of its role in social history. Worthy endeavours, no doubt. But if the authors grew up after the war there will be something missing from their books, something that could only be truly understood by those who had themselves collected cigarette-cards in their youth, and can in consequence tell you, as I proudly can, what a bat does in winter: it splits if you don't oil it. Merry Christmas.

The Times December 24th, 1979

Uncertainty principle

MR WEDGWOOD BENN has claimed that when he was an undergraduate he was approached by 'a certain colonel', who offered him a job. Asked by the infant Benn what the job was, the certain colonel replied that he could not say (he sounds rather more like an *un*certain colonel), but that if Mr Benn was interested in it he would take him to see someone else, who would be more forthcoming. Mr Benn goes on to assert that he 'thought for a moment' and then declared himself unable 'to undertake such a job' (a bit odd, that phraseology, because only a paragraph earlier Mr Benn had been saying that no details of the job had been disclosed, so how he could be so sure that he would not be able to undertake *such* a job is not clear), as he was looking for work in the Labour Movement and hoped one day to become an M.P. At this, he says, the colonel, suddenly becoming very certain indeed, replied 'Oh that is no problem, you could do both jobs.' From this Mr Benn instantly deduced, with the grasp of the finer points of Aristotelian logic that has since got him known as the Wittgenstein of Bristol Trades Council, that the colonel 'knew precisely what I wanted to do *before* he approached me and indeed that must have been *why* he made the approach.'

Mr Benn's refusal, however, meant that he 'was never taken to meet the man who would have explained all'. But that was not the end of the horrid affair, for 'a few years' after Mr Benn had been elected to Parliament the certain colonel came to see him at the House of Commons and 'repeated his invitation to do some work for the Foreign Office' (another odd turn of phrase, as in Mr Benn's description of the earlier encounter there is no mention of the Foreign Office, and indeed only a blank refusal to describe the job at all).

This time, the certain colonel made no mention of taking the fledgling legislator to see an oppo of his for further details; instead, he directed him to 'a certain Labour M.P.'; the amount of certainty in this story, considering that it is about the security services, is most reassuring, and if the Russkis ever get to hear of it it should make them think twice before getting up to any of their dirty tricks, faced as they will be with opponents fairly oozing certainty, brave lads, from every file.

But even that does not close this strange chapter in Mr Benn's early romantic life, for 'many years later I came across the name of the Colonel again in a newspaper story about the security services' (the question of the Colonel's certainty is no longer raised, but he must have been promoted in the interim, as he now has a capital C to his rank), from which Mr Benn, with the penetrating analytical mind that has led him to be thought of as the Niels Bohr of the Holland Park Comprehensive Parent-Teachers' Association, 'could not help wondering how many other people in the Labour Party, in Parliament, in the trade unions or outside, were recruited on the same basis [yet another strange choice of words, since nobody in this story has so far been recruited on any basis] and are still on the Government pay-roll, unknown to all the colleagues with whom they are still working.'

It is easy to mock. It is easy, also, to point out that although we (or, to be precise, Mr Wedgwood Benn) can only wonder about members of the Labour Movement who have been recruited for the British security forces, we do know of two who were covertly engaged to work for security services with their headquarters considerably farther to the East than Queen Anne's Gate, and blushed, later on, to find it fame. But it so happens that I am in a unique position to verify and discuss Mr Wedgwood Benn's story. For I was the certain colonel.

'Colonel', you must understand, was a courtesy title only, much as some of the younger London taxi-drivers like to call their male passengers 'Squire'; in fact, I held no official rank at all, military or civilian, for it was thought better that I should appear on no list, and be referred to in no document. Indeed, my salary appeared on no Estimate, and was always paid to me out of money provided for such ostensible purposes as 'Extra butter for the garrison at Gibraltar'. Yet I was the man, sent by a certain committee of almost unbelievably important (and certain) personages in our public life, to see if Mr Wedgwood Benn could be persuaded to throw in his lot with the gallant men and women who, disguised as members in good standing of the Barnsley No. 4 Division of the Amalgamated Union of Sheet-Metal Workers or the Management Committee of the Ball's Pond Road Ward Section of the Hackney South and Shoreditch Constituency Labour Party, were doing their bit to keep Britain out of the hands of Harry Pollitt.*

On the details of our meetings, however, Mr Benn's memory (understandably after this length of time) is somewhat at fault. It is true that I went to see him when he was but a lad, and no less true that I asked him if he would be interested in a job; it is also true that I did not, because I was not allowed to, specify the nature of the work involved. But I have just checked my own report of the encounter, prepared for my superiors, and I must say that it differs widely from Mr Benn's version. He says that he told me that he could not take a job because he was planning a career in the Labour Movement, but what he actually said (the room was bugged, of course, at my orders, and I quote from the official transcript) was: 'Does it include a fully transferable non-contributory pension-scheme, four weeks off every calendar year plus official Public Holidays, paternity leave as appropriate, right of three warnings of unsatisfactory work before question of dismissal raised, said

---

* General Secretary of the Communist Party when Mr Wedgwood Benn and I were young.

question to be heard by committee comprising one trade union representative, one management nominee and one independent arbitrator acceptable to both sides, removal allowance, disturbance allowance, dirty work allowance, noise allowance, unsocial hours allowance, overtime at time-and-a-half (maximum nine hours a week) and luncheon vouchers? If so, you're on.'

I suggested that these details, though I was far from regarding them as of no importance, could well wait until the general principle had been established, to which Mr Benn replied, with some heat, in the following terms:

Comrades and fellow-workers! We see again, as we have seen so often, the might of capital arrayed in all its naked brutality to grind down the workers' standard of living, eroded as it already is by the wage-slavery which is their lot. Shall we stand idly by and watch it happen, watch the blood of our comrades shed once again, as it has been shed so often in the past? Shall they continue, year after year, to send the finest of our brothers and sisters to the remote penal colony of Tolpuddle? No! Let us instead stand shoulder to shoulder across the path of reaction, sending these jackals of capitalism about their business, and declaring that we shall not rest until they have been dispatched into the oblivion of history, while the working-class strides ever onward and upward towards the sunlit heights of the technological revolution. Do I have a seconder?

Mr Wedgwood Benn, without waiting for an answer to his question, then drew a small whistle from his waistcoat pocket and blew a piercing blast, accompanying it with a cry of 'Everybody out!' I made an excuse and left.

Some years later, I did indeed, as Mr Benn says, visit him at the House of Commons, though I have to make it clear that this visit was in no way connected with my official business (I had reported to my superiors after the earlier encounter that Mr Wedgwood Benn might prove a little too excitable for the kind of work we had in mind), and was merely for the purpose of seeing whether (Mr Benn was my M.P.) I could obtain a pair of seats for the Public Gallery on behalf of my newly married daughter and son-in-law, who were coming to London for their honeymoon and had expressed a wish to visit Parliament. He very kindly obliged me in the matter, and then raised (I had made no mention of it) the fact that we had met before. Somewhat embarrassed, I said that I recalled the meeting, and expressed polite regret that nothing had come of it. Mr Benn leapt to his feet and began to shout, his words being as follows:

> Brothers and sisters! Once again we see how the Special Patrol Group, the Special Branch, the B-Specials and the other hireling lackeys of the fascist junta that rules this country are combining to put down with ruthless brutality the legitimate protests of the working class – crushed as it is beneath the iron heel of capitalism – at the oppression and victimization to which it is subject. All power to the Workers! Victory to the Workers by hand and brain! Workers of the World Unite! Sus laws out, out, out! Workers' control in, in, in!

He then repeated his trick with the whistle, and I repeated mine with the excuse. But I have often wondered what became of him.

The Times December 11th, 1980

The end is nigh

WHAT IS IT that makes *Savage Amusement*, by Peter Flannery (Royal Shakespeare Company) so depressing an
experience and that on this occasion transforms a subjective
reaction like a feeling of depression into a fundamental criticism of the play? The answer to both questions is the same, and
since I think it also offers an explanation of the appalling
standard of most of the 'committed' drama of the past dozen
years, the topic should be worth exploring.

The play's contents, to be sure, are depressing enough. It is
set among squatters in a derelict house in a dying area of
Manchester, and takes place a few years from now, when
matters have apparently moved far; at any rate, shoplifters can
now be informally birched by Tesco's. (In the last breakdown-
of-civilization play I saw, the Decline of the West was signalled by the news that Norman St John Stevas had just been
made Prime Minister for the second time in a month. I tell
you, one dark night we'll all be murdered in our beds.)

With vigilante squads roaming the streets, the electricity
and water being constantly cut off, and the cheques from
Mummy and Daddy getting fewer and fewer and less substantial, the household subsists on what Fitz, the retarded teenager
whose voluminous overcoat conceals a heart of gold (as well
as, to be on the safe side, a pick handle) can remove undetected
from the supermarket. (If you think the continued existence of
supermarkets provides evidence that civilization has not collapsed after all, hear the bad news: *there's no coffee.*)

Gradually, the members of the group weaken in their

resolve. Some slip away, one moves towards inner death, another nears breakdown; only Fitz, who has never had anything in his life, can face a future in which there is nothing.

The characters, of course, reflect the dying cities, abandoned, written off by the authorities, boarded up and burning. Meanwhile, they talk of everything except hope ('If we had really cared enough, would places like Hulme exist?'); the talk is strident, repetitive, and crudely didactic, and includes lectures on inner-city decay, central housing policy, anomalies in the Social Security system and the customs of the South American Indians. Much of it rings false ('These cuts obviously aren't going to be restored'), and the only thing we were spared was a claim that 2 per cent of the population own 200 per cent of the wealth.

Yet, after all, the things that happen in *King Lear* and *Antigone* are a good deal more terrible than the events in Mr Flannery's play, and for that matter than those in the plays of Trevor Griffiths, David Edgar, John McGrath and Howard Brenton. It is no use saying that Shakespeare and Sophocles were better playwrights; they were also better playwrights than the James Saunders of *Bodies*, the Arnold Wesker of the Kahn trilogy and the Tom Stoppard of *Every Good Boy Deserves Favour*, yet we no more leave those plays in a state of uncontrollable *Weltschmerz* than we feel like making away with ourselves at the end of *Hamlet* merely because of the litter of bodies on the stage.

It is not, then, the grimness of the picture presented that makes the spirit sink; nor is it the overt pessimism; it is not even the shallowness of a playwright who describes a situation which exactly symbolizes the uselessness of political solutions and then goes on to argue ('It can be stopped even now, but only by people facing up and working together') for more of them.

What is it that gives, has always given, human beings their ability to undergo the most frightful privations, sufferings, persecutions and even tortures, and remain, deep in their

hearts where the world, the flesh and the devil cannot pene-
trate, serene? What enables the slave to dance in his chains,
Prince Myshkin to take the sufferings of the world on his
shoulders – and Mr Saunders's Mervyn to recognize, through
his pain and his drunkenness, the equivocation of the fiend that
lies like truth?

It is, first and last, the knowledge that though the capitalists
may be infinitely wicked, and so for that matter may the
communists (not that most of our committed playwrights
would criticize *them*, except perhaps for not being left-wing
enough), the part of life they can affect by their wickedness is,
however horribly they affect it, the unimportant nine-tenths,
while the vital – literally vital – tenth is as far beyond the
danger of being corrupted by the things of this world as the
problems of the nine-tenths are beyond solution by the
methods of the same world. In other words, what is wrong
with this play and scores like it is that though all the facts may
be correct, and all the charges valid, yet in terms of the
qualities that make a work of art the plays suffer from the one
defect that fatally vitiates art: *they are not true*. Most of the
playwrights in question, and certainly this one, show no sign
of even suspecting the existence of that tenth of life that alone
gives life and art their truth and their meaning.

Some of the most telling scenes in *Savage Amusement* are set
in a Social Security office, where various monetary benefits are
being refused, to the distress and despair of the denied. When
Mr Flannery, and his fellow-playwrights of the committed
school, stop for as much as half an hour to wonder why so
many people who have no need of such benefits, being amply
supplied with this world's goods and the wealth to buy more
of them, are nevertheless gnawed by a misery quite as sharp as
that which consumes the wretched of the earth they depict,
they may write some plays of real and enduring worth. *A la
bonne heure.*

Pop go the millions

THEY ORDER THESE things better in the United States. Mr Robert Stigwood, the impresario, is there suing a pop group called the Bee Gees for libel, extortion, corporate defamation and breach of contract; his statement of claim demands £124,000,000 in damages. This action, it seems, is in response to one launched earlier by the said Bee Gees against Mr Stigwood, claiming a total of £82,000,000 (£20,000,000 of which is for punitive damages), on the ground that he had used their talents to create his own fortune, an assertion which he has described as 'ridiculous, false, baseless and without foundation'.

Advanced students of mathematics will already have worked out that the likelihood of a settlement is remote, since if the Bee Gees' claim for 82,000,000 jimmy-o'goblins is set off against Mr Stigwood's demand for 124,000,000 oncers, the resultant balancing of the books will leave the former 42,000,000 quid in the hole. I therefore look forward to some delightful litigation which will, with any luck, leave all the parties to both actions ruined, and only the lawyers happy. (Of course, even the lawyers will find it difficult in this case to bake enough bread to mop up 206,000,000 smackers' worth of gravy, but the difficulty will not, I venture to predict, turn out to be insuperable.)

No; the fate of the litigants, together with the rights and wrongs (if any) of the litigation, do not concern me. I am only interested in the extraordinary fact that the American law of tort seems to consist largely of over-egging the pudding. I do not, of course, know whether Mr Stigwood has been libelled, extorted, corporately defamed or breached in the contract; but let us assume, solely for the sake of the argument and in no way as a comment on the merits of the claims or counter-claims, that Mr Stigwood has indeed suffered such wrongs. Has he, I ask, suffered £124,000,000's worth thereof?

On the whole, and by and large, and taking one consideration with another, and viewing the matter in the round, and of course without in any way prejudging the action, I rather think he has not.

I shall return to this point in a moment, but first I have to say, with that scrupulous impartiality for which I am known from one end of my desk to the other, that much the same appears to me to apply, *mutatis mutandis*, to the claim by the alleged libellers, extortioners, corporate defamers and contract-breachers. Again, I make no comment on the issues between the parties, and take no sides. But I think I am entitled to say that, if the Bee Gees have had their talents used to create Mr Stigwood's fortune, a price-tag of £82,000,000 on the wrong that that would amount to does strike me as being somewhat on the high side.

And it doesn't stop there. Mr Stigwood has denied the Bee Gees' claim, and it is not for me to adjudicate between the claim and the denial. But I am struck by the terms with which he rejects their assertions: the charges, he says, are 'ridiculous, false, baseless *and* [my italics] without foundation'. And that, you must agree, approaches closely a point at which Mr Stigwood could be said to be overdoing things. (No doubt the Bee Gees reject with equal firmness Mr Stigwood's charges; for all I know they have described his accusations as 'untrue, absurd, false, empty, without substance, lacking in credibility, easily refutable, unworthy of belief *and* [my italics again, I'm afraid] unconvincing'.)

I suppose there is a certain consistency here: if you are going to demand as damages a sum considerably larger than the total annual G.N.P. of several member-states of the United

Nations in good standing, it will hardly do to put in your statement of claim that the words complained of are 'by no means wholly substantiated, unimpressive in the authorities relied upon, lacking a due sense of balance and in poor taste', nor will it suffice to say that they have caused you 'irritation, inconvenience and a feeling of not having been treated with the degree of courtesy and fairness that is surely the rightful expectation of any citizen in a free country'. What I always say is that if you're going to lay claim to all the gold in Fort Knox it's no good ringing the bell and then shouting 'Penny for the guy' through the entryphone.

What is more, nobody going to law in America ever seems to learn anything by the amply recorded experience of others. Again and again, plaintiffs claiming $100,000,000 and upwards for libel or breach of contract have ended by being awarded five dollars or the price of a hamburger, whichever shall be the smaller; it has long been clear that putting a price tag on the damages alleged in American civil litigation is about as meaningful an activity as working out *pi* to fifty thousand places of decimals, for the courts, very properly, award what they think the injury is worth, irrespective of what it says on the ticket. (That, of course, is where the British system, in which no sum may be mentioned, scores heavily.)

But that brings me back to my earlier point. What would the Bee Gees have had to say about Mr Stigwood by way of libel and corporate defamation, and what would they have had to do to him in the form of extortion and breach of contract, for it to be worth a sum of money which, if it were paid in pound notes laid end to end, would stretch from London to Brisbane, and to what degree would Mr Stigwood have had to use the Bee Gees' talents to create his own fortune for the damage thus sustained by them to amount to a sum which, measured in the same way, would extend from here to Kuala Lumpur?

This is surely a matter, if ever there was one, in which what imagination does could be correctly described as boggling. For without encroaching on the territory of the court's jurisdiction, it is surely legitimate to wonder whether the Bee Gees had £82,000,000's worth of talent for Mr Stigwood to use in the creation of his own fortune, and indeed whether Mr Stigwood has £124,000,000's worth of reputation to be taken away by libel and corporate defamation, even allowing a sizable chunk of the said sum to be accounted for by extortion and breach of contract.

It is not, of course, easy to be sure, but my own feeling is, most decidedly, that the answer to both those questions is No. Whether the court will take the same view of either party or both, I am in no position to say; I am not sure whether it would constitute contempt of court, or for that matter libel and/or corporate defamation, for me to say I hope so, and I will therefore express no such feeling. And it would be impertinent of me, to put it no more strongly, to remind my readers of Dr Johnson's opinion that there is no settling a point of precedency between a louse and a flea; I shall therefore not do so. But nobody has yet devised a way of stopping a man thinking his thoughts, and I am entitled to think mine, provided I don't do it in the streets and frighten the lawyers.

And it must be said that the Bee Gees and Mr Stigwood are by no means wholly to blame in the inflated ideas they have acquired as to their own worth, or for that matter their own talents. For many years now, our world has told them that they are the salt of it, that art had but stumbled, a child in the dark, until they came along to found an 'alternative culture' which would flood the universe with a new and enduring light. If someone tells the writers of this kind of rubbish that they are 'the greatest song-writers since Schubert' (an actual example), it is hardly surprising that they come to believe it, and not much more remarkable that archbishops and cabinet ministers hasten to take them seriously. In time, it comes to seem true, or almost so, and those who have not forgotten that it is false lose the energy to go on saying so. Presently, it is the received wisdom, and gets into the history books, and another victory is recorded for Gresham's Law, while the creators and promoters of the bad money go to court for hundreds of millions of pounds, and think themselves well worth it. Lay on, then, Bee Gees! Lay on. Stigwood! And damn'd be him, like, that first, I mean, cries, 'Hold, enough!'

The Times November 12th, 1980

Putting pen to paper

WHAT A MARVELLOUS remark that was of Andrei Sinyavsky's: 'Balzac and Dumas wrote mountains of books because they had the good luck to own plenty of clean paper.' I think you could tell a man's character and certainly his profession, from his response to it; if you think it is simply nonsense, for instance, you have never written a line more significant than a thank-you note. If you think it is true, you are one of those writers (they range from the greatest geniuses to the lowliest scribblers) who not only know how little literature depends upon inspiration and how much upon simply regarding it as work to be done, but actually put the knowledge into practice. If you think the remark is false, you *may* be one of the world's great creative artists (though I don't think you are, or I would surely have heard of you). But if the effect of the remark upon you was to cause a violent fit of the screaming heebie-jeebies, you are a journalist, and there is nothing you can do about it, short of hanging yourself.

The occupational disease of this trade is a constitutional inability to get down to work a moment earlier than is absolutely necessary, and the lengths to which I will go to prevent myself actually putting anything on to a clean piece of paper sometimes make me think that they will be coming to take me to the funny-farm any day now. I calculate that I have eaten at least 7,000 tons of digestive biscuits in my time solely because the prospect of eating a digestive biscuit seemed to me more inviting than sitting down and hitting the keys of the typewriter.

There are, of course, journalists (it was Desmond Mac-Carthy, prince of procrastinators, who wrote the journalists' terrible motto: There's always another quarter of an hour) who go further, and fail to start writing in time, or even at all, but these are a different class altogether, for the point of my kind, which is the overwhelming majority, is that we have calculated the time necessary to write whatever has to be written with such precision that we always do finish in time. But the ones who don't get the article written at all are the sad cases, and the excuses they have to invent would fill many thousands of Arabian nights. Greatest of all was one thought of by the late John Davenport when he was unusually hard-pressed, even for him, to explain why his book review had not been delivered. 'But I brought it in yesterday,' he said down the phone to the features editor in hurt tones; 'you were out, and I left it on your desk.' A pause, and then he added with an audible start: 'Oh, wait a minute – I remember now, the window was open; maybe it blew out.'

How different from Balzac and Dumas and Sinyavsky. How different from Trollope, who wrote with his watch upon his desk, and clocked up an absolutely unvarying 1,000 words an hour – and no messing, for it was not only 1,000 an hour, but a regular two hundred and fifty in each quarter. If you have never actually written for a living, it is almost impossible to believe that such a method can produce great books, but there are Trollope's to show that it can.*

The kind of journalist I envy is the one who can simply go to a telephone and talk his story down it; Philip Hope-Wallace can even do this with theatre reviews, and many's the time at Stratford-upon-Avon, while I have been struggling to get the *mot juste* down on paper with the minutes ticking away, that I have heard Philip in the next room effortlessly fluting his notice the moment he has got back to the hotel, and without

* 'Great' now seems to me much too strong for Trollope; shall we say 'admirably entertaining'?

first writing down a word of it. The Harold Robbins school of novelists does the equivalent today, of course, when they talk their novels into tape-recorders, and the thought chills the blood even more than Trollope's watch, for how can art be dictated like a letter to a stockbroker? So we feel, but we are falling into that grammatical error that used to be called 'the container for the thing contained', for if *Paradise Lost* could be dictated to an amanuensis, who shall rebuke Mr Robbins for dictating his novels to a machine? (Possibly Mr Robbins's novels are not as good as *Paradise Lost*, but that is another matter.)

Journalists are usually poor letter-writers; I am a very bad correspondent indeed. I have heard it said that this is because of the instinctive distaste we feel at writing something we are not going to be paid for, but I cannot believe we have quite such mercenary subconsciouses; it is more probably because since, in our work, we are always striving to get the greatest possible effect, the essential spontaneity of a letter escapes us. The real creative artist, who does not consciously strive for effect at all (though he may re-write a passage dozens of times), does not have this problem; I believe that it is in this instinctive grasp of the effect of his words that there lies the only sure test of the real artist. When Shakespeare wrote:

> . . . Nay, this my hand will rather
> The multitudinous seas incarnadine,
> Making the green one red

he surely never thought consciously that it was the contrast between the two mighty polysyllables and the musket-fire of the last line that made the passage so effective, let alone that showed him to be a great writer. I am less sure about Virgil's two celebrated onomatopoeias, *Quadrupedante putrem sonitu quatit ungula campum* (in which we can hear, provided we have scanned it aright, the very thunder of the hooves that the line is about), and *Illi inter sese, magna vi brachia tollunt* (in which we hear no less clearly the hammer on the forge); I rather suspect that Virgil did think of the effect first and then juggle words until he found some that would achieve it.

All of which has taken me far from Sinyavsky's *mot*. But he made a better, and less questionable one: 'Paper exists to enable a man to forget himself amid its whiteness.' Say 'art' instead of 'paper', and Mr Sinyavsky's is a considerable achievement, for man has been trying to define art ever since he invented it. A man I met at a party once did even better; he defined love. Unfortunately, I was rather tight at the time, and I forgot his definition before the morning; every time I have met him since, he has refused to repeat it (perhaps we were both tight and he forgot it too). Anyhow, I have filled a considerable expanse of white paper by now.

The Times November 22nd, 1973

Expectation exceeded

THE TAJ MAHAL has a great deal to live up to. So much, indeed, that there can be few thoughtful visitors today who,
knowing something of its reputation, do not fear the betrayal
of expectation. How can *anything* justify the rhapsodies, the
descriptions, the history, the legends, the very photographs?

I confirm that it was in such a spirit, almost with fingers
crossed behind my back, that I paid my two rupees, passed
through the outer arch, and approached the inner, which
serves, when you have advanced to the right point, as a frame
for the picture before you. Fear nothing; the sight that there
swims into view surpasses everything you have heard or seen
or read or imagined, and almost the only intense emotion you
will not experience as the frame fills is disappointment.

They told me that the Taj Mahal is beautiful, and they were
right. They also told me that it is white, though here they were
wrong, for white is almost the only colour it is not, except for
a few minutes immediately after the sun goes down; at that
point all the delicate blues and greys and yellows and pinks are
drawn from it and leave it like a ghost, until it takes on its
evening life and becomes as rich as the moon.

They were right about the beauty, and wrong about the
colour. What they altogether omitted to mention was the fact
that it is perfectly symmetrical. Apart from the flight of steps,
in the front, leading up to the marble platform on which the
whole building rests, it is completely symmetrical in two
senses. Each of the four sides is identical with the other three,
not only in shape and size but in the last detail of decoration;

and each side could be folded over on the central perpendicular, when the two halves would be found to match exactly. The Taj Mahal, in short, is God Almighty's Rohrschach blot, and says much for the attractiveness of the patient's subconscious.

There has been much argument over the identity of the architect; I gather that modern scholarship generally suggests that Shah Jehan designed it himself. If so, Plato's philosopher-king was surely embodied in him, for although I have the liveliest respect for the wide variety of accomplishments displayed by our Heir Apparent, I take leave to doubt if he is quite up to creation of this order. (And on this scale; the other thing they didn't tell me was how enormous it is.)

It floats. And this is not an allusion to the way in which it is reflected in the long watercourse that runs from the entrance to the very foot of the building, though that is indeed a miracle within a miracle, particularly when, at evening, the fountains, evenly spaced down the centre of the channel, are turned on, so that the shimmering reflection of the building turns into a snowstorm, a Seurat, a kaleidoscope, a dancing mosaic. But even without the water, the Taj Mahal would still float.

It sits, as I say, on a square platform, and the huge central cupola, guarded by the four minarets (which draw the eye inward, not out to the corners where they stand) is of enormous size; the façade, too, is a mighty wall of marble, and the arched door and windows, together with the pierced screens and the coloured inlays beneath the dome, ought logically to appear as supporters for the stupendous mass and weight above. Instead, they act as tethers to what otherwise would soar into the sky. It is not just that the architecture is delicate, the weight run off like rainwater or lightning; it really does seem lighter than air, and the dome, as you watch, seems to be made of egg-shell.

Actually, the image we have from the pictures (and even at first glance) of a hemisphere cupola, is an optical illusion; the curve continues well below the circumference, into, and almost to the lower edge of, the decorated 'collar' in which it rests, which must presumably have made the construction even more difficult. There is another optical illusion built into it; the verses from the Koran that surround the central arch on each side are inscribed in lettering which grows larger towards the top, so that from the ground it looks of uniform size, instead of appearing to shrink as it would if it *were* all the same size. This is like the famous 'bulge' in the platform of the Parthenon, which would otherwise look as though it was sagging towards the middle. (I was on the Acropolis at Christmas, shocked to find that you can no longer go inside the Parthenon, and it occurs to me that I do not often see two of the seven wonders of the world within a month. Who first worked out the need for these two devices? And who, incidentally, first noticed that they had been employed?)

The Taj Mahal provokes more questions than those. Every block in the mighty dome, for instance, must be curved to a particular formula, and no curve in any one layer will be exactly the same as in the layers above and below. (The image of the dome is of almost incredible smoothness and regularity.) How was the appallingly complex problem that this posed solved without a computer and other modern tools? (Mind you, every imaginable scientific aid is available to architects today, and the result can be seen in Juxon House, the Hayward Gallery, the north and west sides* of George Square, Edinburgh, and the building in which these words were typed and printed. They had ShahJehan and the Taj Mahal, and we have Colonel Seifert and Victoria Street: *Allah akbar.*)

I found my own reactions extraordinary; at any rate extraordinary enough for me to spend a lot of time thinking about them. The comparison that came to mind was with the Wieskirche, that baroque masterpiece near Munich which I have on occasion gone several hundred miles out of my way to visit. Zimmerman's Christian church seems to be made en-

---

* Now the south side as well.

tirely of light; I dream of one day hearing a performance of _The Creation_ within its walls, and its effect on me – not just at my first sight of it but every time – is a great burst of sunlit joy inside the brain, illuminating the universe from within.

The Taj Mahal, on the other hand, seems to be made of air, and the effect it had on me was to induce a kind of cosmic sadness, which grew in intensity through the hours I spent there every day (I stayed three days in the vicinity), until I began to feel it would kill me; on the last evening, when I turned to leave, with no more time in hand than was necessary to get to the airport, I did not dare to look back through the arch at the framed view as I left, for the fear of being turned into a pillar of marble and for the certainty that I would weep.

This laceration of the heart I also feel when I hear the main theme of the _adagio_ of the Ninth Symphony, when I stand before one of the late Rembrandt self-portraits, and every time I go down the Grand Canal. The obvious conclusion is that those are the things that enable me to hear the secret harmonies of the universe, and the obvious conclusion is probably the right one. If so, I presume the sadness comes from my inability to hear them all the time and at full strength, and if _that_ is so then I can say that I can never have felt the inability so keenly as I did before the Taj Mahal.

On that last day, I sat till the sun went down; as it did, a huge flight of birds flapped slowly before the dome, 'making their course to the rooky wood'. They made a quivering black ribbon for it, gently pulled across by an invisible hand, and when they were gone the building donned its evening garb, the colours more delicate than ever, the lightness more pronounced; and it was time to go. For the next ten days I kept making impossible plans, involving air timetables of ferocious complexity, to get back for a final glimpse before leaving India. It could not, in fact, be done, so instead of impossible plans I made a possible vow: to return.

The Times February 3rd, 1978

For the colour of his hair

THE CASE OF Mr John Saunders is an instance of injustice committed by people who ought to have known better and reinforced by people whose job was to put it right. It has implications far beyond the effects on the victim, striking as it does at one of the fundamental principles of our law, and thus seems to me to be doubly worth writing about.

Mr Saunders is a homosexual. For two years he was employed, as a handyman, at a residential camp for schoolchildren in Aberfoyle, Perthshire. There were no complaints about his work or his conduct, he has no criminal record, and there has been no suggestion that he ever attempted to indulge his sexual tendencies with any of the children who stayed at the camp; these facts are agreed by all parties involved in the matter.

None the less, when the nature of his sexual orientation came to the notice of those who run the camp, by whom he was employed, Mr Saunders was dismissed. He went before an Employment Appeal Tribunal, asking for a declaration that the dismissal was unfair; he naturally wanted the appropriate financial compensation that would follow such a ruling, but his application was also, no doubt, designed to challenge the monstrous assumption that a man (or for that matter a woman) may be dismissed from a job because, and *only* because, of a homosexual nature. The tribunal ruled that his dismissal was not unfair, on grounds as bizarre and disturbing as have been heard since the notorious 1941 case of Liversedge *v.* Anderson, in which the House of Lords, over the noble and impassioned dissent of Lord Atkin, decided that in a statute directly affecting the liberties of the subject the words 'If the Home Secretary has reasonable cause to believe' meant 'If the Home Secretary *thinks* [however mistakenly, absurdly or indefensibly] that he has reasonable cause to believe'.

The members of the tribunal agreed, like everybody else, that Mr Saunders had given no cause for complaint or suspicion. They went further, and declared that there was no evidence to suggest that homosexuals are any more inclined to paedophiliac conduct than heterosexuals. But they then added that there are people who believe that homosexuals are a greater risk to the sexual integrity of children than heterosexuals, and that in deference to that prejudice they would refuse Mr Saunders a declaration that his dismissal was unfair.

Mr Saunders now wants to appeal to a court from the tribunal's decision. I am bound to say that his hopes of relief from the Scottish courts are slim; some of the judges north of Berwick appear to believe that Lord Goddard was a milksop and Judge Jeffreys a sentimental old fool. But what happens to Mr Saunders is only part of the scandal; the greater part lies in the fact that if he does not get legal redress it will have been judicially established that a citizen who is wholly blameless may be punished because some people believe that *other* people, not including the citizen in question, might, in certain circumstances, behave wrongly.

I think the best thing to say about such a prospect is that it simply *must not be*. The prejudice against homosexuals referred to by the tribunal (incidentally, they failed to adduce any evidence of it) has dogged those of the 'wrong' sexual orientation for very many years; ironically, it seems to have increased since the barbaric legal penalties for homosexual acts were removed. But this is no time to be strengthening it.

As I have said before, one charge that can reasonably be laid at the door of many homosexuals is that they fail to understand, let alone take into reasonable account, the depth and origins of the prejudice against them felt by many otherwise reasonable heterosexuals. But that, as I have also said before, is a small failing beside the prejudice itself, let alone beside some of the more revolting examples of its expression and of the effects it has. And what is so deplorable and dangerous about the particular expression and effect of the prejudice suffered by Mr Saunders is that it formally enshrines, in a quasi-judicial context, the principle that the prejudice of parties who are not themselves involved in a case, and indeed whose existence is only assumed, not proved, may be used as a basis for a binding decision.

Now do you see why this must not be? The world, after all, does not exactly lack prejudice. Some people, for instance (Mr Enoch Powell is, or was, one of them), believe that black immigrants are given to the curious practice of thrusting excrement through the letterboxes of white citizens. May we now look forward to the day when an African or West Indian loses a case before a judicial body not because he has done such a thing, or even because others of his colour have done it, but because certain people of a different colour believe that those of his are likely to do it if they are given a chance? You call that fantasy, do you? Pray, what would you yesterday have called the case of Mr Saunders?

The roots of prejudice – sexual, racial, religious, national, political – are long, twisted and old; they will not be rapidly or easily grubbed up. Laws designed to make us love those we hate are doomed to failure, and their proponents to bewilderment and disappointment. But laws designed to regulate our conduct rather than our feelings are another matter, and it is significant that those hostile to laws which prohibit racial discrimination in, say, housing or employment, have always sought to blur this distinction, and to implant the idea that because it is impossible to stop a hotelier feeling revulsion at the thought of a black head on one of his pillows, it is somehow unreasonable to forbid him to put up signs saying 'No niggers here'. But it is not unreasonable; if he accepts the legal obligations of one who holds himself out to provide

accommodation for all who can pay and will behave themselves, the law may indeed insist that he does not pick and
choose, on grounds of colour, among those who seek the use
of his facilities.

So let it be with homosexuals. There is no evidence, *as was
agreed by the employment tribunal which ruled against Mr Saunders*,
that homosexuals are any more likely than heterosexuals to
seduce children in their care (and it is worth stressing that the
children at the Aberfoyle camp were *not* in Mr Saunders's care
anyway – he was a handyman, not a teacher, supervisor or
group leader). That being so, those who ran the camp had no
business dismissing him because of the prejudice of others, the
tribunal had no business ruling that the existence of that
prejudice rendered this dismissal fair, and the Scottish courts
have no business upholding that ruling. I hope they will not.*

The Times April 24th, 1980

* But they did.

Never on Sundry

I AM GETTING A great deal of quiet pleasure out of the row over the suggestion by the Education Secretary, Mr Carlisle, that local authorities should publish the examination results of the schools in their areas, and since quiet pleasure, though very agreeable, is not nearly so much fun as the noisy kind, I think I ought to do what I can to raise the decibel count.

As you would expect if you have been following the story, our old and valued friend A. Spokesman has not been idle; his latest contribution, made on behalf of the National Association of Head Teachers, can serve both as a useful summary of the story so far and as an indication of what passes for thinking in the camp of those resisting the Education Secretary's modest proposal.

Mr Carlisle is accused by our friend of 'being obsessed with statistics', whereas 'cold statistics are quite misleading and can unfairly misrepresent many good schools'. (I am not quite sure how you can *fairly* misrepresent many good schools, but education has rarely been thought necessary for those engaged in providing it, and this may be no more than an illustration of the fact.) But A. Spokesman (or 'A' as he is amusingly known to his friends) goes on to make clear the danger that he foresees from the use of cold statistics.

'You may', he says judiciously, 'have a school in a run-down inner city whose examination results don't appear to be very impressive. Yet the efforts it makes on behalf of its pupils may be just as extensive, at a different level, as those made by a residential area school with a high academic record.' Yes, indeed; quite possibly. On the other hand, you may have another school, in the same run-down inner city, whose examination results appear to be frightfully impressive, but which makes virtually no efforts at all on behalf of its pupils. Then again, you may have a residential area school with a low academic record which makes enormously extensive efforts on behalf of its pupils, a school in a different run-down inner city with a high academic record *and* extensive efforts, two more residential area schools, one of which does, and one of which does not, make extensive efforts, three more schools in a run-up outer city, of which one has a high academic record, one makes extensive efforts and one produces examination results which don't appear to be very impressive, fourteen more schools in various other run-down inner cities, not necessarily one to each, many of which have examination results more (or less) impressive than those of others, thirty-seven residential area schools with academic records varying from very high to very low, a pair of schools – one in a run-down inner city and one in a residential area – which both have headmasters who are drunk from morning till night and have to be shut in a cupboard if their schools are to produce any examination results at all, impressive or unimpressive, sixty-six other schools which . . . but the permutations are endless, and there is little point in continuing with them.

In any case 'A' eventually abandons (not a moment too soon, in my view) the marshy ground of hypothesis for the *terra firma* of dogmatism. 'Parents and prospective parents', he says, 'are entitled to know the academic attainments of the school;' (too kind, too kind) but, 'equally, the school is entitled to state these attainments within the context of the school, its environment, and any other factors which are relevant.' Above all, however, examination results 'should not be available to all and sundry.'

Now here, at last, I am directly addressed, and feel entitled to express an opinion. For although I am not, and would not claim to be, all, I am, you may be interested to learn, sundry. I have been sundry all my life, and have been getting steadily sundrier as the years go by; indeed I doubt if you could find a sundrier man in a day's march. And speaking in that capacity, I must say that in my experience it is very frequently true that people who find it embarrassing for the facts about them and their work to be published do tend, as in the case of the National Association of Head Teachers (A. Spokesman up), to find reasons for banning, censoring and suppressing those facts, and in particular for ensuring that they are not available to all, much less to sundry. But you see, sundry, in democratic countries, are the people in charge, that being a definition of democracy, and the point about democracy is that sundry are entitled to make up their own minds on whatever facts seem to *them* relevant and significant. Countries where somebody else decides which facts are relevant and significant, and permits those facts, and no others, to be published, are not democracies but something quite different.

Naturally, the suppressors, banners and censors in the examination-results row are not usually quite so crass as our friend (who did not fail to say in addition that 'setting out results in a standard form would produce a league table mentality which would be extremely damaging'), but no amount of sophisticated talk about not taking examination results out of context, and regarding them as constituting only one part of a wider basis for assessment, and deploring the concentration on them at a time when most far-seeing educationalists consider them of less importance than was once supposed, will disguise the unlovely truth, which is that those who are protesting against Mr Carlisle's proposal are trying to keep secret important information which the public, also known as sundry, are well entitled to have, and, in the most literal sense, do have an interest in acquiring.

The information, say the censors, might be misunderstood, misinterpreted and misused. I dare say it might; I can think of no information whatever which would be permanently immune from misunderstanding, misinterpretation or misuse, not excluding Pythagoras's Theorem, which to my certain knowledge has frequently led to innocent bystanders being accidentally stabbed in the hypotenuse. But it is also fundamental to democracy that sundry, in being allowed to make their own judgments, are also allowed to come to mistaken or foolish conclusions as well as correct and wise ones, and if people need large quantities of information in order to have a good chance of coming to the latter rather than the former, it seems imperfectly logical for those insisting that more information is essential to combine that insistence with a resolute attempt to provide less.

As a matter of fact, we have been here before, though you would have to be as wicked as I am even to remember, let alone to remind all and sundry. Some years ago, the people running the Advisory Centre for Education announced that they intended to publish, in respect of the public schools, their figures for university entrance – a proposal which would have had, among other effects, that of blowing the gaff in a large way on the widespread but erroneous belief that because the best public-school education is very good indeed, *any* public-school education must be good, whereas the truth is that some of it is quite outstandingly lousy, and that the incidence of lousiness is by no means entirely confined to the less famous establishments. The public schools had three dozen varieties of fit simultaneously, and found an ingenious way out of their embarrassment by copyrighting the information in question; they thus prevented ACE from publishing it, and Dr Smart-Allick and Narkover breathed more easily. But all the arguments that we have been hearing these past few weeks were presented on the earlier occasion in exactly the same form (I believe that A. Spokesman's late father, A. B. Spokesman, was involved), and were just about as plausible and convincing then as they are now. I hope Mr Carlisle will not be dissuaded from pursuing his excellent and useful proposal, and so say sundry of us.

The Times December 9th, 1980

Down Quality Street

A S A BOOK-COLLECTOR, I am of that deplorable species, the magpie. My shelves groan under volumes on so many disparate subjects that anybody attempting to deduce what sort of man I am from the evidence of my library alone, would conclude that I was either the greatest polymath since Leonardo da Vinci, or one who was incapable of keeping his mind on the same subject for more than half an hour at a time. Fortunately, it is not for me to say which; but either explanation will account for the amazing way in which my head is stuffed with such a vast collection of entirely useless knowledge. I know, among other things, that camels cannot walk backwards and horses cannot be sick; that Drury Lane Theatre burned to the ground a fortnight after the first safety-curtain in the world was installed in it; that Beethoven contemplated an opera based on *Faust*; and that the German for one who assassinates the aunt of an African chieftain is *ein Hottentottenpotentatentantentotenattentäter*. I have a book explaining that the plays of Shakespeare were written by the Earl of Oxford; a three-volume bibliography of improper literature; a *catalogue raisonné* of all the airports in the world; fourteen editions of the poems of François Villon; two complete shelves full of books proving, to the authors' satisfaction at any rate, that President Kennedy was not killed by Lee Harvey Oswald; a book about lighthouses; a book about Thuggee; and a history of false teeth.

But I have rarely had a completely otiose bibliophilic pleasure keener than that generated by a little book I have just plucked from the catalogue of the good Mr Steedman of Newcastle-upon-Tyne. It is called *The Fashionable Court Guide*, or Town Visiting Directory; it was published in 1793, and the preface makes clear that it is the second annual edition to appear. (The compiler signs himself simply P. Boyle, and the only thing I can discover about him is that he is not in the *D.N.B.*)

The book consists of, as P. Boyle puts it, 'the address of every person of rank and distinction in town'. There are two lists of these; one is in straight alphabetical order of their surnames, and in the other 'the polite inhabitants of each street are also given in a separate and numerical manner, so that you see at one view, the various circles of fashion, and become acquainted in an instant with the names of those who surround you.' Naturally, what a man who acquires such a book does is to look up, first his name, and second his address. I was not surprised to find that there was not a single Levin, for the Levins have, alas, rarely been among the polite inhabitants of anywhere (the *rude* inhabitants, now . . .), but I was a little put out to discover that although the house in which I live existed then, and its next door neighbours in 1793 contained Matthew Lewis and the Marquis Titchfield respectively (while across the road at No. 39, where my doctor now is, there dwelt Admiral Allen, and at No. 36 General Annesley), my No. 10 was not listed as containing any person of rank or distinction at all.

Such disappointments, however, were heavily outweighed by the opportunity the book has given me to acquire yet more useless information. What shall it profit me, for instance, to know that Charles James Fox lived at 26 South Street, off Grosvenor Square? He is my hero, it is true, but his address is of no importance, yet it is now in my head, and will never leave. (Burke, meanwhile, was living at 6 Duke Street, St James's, and Pitt, reasonably enough in view of the fact that he was Prime Minister at the time, in Downing Street.)

The Duke of Gloucester was at 33 Upper Grosvenor Street,

and the Bishop thereof at 43 Davies Street; Wilberforce lived in Old Palace Yard and Samuel Whitbread in Lower Grosvenor Street; Wilkes is not listed at all, though I would have thought that he had worked his passage into polite society by then.

Sometimes, P. Boyle has been unable to find the forenames of the people of rank and distinction, and lists them by their surnames only, so that 'Pypps, Esq.' is listed at 41, Charlotte Street and 'Foyster, Esq.' at 7 Grafton Street, while at 46 Dean Street, Soho, there lived a couple of sinister-sounding fellows (resurrection-men, if you ask me) known simply as 'Randall and Mogg'.

Sloane Street contained (at No. 91) a Miss Whippam, and (at No. 81) a Mrs Twigg, though whether these were their real names, or whether they were the precursors of that lady whose card I once saw displayed on a newsagent's window-board, giving her telephone number and continuing 'Clarissa Wippley-Roddley welcomes old and new clients', P. Boyle does not say. The Reverend Mr Pennock appeared to live in the British Museum.

One interesting fact to emerge from *The Fashionable Court Guide* is that polite London society in 1793 numbered no more than about 5,000. The first census, in 1801, gave the population of 'London and suburbs' as 864,000 (incidentally, is it or is it not true that, as I have been told, one of the tables in the 1851 census, giving the figures by occupations, in order of the numbers of people engaged in each, ended with the memorable rubric 'Queens, one, Bumboat-women, one'?), so it presumably would not have been much smaller than that eight years earlier. Is 1 to 160 a reasonable ratio for the polite? I find it distinctly on the high side, considering that the *Guide* lists only heads of families and the census, of course, the entire population. But imagine the fuss if somebody tried to revive such a directory today, with half those left out suing for libel, and half those put in protesting that they are opposed to such snobbery!

The Times June 19th, 1973

How to know when you're not wanted

I T IS REPORTED THAT

The owner of a hairdressing salon who punched one of
his staff in the face, dragged him across the salon floor and
kneed him in the groin, said at an industrial tribunal in
Birmingham that he had not dismissed him. But the tribunal accepted a claim that such treatment was tantamount
to unfair dismissal.

The Birmingham Industrial Tribunal will be very happy to
learn that I entirely agree with their interpretation of Paragraph 4, Section 1, of the First Schedule to the Trade Union
and Labour Relations Act 1974. It is true that there is no
generally accepted definition of dismissal, but most people, I
imagine, would feel that it is a matter of intimating to the
person to be dismissed that his continued presence is not
required.

There are obviously many ways in which the information
can be conveyed, the most familiar being the words 'You're
fired'. The fact that there are ample means already at hand for
telling an employee to get his cards need not, however, inhibit
an employer from seeking new ones, and the employer in this
case could certainly be said to have extended the horizons of
dismissal. But the unconventional nature of his approach (and
the approach must anyway be a matter of taste) should not be
allowed to blind us to the facts. The important thing about

sacking a man is to ensure that he knows he is sacked, and an employer who punches one of his workforce in the face, hauls him across the floor, and knees him in the groin, though he might lay himself open to criticism on a charge of severity, could not by any stretch of the imagination be accused of ambiguity, particularly when, as was also disclosed in the findings of the tribunal, he then attempted to drag the employee outside 'so that he could have a real go'. The dismissed man might well have felt that the go his employer had already had was about as real as goes can be, but at any rate he could hardly have been in any doubt that his dreams of working his way up through the firm, possibly ending as a full partner, were at an end.

Nor, as a matter of fact, *was* he in any doubt; it was the employer who insisted that what he had done did not amount to dismissal. The report of the tribunal's judgment does not, unfortunately, give the employer's reasoning, and one can only speculate as to what he thought he was doing, if it was not engaging in dismissal, when he punched the man in the face, dragged him across the floor, kneed him in the groin and then made clear that he wished to take him outside and hurt him.

The trouble with such speculation, however, is that it leaves so very little room for manoeuvre. What *was* he trying to convey, if it wasn't that he no longer required the services of the man at the receiving end? It may be said that we know nothing of the employer's motives in the matter, or of what alleged conduct on the part of the employee had driven him to it. But I cannot see how, if we knew what the man had done or was supposed to have done, this would help us. After all, the question is not whether the employer was *right* to sack him, but whether he *had* sacked him, and unless he was going to argue that the man had on an earlier occasion asked for a lesson in all-in-wrestling and thereafter forgotten that he had done so, I really cannot see how a denial of dismissal, in the circumstances described, could be sustained.

Mind you, though it takes us no further on the main question, it is permissible to wonder just what it was that the worker had done to get his boss into quite such a tizzy. I would remind you that the business was a hairdresser's, and although it is not clear in what capacity the man was employed, it is not unreasonable to assume that he was in the business of dressing hair. But we should not assume too readily that he had absent-mindedly dyed the hair of the Deputy Chairman of the Brierly Hill Watch Committee bright green, or (supposing this to be one of the now-fashionable unisex salons) cut off all or some of the Lady Mayoress's ears. In those circumstances, the vigorous action described would surely have been undertaken in the first instance by the indignant customer, and there is no suggestion that anybody but the boss was involved.

Industrial espionage can, I think, be ruled out. Though an employer would certainly be entitled to feel, and indeed to express, considerable anger at the passing of the details of his firm's secret processes to a rival company, and though it would even be understandable, however deplorable, if in the face of such disloyalty he were to lose control in the manner under discussion, I cannot bring myself to believe that an employee of a West Midlands hairdressing salon was subjected to so very vigorous a rebuke for revealing the firm's newly devised technique of blow-waving, say, to the shop across the road. But if the scope for such activity in a hairdressing salon is limited, the opportunity for conduct really meriting the action taken seems even more so. How *do* you bring the owner of a hairdressing salon to such a pitch?

This is beginning to be a riddle wrapped in a mystery inside an enigma. After all, if a man punches you in the face, drags you across the floor, knees you in the groin and makes it clear that that treatment is only by way of being *hors d'oeuvres* to the feast, it would not be at all unreasonable for you to take him to law. But surely a summons for assault, not to mention battery, would seem the appropriate remedy, rather than a claim for wrongful dismissal? Are we to understand that the dismissed man was complaining not at the *manner* of his dismissal, but at the dismissal itself, so that he was directly or implicitly seeking reinstatement? If so, reason totters on her throne, for surely a man who has been bitten in the left leg by a tiger, and deduced from the beast's demeanour that it is keen to devour him altogether, would not, following so narrow an escape, be eager to meet the creature again, taking such eagerness so far as to initiate legal action, the effect of which would be to bring about just such a meeting, before some court of fur and feather?

But this is taking us far from the subject of our original inquiry, which was concerned with the thought-processes of a man who makes a determined effort to convert one of his employees into steak tartare and then denies having meant by such action to dismiss him. 'It was almost immaterial', said the chairman of the industrial tribunal which ruled that the action was indeed tantamount to dismissal (and unfair dismissal, too), 'what he did after that', and a more admirably concise summary of a situation I never expect to see. It may be, of course, that if the employer, even while he was bashing the living daylights out of his employee, had been careful to keep shouting, 'But I'm not dismissing you, you know – indeed (take *that*) so anxious am I to retain your valuable services (*and* that) that I am considering (I bet *that* hurt) offering you a substantial increase in pay (just you wait till I get you outside), provided that it is well within the terms of the Social Contract (I haven't finished with you yet, not by a long chalk), so perhaps we might open discussions on a productivity deal (as soon as I've pulled your head right off your bloody shoulders)', the tribunal might have had no option but to uphold his contention that his action did not amount to dismissal.

Fortunately, no such nice question of law arose. On the other hand, the principal mystery remains. A man punches another man in the face, drags him across the floor, knees him in the groin, makes it clear that he considers the treatment inadequate, and then denies that he intended to convey a dislike of the victim's company sufficiently strong for him to wish to dispense with it altogether. His denial was found unconvincing. Can he really claim to be surprised?

The Times June 2nd, 1978

As to the manna born

'STOP THE FARES rise!' cried a poster on a wall I was passing the other day. An excellent suggestion, I thought, and stopped to read further, though as it happened there was not much further to read, for the solution to the problem was as succinct as the statement of it. 'Demand more government aid to London!' it urged, and that was all.

I am aware, and I face the knowledge with a heavy heart, that this country has come to such a pass that many of my readers did not immediately spot the fallacy in the poster I have quoted, and that even now I have said that there is a fallacy in it some will not spot it until I explain. (That in itself is matter well worth comment, for it would once have been otherwise, but the route by which we reached our present pass is not the substance of my song today, and will only be touched upon in a grace-note or two.)

Now 'aid', in the context of stopping London fares from rising, must, of course, mean money; what is demanded, therefore, is 'government money'. But what exactly is government money? Obviously, those responsible for demanding it are not thinking of the personal fortune possessed by the Benn family, or of the money Mr Wilson made from his memoirs; the money owned by members of the government is not what is meant by 'government money'. What is referred to is money raised from taxation under legislation passed by this or previous governments. This, however, is obviously not 'government' money before it is raised; it is ours, and it is taken from us, by law. But then it can hardly be called 'government' money after it has been taken from us, either, though it might possibly be called 'public' money with some justice provided it is clearly understood by all concerned what 'public' means in the context.

No doubt I am making heavy weather of a minor exercise in semantics, but I believe I am doing so to some purpose. For if those who put up the poster had wanted to be strictly honest with their readers, or at any rate to leave their readers in no doubt as to what exactly was involved, the exhortation would have read not 'Demand more government aid to London!' but 'Demand that other people should pay *their* money to keep *your* fares from rising!'

Put like that, of course, it would raise all the questions it carefully refrains from asking in its present form. 'Government' money is a bland, featureless substance; nobody has ever owned it, let alone loved it and cared for it. 'Government' money was not created by labour, thrift or even luck; it was just found in heaps on the floor. 'Government' money can properly be used for any purpose; no question can arise, in the case of 'government' money, as to whether it should or should not be spent; and above all, 'government' money is limitless.

In a sense, of course, we have reached, by constantly telling ourselves that the state must do more and more and individuals less and less, a point at which 'government' money actually *is* limitless, in that if no more can be raised by taxation it will simply be printed. But even in less notional terms the idea that 'government' money somehow undergoes a subtle but profound change on leaving our pockets (which is, after all, where it comes from) has taken such a hold that Chancellors of the most honourable and upright character, holding the most rigidly orthodox views of public finance, have seen nothing odd in saying – when presenting their Budgets, for instance – things like: 'I can afford to be a bit more generous here', or: 'This concession will cost £200 million in a full year'.

But it is even worse than that. The depths to which we have sunk in the perversion of language and the thought it expresses could be seen all too clearly in the House of Commons only last week, during the discussion over the proposal to let old age pensioners have television licences free or at reduced rates. This repulsive and patronizing suggestion was supported by Labour, Scottish Nationalist and Conservative speakers; even the official Opposition speaker in the debate, though he did suggest that it might be better to give pensioners more money rather than benefits in kind, seemed half-hearted about it, and only Mr Galbraith attacked the idea at its odious root.

And *isn't* it odious? Is it not odious, and worse than odious, that we are now so steeped in the idea that the state must do everything and the individual nothing that we throw old people such bones as free television licences and free bus travel and cheap tobacco, rather than giving them more money and allowing them to spend it on what they like?

And, of course, as soon as we ask that question the larger question of subsidies arises. Very poor people, it is widely agreed, cannot afford butter. So we give money, not to them, but to the butter. Bread, too, is paid to bake itself more cheaply: but the idea that poor people might like the equivalent in money, so that they could spend it on biscuits – or beer, for that matter – is considered ridiculous. And now we are urged to 'demand' that others should pay their money to keep London's fares down. (And what of Birmingham's fares, and Manchester's, and Weston-super-Mare's – do they not rise, too? And if so, should not 'government' money be used to keep them down also?)

Representatives of the T.U.C. met the Prime Minister and the Chancellor on Monday, and – well, as Alan Hamilton put it in his report of the meeting:

> Selective reflationary measures but no reduction in the level of wage increases were urged on Government ministers . . .

Elsewhere, the figure involved in the 'selective reflationary measures' has been estimated to be £2,000m. *Two thousand million* buckets of petrol are to be flung into the raging furnace of inflation, and – I quote Mr Hamilton again – the T.U.C.

> offered no hope that the guidelines for keeping pay increases within the social contract could be tightened, and ministers appear not to have pressed the point.

Well, no doubt Mr Healey will not agree to 'reflationary measures' (the English for which is 'inflation') amounting to £2,000m. Shall we say £1,500m.? All right, split the difference – £1,875m. For what we have here is made of that fabled substance – said by many Biblical scholars to be the 'manna' referred to in the Old Testament – *government money*, and therefore does not have to be earned, let alone paid for, in the ordinary way. Unemployment is rising: increasing the rate of inflation is one way of causing it to stop rising, or to rise more slowly: therefore 'government money' must be spent to increase the rate of inflation.

That may seem like a digression, but it is not. What we are in the grip of, apart from inflation and raving lunacy, is the tendency to believe that at all levels and in all fields, the state will provide, and the individual need not therefore bother too much to do so. The state will provide, that is, with 'government money', which will be either money taken out of other people's pockets, or money which has simply been printed, and which will therefore lessen the value of the money remaining in all our pockets. 'Reflationary measures but no reduction in the level of wage increases'; or, to put it another way, 'Stop the Fares Rise! Demand more Government aid to London!'

So it will go on until reality asserts itself, or until we decline altogether into a condition in which we will do nothing at all for ourselves, but insist, or at least (and perhaps it would be even worse to do so) agree, that the state must do it all. But we know, do we not, of what kind of society the hallmark is the failure to remember that 'the state' is composed only of us and nothing more, and that the whole can never be greater than the sum of its parts? In the end, we may come to that – not by revolution or coup or the breakdown of society, but by nothing more sensational than the slow drip into our veins of the belief that the cure for a lack of money is 'government aid'. That poison has already spread far through our system; and there is still no antidote in sight.

The Times February 26th, 1975

Beyond the Pale

The Old Country by Sholom Aleichem★
Tevye's Daughters by Sholom Aleichem★
The World of Sholom Aleichem by Maurice Samuel★

THIS IS WHERE the fine folk with their airs and graces, not to mention their stately homes and indeed their hyphens, have to listen, if they want to learn something, to me, Bernard from Camden Town, grandson of Yossl the Tailor (and a sadly unsuccessful one, I may say) and of Yossl's wife, Bathsheba. For the world portrayed in these three books is the world of my grandparents, who came from Russia, two droplets in the huge wave of emigration at the turn of the century, who always, to the end of their long lives, referred to the land they had left fifty years before as home, and whose stories of life in Nezhin, their native village, were cut from the very same cloth as these tales of Kasrilevka and Zolodievka, Yehupetz and Boikerik, and all the other tiny settlements in the Pale to which the Jews in late Tzarist Russia were confined.

Indeed, one of my grandparents' stories of their own experiences (in which the thugs who were coming to the village to institute a *pogrom* were delayed on the way and arrived after the Cossacks – themselves no mean anti-semites, but on this occasion on the side of law and order – had ridden into town, to end by whipping the hooligans through the streets) is virtually identical with that recounted in *Tevye's Daughters*

★ Vallentine Mitchell, 1973.

under the title 'A Wedding Without Musicians'. (I used to read the short stories of Sholom Aleichem to my grandparents in translation – my grandmother never learned to read or write in any language, and my grandfather found written English a struggle – often, just to make the whole clash of worlds even more bizarre, during air-raids.)

Sholom Aleichem (his real name was Rabinowitz, and his pseudonym is the standard Hebrew greeting, meaning 'Peace be with you') is undoubtedly the greatest and most celebrated writer who ever used Yiddish, which was, incidentally, his native language, as it was that of my grandparents; Hebrew was the language of the Scriptures, not for use in ordinary speech or writing, and Russian was an altogether foreign tongue. He made the long journey to a new life at much the same time as the many millions who poured out of the East in search of a land free from persecution (some of them found it in Germany and settled there, may they rest in peace); he went to America, and there set about recording for posterity a way of life that was just on the point of vanishing for ever. He achieved an extraordinary international reputation, being read throughout the world, wherever the refugees of the new Diaspora had settled, and when he died in New York, during the First World War, 15,000 Jews filed through the little room in which he lay in state like a king, and ten times as many lined the route to the cemetery on the day of his funeral.

In the world he described, emancipation was a word of disapproval, not of praise (Maurice Samuel's wandering and sentimental, but valuable, study of Sholom Aleichem's background records that Moses Mendelssohn, grandfather of the composer, was regarded with suspicion amounting almost to horror because he translated the Bible into German for the use of those Jews who had forgotten their Hebrew), and the only absolutely unforgivable sin was apostasy.

This last view was not based on dogma so much as on an instinctive belief that their religion was the cement that bound the Jews of the Pale together, that gave them their unique identity and their *raison d'être*. Nor is that a mere figure of speech; these people believed that they were on earth to love and worship God, through whatever tribulations it pleased Him to visit upon them. And since one of their two chief forms of expressing that worship (the other, of course, was continual prayer) was to help their neighbours, the instinct was correct; it is significant that, despite the private rejection of the faith of their forefathers by much of the present Israeli political leadership, and their public rejection of *yiddishkeit*, there is no disposition on their part to secularize the State, for Judaism is felt to hold Israel together as it held Kasrilevka, and for that matter my grandparents' Nezhin.

That is why Tevye the Dairyman (turned decades later into the hero of 'Fiddler on the Roof')bears resignedly the varying fates of all his seven beautiful daughters, except one. The eldest refuses the 'good marriage' arranged for her, and marries instead the penniless tailor; the next marries a revolutionary and follows him to his prison in Siberia; another eats her heart out married to a wealthy speculator whom she does not love; another commits suicide. Only Chava, who marries a gentile, breaks her father's heart by doing so, and Sholom Aleichem must have realized that the parting was unbearable, for he brings her back, repentant, in a later story, to join what remains of the family as they set out on the first stages of their symbolic journey into perpetual exile.

The gallows-humour that has come to the aid of all persecuted peoples is much in evidence, of course, throughout the tales; even more prominent, however, is the amazing optimism that has sustained this particular people through so many dreadful centuries (I have heard devout Jews, taxed with the terrible indictment of their God represented by the Nazi holocaust, explain – and most profoundly believe – that His infinite goodness and mercy are clearly demonstrated by the number who survived).

Thus, in the world of the *shtetl* (the little enclosed village in which Sholom Aleichem's characters lived, and which was a way of life and a philosophy as much as a geographical place), people do not reflect that life could be better, for there are an infinite number of ways in which it could be better to an infinite extent; instead, they reflect that it could be worse, and count their blessings. Even their envy of those more fortunate than themselves is a mask: 'If I were Rothschild,' they sigh, but they admire the great ones instead of resenting them. And a Jew in trouble is a Jew in trouble, wherever he may be; one of the most touching stories in *The Old Country* is 'Dreyfus in Kasrilevka', in which people who have scarcely heard of France follow the fortunes of the *affaire* with the fiercest passion ('. . . the anguish and pain that Kasrilevka underwent, Paris will not experience until Judgment Day . . . '), and when they learn that there were 'some good people who undertook to show the world that the whole thing had been a plot', they elevate Zola to sainthood.

To a *déraciné* like myself the world of Sholom Aleichem, for all its familiarity at second hand, is not only remote, but stifling, bounded by a religion I have never had, a cultural tradition I have lost, and an attitude I have rejected. Yet as I renew acquaintance with his vast, Dickensian gallery of characters (I am sorry there is nothing in these collections about my – and my grandparents' – favourite, Stempenyu the musician), I am glad that they have touched my life too, and that the blood of the Pale flows in my veins.

Observer June 17th, 1973

My counter proposals

I'VE HAD ENOUGH of this nonsense; I propose to buy Harrods myself. The place is by no means what it was (thousands trampled to death on the first day of the January sales, and wire baskets in the Food Hall) but I really am not willing to allow it to be torn in pieces by the likes of Sir Hugh Fraser, Mr Tiny Rowland and Professor Roland Smith. I don't like the cut of any of their jibs, least of all the Professor's (a Professor of 'Marketing', if you please, as a man might boast of a Doctorate in tearing telephone directories in half, and Chairman of a company calling itself 'Silentnight Holdings', which probably makes Christmas cards of a particularly repellent kind), and the packing of meetings, rescinding of resolutions, questioning of dismissals and threatening of legal action remind me of nothing so much as the affairs of the London Freelance Branch of the National Union of Journalists, more than which I can hardly say. And another thing: there have been allegations, in the course of the struggle, of electronic and other forms of surveillance, which seem to me to call urgently for an addition to Whitehorn's Doxology ('Never eat at any restaurant called Mom's, never get into a poker game with anyone called Doc, and never go to bed with anyone whose troubles are worse than your own'), in the form 'Never have anything to do with a situation in which the people involved are bugging their allies instead of their opponents'.

I shall buy Harrods, then. Sir Hugh and Mr Rowland will, I imagine, prefer to accept defeat gracefully and take themselves off to pursue their other interests, but I am willing to offer the

Professor a job in which he can put his theoretical knowledge of marketing to practical use; I shall start him behind the counter in Haberdashery, and if he gives no cause for complaint promote him to Soft Furnishings. (Lady Diana Cooper, Whom God Preserve, once assured me that the unsolved mystery of the etymology of the word 'haberdasher' had yielded to historical analysis. It came, she said, from the cry of immigrant German pedlars who, adorned Autolycus-like with trays of pins and ribbons, would shout their wares to the passers-by in the form '*Ich habe das hier*'. But I shall stand no nonsense from anyone, whether on the staff or the board of directors. From now on, Harrods is going to be run my way.

The first thing to go will be the wire baskets; *somewhere* in England there has to be a shop that isn't a supermarket, and it might as well be in the Brompton Road. From now on, customers who want food will get it from behind a counter, where it will be served by ladies and gentlemen of respectable appearance wearing clean white overalls. What is more, there will be no damned nonsense about pre-packing; a customer wanting half a pound of butter will see the assistant turn to a huge block of the stuff, a deep, golden yellow in colour, dig a chunk out of it with a wooden implement rather like a miniature cricket bat, the blade about five inches long, and then perform a ritual which nobody alive has seen carried out since before the Second World War.

If you have tears of envy, prepare to shed them now. Once upon a time, this is how it was done; it is one of my earliest memories, and I treasure it as I treasure the original taste of original bullseyes and other delights long since gone down the memory-hole of oblivion. The assistant, having dug the butter out, produced a second little cricket bat, and with deft slappings and pattings gradually worked the unformed lump of butter into a neat rectangular block. (He had weighed it first, of course, and added or subtracted, accordingly, to its mass.) He then wrapped it in greaseproof paper, tucked the ends in neatly, and handed it over. But before he did so, he took another wooden implement, bearing the incised image of a flower or other symbol, and marked the butter with it as an American rancher branded his cattle.

Now, now, do not suppose that you have caught out your uncle Bernard with the question you are about to ask: how could the assistant so rapidly 'work' the butter, hard as it must have been from the refrigerator? Children, hear the amazing news: *it wasn't refrigerated*! Soft and malleable, it yielded to the manipulation of the butter-pats. And that is the way it is going to be in Harrods from now on, as it was in days of yore.

And that is only the butter question settled. In the tea department, the assistants will blend your mixture before your eyes; next door, in coffee, they will go so far as to roast it. Upstairs, plastic of all kinds will be cleared out of every department, with the single exception of bakelite, kept on (if, indeed, anything is made out of it any more) for sentimental reasons; more, even aluminium will be viewed with suspicion, and admitted only on sufferance. No pillows other than those filled with the finest down will be sold, no milk chocolate will be available, no gramophone records of any music later than Monteverdi will be stocked. Do they say that the Yamaha piano is as good as any other make? Let them say it elsewhere; we'll have no such fancy modern gewgaws in my music department, which will be full of Broadwood, Blüthner and Bechstein, Steinway, Bösendorfer and (assuming it is still made) Pleyel. Are paperback books fashionable? Then so much the worse for fashion; there will be none but casebound in my shop. (Does the Harrods' Library still exist? If so, it will be lovingly preserved; if not, revived.)

There will be no tailoring but bespoke, no sheets but silk or the finest linen, no pictures but originals, no toys but those of wood and clockwork (*clockwork*, you little pests – you wind it up, with a key), no carpets but Bokhara, no furniture but mahogany, no dinner napkins but they shall be double damask.

And of course, it will pay. Crowds will throng every floor, come to shop at a place where the shopping itself is real, as well as the goods shopped for. There will be no sales, partly because I do not approve of them, and partly because there will be no need of such aids to good shopkeeping; if it comes to that there will be no electronic cash-registers, only an old-fashioned wooden till. Scrubbing-boards, meatsafes, Prince Rupert Drops, liberty-bodices, spats, swordsticks – all these forgotten items of merchandise will be available, and we – proprietor, customers and staff – shall pass the time fleetingly, as they did in the golden world.

And in the chemist's, they will do up the purchases, be they no more than a piece of carbolic soap and a tin of tooth-powder, in brown paper fastened with pink string and sealing wax. You've never seen them do that in Boots, eh? No, I don't suppose you have. But you shall see it done in Harrods, any day now. Eat your heart out, Selfridges.

The Times February 4th, 1981

The sport of kings

HAS SPAIN, I ask myself with little hope of getting any kind of helpful answer, not got enough trouble without finding herself awash with dubious claimants to her dubious throne? Or, to put it another way, have not Spaniards got enough excuses for killing one another without adding dynastic reasons of a more than ordinarily incomprehensible order?

My questions are prompted by the bizarre events that took place at the weekend halfway up a mountain in the western Pyrenees, where enormous numbers of Pretenders to the Spanish throne gathered to do a bit of outdoor Pretending – it was a sunny afternoon – and one man (not himself a Pretender, apparently) finished the day heavier than he had begun it, by the weight of a couple of ounces of lead in his heart.

On the dynastic rights and wrongs involved I do not presume to have views:

> The question's very much too wide,
> And much too round, and much too hollow,
> And learned men on either side
> Use arguments we cannot follow.

Suffice it that one of the chief Pretenders calls himself Prince Carlos Hugo, no doubt as a man might be called Duke Ellington or Earl Hines (or for that matter, I suppose, Baron Weidenfeld). Another, it seems, signs in as Prince Sixto, a name which sounds like that of a comic Hottentot chieftain in a children's strip-cartoon. Both claim to be the only rightful occupant of the Spanish throne, as does the one who has actually got his trousers on it at the moment, Juan Carlos. Others are expected to announce their candidacy from time to time; intending applicants among my readers should write to the Spanish Embassy for the appropriate form, which must be filled in in duplicate and returned accompanied by six Tio Pepe labels and the completion, in not more than ten words, of the slogan: 'I want to be King of Spain because . . . '

For the man who ended up dead, the encounter at Montejurra was no joke. But the deeper truth of the matter is that the affair was no joke anyway, though when the followers of one pseudo-King of Spain march up a mountain intending to hold a rally at the top, only to find themselves ambushed on the way by armed adherents of a rival pseudo-monarch, a chuckle or two over the sherry should not be condemned too harshly, particularly when it is learnt that the two dogs fighting over a meatless bone are actually brothers.

It is obviously a wise and potentially fruitful plan for Spain, as she makes her way cautiously from the rule of Franco towards democracy, to do so under the nominal direction of a king, even one tainted by the fact that he was appointed by Franco himself. All those years of playing Vittorio Emanuele to Franco's Mussolini have proved worthwhile, and the first stages of the transition have gone off with – considering how long-lasting, how brutal, how corrupt and how utterly devoid of any unifying vision the dictatorship was – astonishingly little trouble. It remains to be seen how far, if at all, either the King or the Prime Minister, let alone both, mean what they say about freeing the Spanish people (certainly the provisional plans for a free Parliament and real elections offer great hope for their good intentions, and also for their political skill), and whether, even if they mean every word of it, those forces, of right and left alike, which are implacably opposed to democracy in Spain, will allow them to put it into genuine practice.

But let us assume the best, and foresee a time – five years

away, perhaps? – when Spain will be as free as any Western democracy. Is it seriously supposed that she will remain a monarchy for more than a further transitional period after that? Once the Spaniards have acquired the habit of governing themselves, they will hardly be long interested in maintaining an institution which for them, in its political aspects, suggests nothing so much as the celebrated definition of a mule: a creature without pride of ancestry or hope of posterity.

God knows, the centuries of Spanish monarchy produced enough brutes and imbeciles to convince even the most devout royalist that inheritance is not the ideal method of selecting those who reign over us; by all accounts, the present incumbent is a decent and respectable man, and in any case the tangled genealogy behind him suggests that he is in little danger of succumbing to the Curse of the Hapsburgs in any of its wide variety of forms. But that makes the likelihood of the monarchy enduring smaller, not greater, for a Spanish king whom his people can envisage painted by Velazquez or Goya might awaken all the ancient echoes of that ancient echoing land; one who could hardly hope to be given a sitting by Salvador Dali is unlikely to fire their imagination in quite the same way. The Earl of Warwick had something of a reputation as a king maker, and Napoleon filled a throne or two in his time; but admirable though Woolworth's is, I hardly feel that if it sold kings they would have quite the same *cachet*.

Nevertheless, let us make a further supposition; that Spain becomes a democracy, that the monarchy becomes an entirely constitutional one, that Juan Carlos plays no more directly political a role than our own Queen Elizabeth. In that case, what in the name of Don Quixote de la Mancha would anybody else want to be King of Spain *for*? After all, the Woolworth's analogy is two-sided; given the chance to be Philip II, and send an Armada to conquer England for the true faith, many a republican's faith might waver: is it not passing brave to be a king, and ride in triumph through Persepolis? But the chance to be Gilbert's King Calamity Pop von Peppermint Drop is by no means the same thing. Even many constitutional monarchies, after all, can look back on centuries of unbroken succession; the Spanish throne has at times resembled nothing so much as a revolving door, and its present standing as an obvious constitutional device and nothing more can hardly be expected to restore its glory.

Very well; let us go one step further and believe that even in the circumstances outlined the chance to wear a bit of tatty ermine and a cardboard crown with glass beads stuck all over it to represent diamonds proves to be the last infirmity of ignoble mind, and that Graf Rudi and Graf Bobby, fresh from pushing one another off mountains, should nevertheless apply for the job.

Are they not likely, in those circumstances, to be told that, as claimants to the Spanish throne, they rate rather below the most unmemorable bullfighter who ever ran out of the ring when the bull was let in? Is it not probable that they will be urged to go to London and apply for a job waiting at table in a Spanish restaurant in Soho? What was it Charles II was supposed to have said to his brother? 'No one will kill me to make you king.' I cannot believe that if Spain wants a king she will wish to exchange the present conscientious, hard-working and uninteresting one for a couple of buffoons whose idea of majesty is to go horsing about on mountains, sticking out their tongues at one another and each claiming to be a much kingier king than his rival.

There is a line of Chesterton's about France: 'Your foul dead kings all laughing in their graves.' Well, Spain too, has had some foul kings in her history, and some foolish ones as well, some of whom are more likely to be weeping than laughing at the spectacle of Prince Groucho and Prince Harpo puffing their way up the Pyrenees to establish imaginary claims to a precarious throne, and getting some poor devil shot dead in the process. 'Under which king, Bezonian?' I do not know what rude noise is the Spanish equivalent of a raspberry; but I

daresay that many a Spaniard, raising his head to hope at last
that the long night of his country is ending, will read the news
from the toy kings of the Pyrenees, and make it.*

The Times May 12th, 1976

---

* This column seriously under-estimated both the character of King Juan
Carlos and the strength of the nascent Spanish democracy. But not, I think,
the absurdity of Prince Sixto and his chums.

For those who very nearly made it

I SEE THAT A disused railway signal-box is for sale, though what the purchaser is supposed to use it for I cannot imagine. I once had dreams, when I read of a defrocked church that was on the market at £10,000 or so in Germany, of buying it and running it as a scandalously heterodox place of worship, in which services of revolting opulence (the communion wine, as I recall, was to be Mouton-Rothschild 1924) would be held; but not even I would see much point in throwing the lever that sends the 11.32 from London to Wolverhampton on a wild-goose chase to Bournemouth when the line is for ever empty and the tracks weed-strewn, and not even a ghost train ever passes. On the other hand, whenever I read of a railway signal-box in any connection, or even see one from the window of a train, I am reminded of a story told to me many years ago by the late Gerald Barry, well known as an outstanding newspaper editor, but less well known (though hardly less worthy of honour for it) as the man who thought of removing the peel from a lemon in a single piece and putting the resultant long, yellow snake into the vodka bottle, thus flavouring it most agreeably in advance.

Anyway, Gerald was in his club one day when he was cornered in the bar; too gentle and considerate a man to make an excuse and leave, Gerald prepared to suffer, though the cornerer in question was from that most terrible category of bores, the railway enthusiast.

The enthusiast in question wasted no time on small-talk. 'I've just written', he announced without preliminaries, 'another series of articles for the *Railway Review*.' Gerald did not know, or for that matter care, that the man had written a first series, let alone a second, but he made polite enquiries as to the subject, receiving the memorable reply (well *he* had remembered it for several years, and I have remembered it myself for another dozen or so), 'Some smaller English signal-boxes.'

As a conversation freezer, that is something of a nonpareil. But Gerald had the same kind of profitlessly speculative mind that I have myself, and when he told me the story we fell to speculating uselessly on the human tragedy behind his inter-locutor's simple words.

'Some smaller English signal-boxes'; to most people, the title will mean no more than what it says. But to Gerald and me it opened a window on the world of a disappointed and embittered life, and we reasoned thus. The railway-lover had, in his youth, conceived of a plan as audacious as it was imaginative, nothing less than the compilation of a complete *catalogue raisonné* of all the signal-boxes of all the world's railways, from the mighty computerized monsters of Milan or Essen to the tiniest branch-line structure in rural Bulgaria.

The years went by, while notes, drawings and photographs accumulated. But, after all, there was a living to be earned, a family to be brought up, other duties to be attended to, and one day there dawned the realization that no man could accomplish, in a single life-time, the immense task. The scale of the enterprise would have to be reduced.

Let us suppose that the first thing to be abandoned was the work's global comprehensiveness. Out went his notes on the pagoda-shaped signal-boxes of the Wusan–Hangchow line, out went the ground-plans of the Gaudí-influenced signal-boxes on the Malaga–Cordoba stretch, out the 'dug-out' signal-boxes of Flanders, so clearly derived from the familiar shapes of the First World War. Henceforth, it was to be 'English Signal-Boxes' by which his name would go down in history, or at least railway history.

More years pass; life presses no less keenly; once again there has to be a tightening of the belt, a trimming of youthful ambitions. Now it is 'Smaller English Signal-Boxes'. And even that is not the end; finally, the great work, which would have taken a couple of yards to shelve, is reduced to '*Some* Smaller English Signal-Boxes'.

It is better, we are assured, to have loved and lost than never to have loved at all. To travel hopefully, we are further persuaded, is better than to arrive. If it comes to that, I have heard that mony a mickle maks a muckle, but since I am by no means certain what the remark means, I am in no position to form an opinion on the subject. It may be generally conceded, however, that those who do not quite reach the highest flights of eminence, of success, of happiness, are not simply to be thrust into outer darkness. If somebody has to win a race, somebody else has to come second, and coming second is not an altogether empty achievement. Mallory and Irvine nearly reached the top of Everest; do we honour them the less for that 'nearly'? It used to be – may still be – a practice among certain former students to carry visiting-cards on which they were described as 'Failed B.A. Oxon.'; we may smile at the bearer of the card, but at least he did go to Oxford, and what is more, though he failed, he tried. And there are others who can be commended even though they fall short of complete success, such as Victor Borge's uncle, who invented a soft drink that he called 'One-Up', which failed to attract popular taste. Nothing daunted, he improved the formula and marketed the result as 'Two-Up', only to find that this pleased not the many either. He tried again, with 'Three-Up' and a like result, then 'Four-Up', 'Five-Up' and 'Six-Up'. Then he died. 'He never knew', said Mr Borge, 'how near he came.' (And let us not, while we are on the subject, forget the man who writes those political verses in the *New Statesman* that very nearly scan.)*

And yet the Oxonian would rather have passed his exams,

---

* Mr Roger Woddis. He now writes similar verses for the *Radio Times*. But he still hasn't got the hang of it.

the runner-up would rather have run first, the view from the second rung of the ladder is not so charming as the view from the first. And so, surely, it must have seemed to the signal-box man. He was, as it happens, a man who achieved considerable distinction in his professional life, but I remain convinced that that gave him not one-hundredth part of the satisfaction he would have derived from completing his immense and exhaustive study. It was not to be, and a series on 'Some Smaller English Signal-Boxes' is all that remains to show where vaulting ambition o'er-leaped itself. Oh the little more, and how much it is! And the little less, and what worlds away! As far, indeed, as the fascinating spherical signal-boxes of Arizona (so shaped to present maximum resistance to erosion by sand), which are now doomed to perish, in the fullness of time, without ever being recorded for the wonder and enlightenment of future ages.

The Times November 24th, 1978

Stage coach

'I CANNOT GET USED', wrote Logan Pearsall-Smith, 'to this vanishing-trick my own friends have taken to playing.' Fortunately, my friends have not yet, on the whole, started to play it. But my heroes have been doing so for a long time now, and the latest was last week, when Carl Ebert died.

And who, the young will ask, was Carl Ebert? Carl Ebert, *meine Kinder*, was the greatest opera director of my lifetime; perhaps the greatest there has ever been. And when you consider that the whole of the modern 'producer's revolution' has taken place since I started going to opera, that Zeffirelli, Visconti, Ponelle and the Wagner grandsons all did their first opera productions within that time-span, you will see that my claim of pre-eminence for Ebert is a considerable one. But it is not made lightly; and I believe it is justified.

The facts are fairly simple. Ebert came to this country from Germany soon after the Nazis came to power. By one of those accidents of history that go far towards showing that there are no accidents, he was one of four men, three of them fellow-exiles from Nazidom and the fourth one of the most English Englishmen who ever lived, whose paths met in 1935 at a spot in Sussex of which until then nobody but its inhabitants had ever heard, but which the collaboration among that quartet was to make known throughout the civilized world. The place, of course, was Glyndebourne, and the other three men were Fritz Busch, the Glyndebourne Opera's first conductor, Rudolf Bing, its first general manager, and John Christie, its owner, inspirer and *genius loci*.

Ebert, who started as an actor (he used occasionally to take the speaking part of Pasha Selim in Glyndebourne productions of *Die Entführung aus dem Serail*), had already made a notable mark as a director in his native land. But it was at Glyndebourne that he made the reputation that was to carry his fame and his influence into virtually every operatic centre in the world.

Of those now legendary pre-war performances I cannot, of course, speak from first-hand knowledge, though some idea can be gained from the recordings; if you are inclined to believe that those who speak in raptures of that Golden Age tend to exaggerate, I invite you to listen to John Brownlee singing *Finch'han dal vino*, when you will, as solicitors advertising for missing heirs say, hear something to your advantage. But I first encountered Ebert's work in 1947, at the first Edinburgh Festival; the Glyndebourne Opera had been re-formed, but it had not yet started giving performances in its own home, and the seasons it did at Edinburgh before the Sussex ship was relaunched hit me with a revelatory force. That first year they did two productions, both directed by Ebert: *Figaro* and *Macbeth*. If I close my eyes I swear that I can, a third of a century later, conjure up not just the general impression, but single details. Indeed, I shall give an example, not to justify my claim but because it is symbolic of Ebert's genius, for reasons which I shall also give. In *Non più andrai*, Figaro has set Cherubino marching about the stage with a besom over his shoulder to represent the gun he will shortly be carrying. Suddenly, Susanna has an idea; she goes to a cupboard, rummages through it and emerges with an immense busby. She falls into step behind Cherubino and, seizing her opportunity, claps it on his head.

Any imaginative director could have thought of that; what followed was pure Ebert. Cherubino had no mirror, and therefore did not know what thing now surmounted his head. He put up his hands to feel it; clasped the sides; then, in wonderment, walked his fingers further and further up the thing, eventually standing on tip-toe as if it would help him reach, until his hands finally got to the top and met over the crown, at which a smile, half-fearful, half-proud, spread over his face (I can even remember who sang the part on that occasion – Giulietta Simionato). Ebert had simply listened to the music; even as Figaro is mercilessly teasing the amorous young sprig, Mozart is telling us that, so far from his induction into military life being an unqualified disaster, it will in fact give him *more* opportunities with the girls, not fewer, and the hat will make him look even more of a dashing young fellow.

I saw, over the years, three more productions of *Figaro* by Ebert, all of them more than once; and all of them, as indeed all of his work, were full of similar understanding so perfectly translated into action. Indeed, I remember another moment from that very same scene in one of the other Ebert *Figaros*; this time there *was* a mirror on the stage – a cheval-glass – and as Cherubino was marched past it, this time arm-in-arm with his tormentor, he suddenly caught sight of himself, tore his arm out of Figaro's, and stopped to admire his appearance: *Narcisetto, Adoncino d'amor.*

I could never think of Ebert's business as business; it had that true organic quality, growing naturally out of the demands of the music and the drama, which makes the audience feel that it could not have been done any other way. That is easy to say; and it is said of far too many directors, being quite unjustified in many cases. But of Ebert, whose artistic integrity was absolute, it was always true, and even in the rare productions (I can only think of one, as a matter of fact, his *Barber of Seville*) in which the style had coarsened and broadened, the fault was an error of judgment, not a failing in dedication or purity of intention. And that those principles *never* fail can be said of very few indeed. No one, for instance, who saw the Zeffirelli productions of *Tosca* or *Falstaff* will deny that the director had acted throughout as the selfless servant of the operas; but who will have the temerity to say the same of his catastrophic version of *Don Giovanni*?

Ebert closed his career as artistic director at Glyndebourne (though he returned to do one or two guest productions later) still looking forward: for his farewell he chose, not one of his and Glyndebourne's beloved Mozart operas, but *Der Rosenkavalier*, which had never before been given there, and it remains the finest production of the work I have ever seen. But I think that the Ebert production I loved, and remember, best was the Glyndebourne *Entführung* that he did in the mid-1950s. One of the reasons for its perfection lay in the designs of Oliver Messel, which certainly constituted *his* greatest achievement; but that fact itself emphasized Ebert's success with the opera, for the sets and costumes were as perfectly and naturally integrated into the music and the text as was Ebert's direction. The result was the nearest approach to the full realization of that *Gesamtkunstwerk* of which Richard Wagner dreamed ever achieved on a stage since I have been looking at stages and achievements, in this country or elsewhere.

And now he is gone. He had retired completely long since, of course, and lived quietly in California. But until not many years ago, his shock of white hair could occasionally be seen among opera-house audiences, and now it will be seen no more, for in the celestial opera house in which he is even now being appointed artistic director his place will be behind the scenes, collaborating with Fritz Busch, Oliver Messel and John Christie on productions of the endless stream of new operas that Mozart is writing for them. May he there rest in as much peace as the life of an opera house allows its dedicated servants. He will not ask for more.

The Times May 22nd, 1980

Souls

NOT LONG AGO, Pam Gems, in *Franz into April*, gave a direct account of a psychotherapeutic method in action; her play was woven from her characters' search for meaning that the treatment they were undergoing was designed to supply. Before that, there was the haunting *Abigail's Party*, in which the search was more desperate because unarticulated, and the portrait of the seekers more valuable because there were no solutions on offer. In Olwen Wymark's *Find Me* the search is narrowed down to a single point, yet the need to explain Verity's affliction is a metaphor for a wider need; Julian Mitchell's *Half-Life*, though more superficial than these, has something to say about a man who feels his life has been wasted not because it had no meaning but because he failed to search for the meaning it must have had.

All these plays obviously reflect the increasingly urgent search going on in our society – more intensely, more widely and in a greater variety of forms, than ever before – for something that will explain to the seekers why, though content, they are nevertheless dissatisfied; though affluent, poor; though secure and befriended, afraid and alone; and though undoubtedly alive, most certainly dead.

Now we have, at Hampstead, the latest contribution to this extraordinary debate: *Bodies*, by James Saunders, which is itself an extraordinary debate between two couples who have exchanged partners, returned to their original pairings, and are now engaged in totting up the balance-sheet of their lives.

The first Act shows them separately; in the hands of a less

skilled playwright it would be dangerously static (much of the text is delivered in soliloquy), a quality emphasized by the inappropriately abstract setting. But patience and attentiveness are well repaid; gradually, the mosaic takes on shape and colour. David had an affair with Anne; Helen, in revenge, flung herself at Mervyn. When the marriages were re-formed, David and Helen went to America where, after breakdowns, they encountered one of those psychotherapies that proliferate there along with new religions, through which they achieved stability and harmony. The others are still trapped in their mutually destructive neuroses, and in the second act (the stage lights come up full – there is to be no evading the point) battle is joined after a foursome dinner; a counterpoint is provided by the fact that Mervyn, who is a headmaster, is awaiting news of a pupil brain-damaged in a suicide attempt and due to be disconnected from his life-support machine while the talk proceeds. (The theme of the boy is introduced early and casually, placed like a detonator to be fired later.)

The 'cured' couple are smug and certain; I wrote down 'lobotomized' a few moments before David said, 'You completely misunderstand . . . It's not a lobotomy we've had.' The others quarrel, the wife in flight from the danger of self-knowledge, her seeing husband unable to bear it without whisky. The trigger for his inexorable collapse is his inability either to dent the healthy completeness of David and Helen or to engage his desperately needed wife in his battle. Hear the cured David:

> I still have to live in the world. It puts on a front, you know, a mask. After the therapy you see past that. You look at a smiling face and see the muscles holding the smile in place, you see through the eyes to the anger and resentment and fear. People are hanging on for dear life and *smiling*. We're in extremity, Mervyn. We really are.

Now if you emerge from the Hampstead Theatre believing that Helen and David have found the answer – or even *an* answer – you have missed the point. *Bodies* is a play about four trapped people, not two, and the pain of the neurotic pair, which drives the husband, at any rate, to go on seeking, is more creative and understanding than the contentment and integration of the others.

For more than three centuries our world has been proceeding towards that conclusion, and at last the revolt has begun. *Bodies*, though it is not a tract but a play, and an uncommonly literate, amusing, dramatic and interesting play, too is explosive ammunition for the battle, and anyone capable of being interested in the world beyond 'the body, the environment and the now', which is all David and Helen believe in, will find it a rich and rewarding experience. We have not heard the last of *Bodies*, and certainly not of its theme.*

If you listen to our committed playwrights, you can hear in their plays, amid the anger at the availability of South African orange-juice, the protests at the C.I.A.'s brutal suppression of the legitimate aspirations of the people of Welwyn Garden City, the demands for the nationalization of the means of production, distribution and exchange, and the call for the immediate overthrow of all political, educational, financial and religious institutions (together with the summary execution of those in charge of them), one constant theme.

What they wish us to understand is that they are engaged not in the effete business of entertainment, but in the practical work of changing the system, in order to effect a more just and equal distribution of power and wealth, reverse inner-city decay, provide recreational facilities for young people understandably estranged from our consumer-orientated society, and reduce the wasteful expenditure on defence demanded by the military-industrial complex.

And yet I doubt if many of the committed playwrights in question will trouble to see James Saunders's *Bodies*, to which I

---

* At any rate my readers had not.

have just paid a second visit. For *Bodies* really is about changing the system; more, it could even help to bring about such a
change. Not by convincing the authorities of the urgent need
to enforce the closed shop throughout industry and prohibit
the use of sexist expressions in the media, but by its understanding of the truth that the only way in which the transformation of society will ever be accomplished is by the
transformation of individuals from *within themselves*. For that
is what *Bodies* is about.

Now the subtlety, skill and insight of this masterly author
are enough to guarantee that the play's weight is evenly
distributed. He is not saying that neurotics need expert help
and that those who get it are better off than those who do not,
yet what we actually see to begin with is that the 'cured' couple
really do have (the husband, significantly, more than the still
watchful, even still doubting, wife) a calm and stability that
the other two lack. We cannot just dismiss the therapy they
have had as a kind of lobotomy, and even if we do we are left
with the undeniable fact that the 'uncured' wife is almost
catatonic within concentric rings of fear and despair, unable
even to shout across the barrier for help, and her husband, who
is at any rate conscious of his pain, has to get stupendously
drunk in order to bear it.

For what Mr Saunders means is that therapies, gurus,
religions, meditations and the whole gigantic gallimaufry of
nostrums now available, and eagerly sought, *as never before in
all history*, are nothing but means to an end, the end being that
longed-for reconciliation of the warring part of the human
psyche, which alone can offer an answer to the increasingly
insistent question that will let none of us alone: why, since we
have got everything, have we most manifestly got nothing?

To this question Anne has willed herself to be deaf; David
has achieved certainty, but at terrible cost; Helen wonders, and
wonders why she wonders; Mervyn in his agony is the only
one who is fully alive, and who sees the price David has
paid.

No more searching through the dead past looking for value; no more chasing after meaning, no more attempting the impossible, no more seeking the delight not of this world and no more disappointment that it seems always just out of reach; no more struggle, no more torment, never again need anyone die for a cause, or a friend, or give himself to a stranger for no good reason . . . There'll come a voluntary burning of pernicious books by reasonable people, the end of the old neurosis. And the surviving nuts will stand warming their hands at it, watching the smoke rise, with irrational tears running down their cheeks, and nothing left to sustain them but a memory of a dead faith, and no way to express their feelings but an empty rhetoric.

That is what Mr Saunders is challenging, and the very fact that his challenge can be made shows that it can also be successful. Helen and David have not found salvation, but they, like Mervyn, knew they had to seek it.

Human beings are not predictable. Nowadays, few would deny that, but not everybody has yet realized that it is the most important thing in the world. In every heart there are secret chambers, wherein are kept the qualities which make every living soul unique, and which demonstrate daily and hourly that solutions designed to fit everything will fit nothing. Pope was wrong; Bentham was wrong; Marx was wrong; Freud was wrong. Cervantes was right; Dostoievsky was right; Whitman was right; Heisenberg was right. Hear Mervyn again:

What if the quality that sets man above the rest of the animals, if that's where we want to be, is not the ability to make fire or words or weapons but the blessed gift of irrationality, the God-given capacity to be wilfully illogical, to be – *absurd*.

Mervyn is right, too, and his tormented soul will yet be saved; 'I tell thee, churlish priest, A ministering angel shall my sister be, When thou liest howling.' That is the truth that *Bodies* proclaims, and that millions today yearn for. Over the grave of Lazarus, the earth stirs.

We talked about it for hours afterwards, asking what was going to happen in Act Three, or what Helen and David said to each other on the way home, just like poor Mervyn Griffith-Jones insisting that Lady Chatterley would have left Mellors if he had proved sexually unsatisfactory later.

How often is there a play that is worth discussing seriously at all, let alone in depth and details? *Bodies* (which takes further the argument of *Abigail's Party*, in that here the people are aware of the problem, whatever their varying solutions to it) is a play which, when we have laughed at its wit, been held in the grip of its drama and revelled in the colours and layers of its language, still raises echo after echo in our minds and hearts. Which is not surprising, for it is in our minds and hearts that it is taking place.

Sunday Times February 26th and 19th March, 1978

Playing with fire

TODAY, THE BRITISH Olympic Committee meets to decide whether to advise British athletes to participate in the Soviet Propaganda Games in Moscow, or to recognize that the Soviet Union, by her breach of some *ten* of the provisions of the Olympic Charter and her invasion, subjugation and occupation of a formerly independent state which was itself a member of the Olympic Movement, has put herself outside the comity of sporting nations. Ought the Olympic competitors of states not obliged, by the fact of their own vassalage within the Soviet Empire, to do whatever the imperial power demands, to provide the sanction of their attendance at a show which, for the host country, is to be used *only* as a means of furthering the aims of Soviet tyranny?

I think the Committee should advise British athletes not to go to Moscow, and today I want to present the arguments in support of that contention. And to begin with, let me offer three quotations from official Soviet sources. The first is from the most recent (1979) edition of the Soviet Government's *Handbook for Party Activists*, which contains the rules for those Soviet citizens who are specifically charged with the advancing of Soviet interests within their country and around the world.

The decision to offer the honoured right to hold the Olympic Games in the capital of the first Socialist State was convincing proof of the universal recognition of the historical importance and correctness of our country's foreign policy . . .

The second quotation is from an official handbook, called *Soviet Sport – Questions and Answers*, published in Moscow (in English) by the Novosti Press.

The view popular in the West that 'Sport is outside Politics' finds no support in the U.S.S.R. This view is untenable in our country . . . When, for instance, Soviet representatives call for the expulsion of the South African and Rhodesian racists from the Olympic movement this is, of course, a political move . . . So whenever someone says that sport lies outside the framework of political relations, we feel their remark is not a serious one.

As a matter of fact, I have never thought that Lord Killanin's remarks on the subject of sport and politics have been very serious, but it is useful to have the Soviet Union's justifiably contemptuous view of him and his case so clearly expressed.

The third quotation is from a speech made at the time of the Chinese invasion of Vietnam. This is what the speaker had to say about aggression:

No peace-loving country, no person of integrity, should remain indifferent when that sort of thing happens, when an aggressor holds human life and world public opinion in insolent contempt.

That statement was made almost exactly a year ago today by Mr Kosygin, the Soviet Prime Minister. In a sense, the whole story is summed up in my three excerpts: two demonstrate that for the Soviet Union the Games constitute only an opportunity for political action and propaganda (itself a breach of the Olympic Charter), and the other demonstrates no less clearly the baseness and corruption of those whose army is at this moment in military occupation of Afghanistan after military aggression against that country, and who are, in the fullest sense of the phrase, 'holding human life and world public opinion in insolent contempt'.

And that is the country which is to be rewarded for its breaches of the Olympic Charter and programme of armed conquest of independent states by being encouraged to claim 'universal recognition of the historical importance and correctness of the course of our country's foreign policy'. And faced with the implications of the Soviet Union's manifest unfitness to be allowed to hold the Games after her invasion of Afghanistan, all Lord Killanin, Chairman of the International Olympic Committee, can say, is that other means should be found 'to resolve ideological differences'.

Whatever happens to the Olympic Games, this year or in the future, if weasel words of that kind prevail, then our world is doomed, and deserves to be. Just so might some appeaser in the 1930s have said of efforts to stop Hitler's aggression that means other than resistance to it should be used 'to resolve ideological differences'. The rattle of the chains from the Soviet concentration-camps, the screams of the tortured in their psychiatric prisons, the rumble of the tanks on the roads of Afghanistan, the tears of the captive peoples of the Soviet European Empire – these things are presumably 'ideological differences', which must be 'resolved' (by, I take it, ideologues), lest the appeasers should have to admit the truth about the way in which rulers like the Soviet ones use sport as an instrument of ideology exactly as they use the censor's pencil, the jailer's key and the soldier's gun.

If the appeasers admitted that, of course, they would have to admit much more; that the Soviet Union was ineligible ten times over, under the Olympic rules themselves, to stage the Games, long before the invasion of Afghanistan was contemplated; that the claim that the I.O.C. keeps politics out of sport is false; and that the shameful pleasure of strutting in the Moscow limelight is more enticing than the stern dictates of honour.

These things the I.O.C. cannot admit. Within *one week* after refusing to cancel or postpone the Moscow Games, a refusal based on the claim that such an action would be an impermissibly political one, the International Olympic Committee expelled the Taiwan team, on *entirely* political grounds. Taiwan's claim to call herself 'The Republic of China' had naturally displeased the Chinese Government in Peking, so Lord Killanin and his committee duly obliged with the political decision required of them. They did the same at Montreal, too, when the Trudeau government excluded the Taiwanese for the same political reason; the I.O.C. ratified the decision. No less exclusively political was the expulsion from the Olympic movement of South Africa (Lord Killanin's insistence that the Soviet Union must at all costs be allowed to keep the Games is now particularly odious in view of the grossly racialist character of that country's policies). I am not here concerned to discuss whether Taiwan should be allowed to call herself the Republic of China, or whether South Africa ought to be allowed to participate in international sporting events. These are matters on which there can clearly be two opinions; but only one is possible when it comes to the falsity of the I.O.C.'s claim that it cannot, and does not, take political decisions.

It is time for a fourth quotation. Who said this in March, 1936, when the Terror was getting under way in Germany, when the whole array of anti-semitism was being put into force there, when rearming for aggression was Hitler's chief and unconcealed concern – and when preparation for a colossal Nazi propaganda show at the Berlin Olympics was going busily forward?

These games . . . play a real part in creating a better understanding between the nations of the world . . . it would be nothing short of calamity if this country, to whom the world often looks for a lead, were not fully represented . . . the Germans are deeply conscious of the obligations which they have entered into by undertaking to hold them in their country.

The voice is that of Lord Exeter; he wrote those words in a letter to this newspaper, published on March 9th, 1936, and he can at any rate now claim to be consistent in his folly.

Let me sum up. The Soviet Union, contrary to the letter as well as the spirit of the Olympic Charter, uses the Olympic movement for propaganda purposes, pays her Olympic athletes, discriminates among athletes on grounds of race and political opinion, does not abide by the rules for freedom of communications, allows her Olympic Committee no independence from the State – indeed makes it an integral part of the State machine – and concludes the list of offences against the Olympic rules by invading and occupying a country which is a fellow-member of the Olympic movement. Today, the British Olympic Committee meets to decide whether to ratify those breaches of the rules and of the decencies alike; its present policy is to do so, and this is the last formal chance it has of deciding instead to abide by the Olympic Charter.

Now suppose the members of the Committee do decide that the Charter does not matter, that aggression does not matter, that the fielding of an entirely professional team does not matter, that censorship does not matter, that racism does not matter – that *nothing* matters beside having fun in Moscow. I fear they *will* so decide; nothing in the conduct of Sir Denis Follows suggests any other course of action, and those affiliated sports associations whose members are opposed to attending the Games in Moscow are, so far at any rate, clearly in the minority. What then?

Why, then, it behoves me to ask our athletes, severally and collectively, what makes them think that they are exempt from the general obligations of human beings not to behave like brutes? Why, because their splendid bodies can run faster or jump higher than other people's, do they suppose that they need not mind about helping tyrants to further the work of tyranny? What do they mean when they say (as some already have) that it is 'up to the politicians' to take action over the Moscow Olympics? Do they not even understand that in a democracy *we* are the politicians, the ones at Westminster being only our representatives? Do they admit no obligation to their common humanity with those whom their Moscow hosts oppress? Does it not matter to them that no Jew who has expressed a desire to emigrate from the Soviet Union, no man or woman who has been caught reading a forbidden book about freedom, could be picked for the Soviet Olympic team, that those athletes who *are* picked for it will be spied upon night and day in the Olympic Village by K.G.B. men, that the athletes who come from free countries like ours will be used by the Soviet Union not as examples of fine sportsmen and women, but as men and women who have come to Moscow to offer 'recognition of the historical importance and correctness of the Soviet Union's foreign policy'?

No man is an island; not even if he is an athlete. Any man's death diminishes me; even if I am an athlete. Send not to ask for whom the bell tolls; even if you are an athlete, it tolls for thee. Each athlete, once the political decision to go to Moscow is taken, will have to decide for himself or herself whether to acquiesce in it. Let none be under any illusion: by going to Moscow and giving the Soviet Union a victory for propaganda following a victory for aggression, they will be condoning tyranny, disgracing themselves and betraying the ideals of sport. They may, it is true, win medals, of gold, silver or bronze. But not all the skills of alchemy will ever transmute their prizes into anything but tarnished badges of shame.

The Times March 4th, 1980

Credo quia impossibile

The Monument: The Story of the Socialist Party of Great Britain
by Robert Barltropp*

ONE OF THE nicest things I know about Britain is that
organizations like the S.P.G.B. can exist, and when I say
'organizations like' the S.P.G.B., I mean the S.P.G.B., for
there is nothing else like it, and when I say I am glad it can
exist, I do not mean that I am glad we live in a society free
enough for such glorious nonsense to be freely promulgated,
though obviously that *is* cause for rejoicing, but that what
truly warms the heart is the glimpse its existence gives of
richness, variety and eccentricity that make up our extraordinary nation.

The S.P.G.B. was originally a fragment of the cosmic dust
resulting from the 'big bang' of Marxism in the nineteenth
century. The proliferation of socialist, utopian and millenarian
sects around the end of Victoria's reign was largely the result
of the passionate intensity with which almost every individual
in them maintained that there was but one true faith and that
he alone held it; the S.P.G.B. originated with a group expelled from Hyndman's Social Democratic Federation for
some inconceivably obscure variety of deviationism, and is
unique not just in that it is the most extreme of all the
Impossibilist sects but because it has remained absolutely

  * Pluto Press, 1976.

unchanged in its beliefs from 1904 to the present day.

The original declaration of aims stated that the S.P.G.B. was 'hostile to every other party' and that it was 'determined to wage war against all other political parties, whether alleged labour or avowedly capitalist.' And to this position it has adhered ever since, with absolutely literal fidelity; it is perfectly fair to say that its members believe that there is *nothing whatever* to choose between the Labour Party and the National Front, or between the Communist Party and the Tories.

The S.P.G.B.'s position is simple, and always has been. Marx was right; the S.P.G.B.'s interpretation of Marx is right; there is no possibility of anything at all happening to improve the lot of the people until, overnight, they seize control of their own destiny and enact Socialism; none but the S.P.G.B. can convert them to that view. It follows that all attempts at reform of any kind must be implacably resisted, partly because they are all devised by the capitalist class to further their own ends, and partly because they delay the dawn.

Thus, its members are immovably opposed to the Welfare State; they have opposed the introduction of holidays with pay because these only refresh the workers for more exploited labour; when they put up candidates for local councils or Parliament (and they have always been very dubious about doing so) they spend much of their electioneering time insisting that only voters who are 100 per cent supporters of everything they stand for may vote for them; they fought against the introduction of safeguards for factory machinery because it might put off the day when the downtrodden (and, presumably, mutilated) workers take over the means of production, distribution and exchange; they refused to accept advertising in their paper (the *Socialist Standard*) though they have always been desperately poor, because advertising is a filthy capitalist habit, *despite the fact that at the time they took the decision they had only ever had one advertiser, and he was the Party member who printed the Party journal at ruinous cost to his little printing business, which he wanted to see survive solely so that he could go on producing it for his comrades*; and one member, hardly exceptional among his fellows, 'would have no furniture because (he said) capitalists sent bailiffs to take such things away from working people, and so his family used orange boxes instead.'

It is not difficult to guess what this Impossibilism has led to, again and again, throughout the Party's history: a succession of atrocious purges and heresy hunts, of a medieval intolerance and ferocity, within the ranks of the Elect. Again and again, their best men have been thrown out for daring to suggest the tiniest variation in the interpretation of Holy Writ; whole Branches (sometimes amounting to a substantial proportion of the entire membership, which has rarely been more than a few hundred) have been expelled; and every time there was a vote on an expulsion, those who had voted against it were themselves forthwith expelled, followed by any who had voted against *their* expulsion.

Until very recent times, the S.P.G.B.'s story has been largely composed of some marvellously colourful figures; there was Moses Baritz, for instance, who, barred from a meeting of a rival organization, 'climbed on the roof with a clarinet, poked it into a ventilator shaft, and blew piercing unbearable *obbligatos* into the hall until they let him in.' And there was Tony Turner, whom I heard speak many times, and who was certainly the greatest soap-boxer I can remember (he once spoke, in Hyde Park, from early morning until late at night, without a break).

The author is himself a lifelong member, though he left the Party for some years, and may well be expelled for heresy because of this book; it is written with an honesty that is beautiful to contemplate, a self-taught style of extraordinary grace, and – *anathema sit! anathema sit!* – considerable humour. He tells a tale of gorgeous absurdity; of a Party which expelled a member for turning up at a meeting, during the Second World War, with his gas-mask, because the Party had ruled that the war was about nothing but capitalist rivalry; a Party with a faction which argued that 'vegetarianism was a capitalist plot to lower labour costs by making the working class feed on grass'; a Party which, facing financial extinction, was saved by a large donation from a ninety-two-year-old sympathizer with a cat called Karl Marx; a Party which has survived for seventy-two years by an implacable refusal to recognize any form of reality. I hope it goes on refusing for another seventy-two years at least, for when it dies England will have lost a monument indeed.

Observer April 18th, 1976

Not to be sneezed at

ALDUS BOOKS HAVE announced the forthcoming publication of a book by Mr John Trueman, called *The Romantic Story of Scent*. In their announcement they say that since it is almost impossible to describe a fragrance in words they:

> have given the reader the scents themselves. Eighteen labels on the jacket flaps – each of which can be peeled off and stuck on the appropriate pages of the book itself – correspond to the eighteen scents described. A tiny scratch on the label releases the fragrance, not just once, but through rereading after rereading. Each label is coated with an invisible film consisting of millions of tiny capsules, each of which contains fragrance. This newly-perfected process of micro-encapsulation enables the reader actually to smell the scents while reading about them . . .

Now that is all very well (and incidentally reminds me that there used to be – still is, for all I know – an American magazine that added realism to its advertisements by attaching to them samples of the goods advertised, so that each issue was several inches thick, containing as it did snippets of fabric, miniature lipsticks, envelopes full of cornflakes, sachets of liquor and the like, though I cannot remember what they did when they had an advertisement for Rolls-Royces, industrial ovens or pedigree bulldogs), but I have an uneasy feeling that these enterprising publishers have not thought the thing through quite far enough.

To start with, what are they going to do about Miss Barbara

Cartland's next romantic novel but three, if it should contain, as it well might, such a passage as this?

> Fiona's heart was beating wildly as Julian gently drew her into his arms. She could smell the rough tweed of his jacket and the reassuring scent of his cigar, which he had thoughtfully taken out of his mouth before kissing her. Behind them, the breeze stirred the bank of violets; in front of them, it stirred the bed of peonies; to their left, it stirred (oh, *what* a busy breeze it was!) the field of clover; to their right, the pigs grunted in the sty. There was a crash; she realized she had dropped her basket and smashed a bottle of eau-de-cologne, another of Château Latour 1947 and the phial with old Mrs Blenkinsop's specimen that was due to be taken to hospital for analysis. Julian's trousers burst into flames, and a passing Chinaman lit a joss-stick. Far away, Sir Jasper spread some more anchovy paste on his digestive biscuit, and twirled his waxed moustache. His wife was sick into the kedgeree, and the undertaker's men entered to remove the butler, who had been dead for some days.

The resultant conflict of odours would be more likely to get the publishers prosecuted for causing a public nuisance than to turn the work into a best-seller, and I know whereof I speak, for the first newspaper job I ever had involved my going once a week to the printers, which was situated next door to a factory making soap, cosmetics and scent, the whole area being steeped as a result in a pong that was almost unbearable, despite the fact that each constituent part of it was guaranteed to make the user smell sweet as any rose, or possibly sweeter.

And that does not exhaust the possibilities, either. Take the book on scent itself, with its eighteen varieties of smell. Suppose that a married man should have to stay away for the night on business, and suppose further that in the train coming back he should while away the journey by reading *The Romantic Story of Scent*, following the publisher's instructions carefully. He arrives home, and flings open the door with a cry of 'I got the Fiddle and Dee contract, darling – this will mean promotion, with any luck!' His wife, delighted, rushes to embrace him, and is assailed by the combined scents of lily-of-the-valley, stephanotis, lavender, attar of roses, verbena, parma violet, mimosa, sandalwood, wild fern, rosemary, orange-blossom, pine, magnolia, jasmine, carnation, musk, lilac and frangipani. He would not only face the prospect of his wife instantly packing her bags and going home to mother; he would be lucky if, after the divorce, she refrained from selling a series of articles to one of the less expensive Sunday newspapers under the title 'I married a monster'.

And, of course, it will not stop there. Those very newspapers, rubbing their hands at yet another headline reading 'Axe-fiend slays nine', will take to sticking a micro-encapsulated label on every copy, a scratch at which will release the powerful smell of human blood, though what they will do if the headline is 'Axe-fiend slays nine in brewery as gas-leak threatens rubber-galosh factory' I cannot imagine, or rather I can. As for other books thought suitable for the treatment, it is all very well saying that it would be limited to cookery books, encyclopaedias of wild flowers, catalogues of fertilizer manufacturers and the like, but sooner or later some clown will commission a history of those hot-dog stands that infest London, the stench from which has frequently brought me to my knees when I have been a quarter of a mile away and upwind into the bargain, and we shall be afraid to get into a bus in case one of the other passengers is reading it.

Next, of course, the other senses will be catered for. War books will be supplied with miniature tape-recorders on each page, and the noise of bombs and guns will deafen everybody for miles around; the *Guide Michelin*, recording the specialities at Père Bise, will encourage its readers to lick a micro-dot in the margin and taste the *poularde braisée à la crème d'estragon*; improper novels, when they come to the bit where the hero tears the clothes off the heroine, will print the crucial page on real knicker-silk.

I believe, incidentally, that some theatrical and film producers, in a misguided attempt to add verisimilitude to the work on offer, have tried pumping the appropriate smells into the auditorium, as called for by the story, only to find their plan going badly awry, as they had failed to devise any means of removing each smell from the place before the next one was due, so that as the heroine was unwrapping an exquisite gardenia which had just arrived with a note from the hero, the audience was still being regaled with the kippers that had been consumed in the previous scene. Let Aldus Books be warned by this horrid example, and abandon their plan. It is not always true, and they may discover as much to their cost, that if you take care of the scents the pounds will take care of themselves. In short, I smell trouble.

The Times May 15th, 1975

Yours faithfully, Cicero

THE CICERO PROBLEM is a very intractable one. In essence, true, it is simple, and can be reduced to a single question. The trouble, however, is that the question is almost impossible to answer. It is: do we like him or do we not?

The question must be kept carefully distinct from others that present themselves, and that on a cursory inspection seem to be the same, or at any rate indissolubly linked. Thus: do we trust him? I think we certainly do. Do we wish to sit next to him at dinner? On the whole, I think we do not. Was he, on balance, a Good Thing? Surely yes. But do we like him? Do we warm to him? Do we sympathize with his predicament and his weaknesses, do we cheer him on against Catiline or Clodius, do we feel involved with him, do we, when his slave delivers a note asking if he may drop round, immediately experience a sensation of pleasure and anticipation?

I really do not know, and my doubts are not, as they would be in the case of many another man, tantamount to an answer in the negative; without actually having had the benefit of a first-hand acquaintance with him, I think it is impossible to say for certain whether I like him or not. And the question has presented itself to me very directly because I have just read Professor D. R. Shackleton Bailey's complete translation of Cicero's letters. These are divided into his letters to Atticus (which was strictly a nickname, derived from the Philhellenism of Cicero's friend and correspondent, who was born Titus Pomponius), and his letters to his other friends and his family. Professor Shackleton Bailey published a vast scholarly edition of the Atticus letters a decade or so ago; he has recently followed this with a translation of the rest of Cicero's extant correspondence; both sets of letters have been published in three volumes in the Penguin Classics;* I have just read the lot; and I still do not know whether I like Cicero or whether I don't.

If I do not, it is not for lack of material or interpretation of it. There are 909 letters in all (far more than survive from the correspondence of any other figure of classical antiquity – indeed, fifteen centuries were to elapse before a greater epistolary vein was mined, in the letters of Erasmus); the earliest dates from November 68, the last from July 43. Cicero was thirty-eight when he wrote the first; the last was written five months before he was killed in the aftermath of Octavian's march on Rome and uneasy alliance with Antony and Lepidus. The editing is throughout a model of sympathetic yet rigorous scholarship; Professor Shackleton Bailey even corrects Cicero's misjudgments when there is evidence that they were baseless, and his three comprehensive glossaries, of persons, places and terms, almost *but not quite* make up for the lack of an index.

But I still do not know whether I like Cicero. Paradoxically, I like him when I leave my emotions out of consideration. He took on the unspeakable Clodius (the one who infiltrated the sacred feminine rites in Caesar's own house) for the same reason that he took on Catiline; they were both dangerous blackguards and deserved to be driven from Rome. Unfortunately, the delicate balance of power when it came to Clodius was suddenly tilted against Cicero, and it was he who had to flee the capital, while the triumphant degenerate had Cicero's very house pulled down. It is impossible not to sympathize with Cicero throughout the struggle, nor to rejoice when he is re-enfranchised, compensated and – ultimately – revenged. But I am nagged by a feeling that my sympathy is derived

* Penguin, 1978.

from the fact that Cicero in this matter was a victim of injustice, rather than from a true fellow-feeling.

And there is, undeniably, much to be said on the other side. Cicero's best friend (Atticus, I take it) could hardly deny that there is a sense of self-satisfaction about him that is unappealing:

> I happened to be absent when the decree was voted . . . I administered what I felt to be a highly impressive rebuke to the Senate, speaking with no little weight and fluency in a not very respectable cause . . . and I have not only borne with it but lent it my eloquence . . . But there was the gravest danger of a complete break between Senate and Knights . . . Here again it was I who stepped into the breach. Through my efforts they found the Senate in full attendance and in generous mood . . .

The tone, even down to that mock-deprecating qualification ('in a not very respectable cause'), is that of Macaulay, and I am perfectly certain that I don't like *him*. Moreover, there is a coldness about Cicero, an air of feeling nothing but the correctness of certain emotions at certain times, that makes me uneasy. There is a letter from Servius Sulpicius Rufus to Cicero, telling in the sparsest language of the murder by a madman of a mutual friend of theirs. It includes virtually nothing but the facts, but it has a directness and simplicity that make it more moving than anything I could feel from Cicero's side of any of the correspondence. His political caution, it seems to me, was another side of his personal aloofness; he tried to remain on good terms with most of the factions (except Antony's) as the Republic crumbled, and his skill in doing so was matched by his skill in keeping his deeper emotions concealed – to such an extent, indeed, that it is difficult to resist the conclusion that he hadn't got any.

And yet there is much on the other side. He was devotedly loyal to his friends, his allies and his political patrons; he was a brilliantly evocative parliamentary reporter (his accounts in these letters of the Senate's proceedings are at times positively Hansardian in their completeness); he was clearly a true repository of Roman honour; though a dangerous foe, he was not on the whole vindictive – even in exile, he is contemptuous of Clodius rather than full of hate for him, and his account of his restoration to position and fortune is remarkably free of rancour or gloating; he was alert and alive to the last, inquisitive and receptive; he was certainly brave; he is never boring, at any rate in his letters (I have the feeling that his speeches would have been another matter); he was obviously a superb lawyer, though some say that that is not in itself the very highest praise one man can bestow on another.

I would very much like to have known him, and this is a conclusion I have come to after reading his correspondence. There is no reason to suppose that he had any thought of publication when he wrote the letters, though in those troubled times he had always to bear in mind that they might fall into the wrong hands, so that he is always saying less than he means, trusting to his correspondents to fill in the gaps (it is one of the many merits of Professor Shackleton Bailey's editing that he explains an enormous proportion of Cicero's hints and veiled meanings); if the letters did not often come from his heart, they clearly came from his mind without thought for their effect on posterity.

And what is that effect? I still do not know, for a wish to have made his acquaintance is not the same as a feeling that I would have liked him if I had done so. I comfort myself with the reflection that Shakespeare shared my uncertainty; Cicero, in his only scene, plays an equivocal role:

> Indeed, it is a strange disposéd time:
> But men may construe things after their fashion,
> Clean from the purpose of the things themselves.

And in the only two important references to him he is portrayed first as cannily speaking Greek to a largely Greekless audience, and second as being of little use to the conspirators, for the most significant of reasons:

> O! name him not: let us not break with him,
> For he will never follow anything
> That other men begin.

Not that that alone would make him unlikable, even if Shakespeare is being fair to him. Anyway, I have had a good time with his correspondence, and that, if he is anxious for my approbation, will have to suffice him.

The Times March 18th, 1980

Looking on the bright side

IT IS WELL known that no news is good news; what is less widely understood is that good news is bad news. And this particular bit of truly significant news has not yet, apparently, penetrated to China, where the authorities have decreed, according to a report by the *Daily Telegraph*'s inquisitive and entertaining Peking correspondent, Graham Earnshaw, that only good news is to be reported, and that stories of such negative matters as crime and corruption are no longer to be published. Stories of upright citizens labouring tirelessly are the in thing; a lady who worked in a factory tirelessly labouring at the production of toothpaste for the state and, when she died, bequeathed all of which she died possessed to the said state, has been posthumously and publicly canonized, as have two men who were drowned while trying to rescue a girl who had fallen into a river. (I am not sure that the newspaper which reported the latter story had fully got the hang of the new rules; surely it could have better filled the space with accounts of girls who had not fallen into the river in the first place.)

It won't work, I'm afraid. The heirs of Mao are only the latest in the long line of those who have dreamed the same dream; that if you do not draw attention to the darkness, it will turn to light of its own accord. The hunger is constantly making itself felt in this country, too; it's a poor month that doesn't see a letter in one newspaper or another complaining that the press prints only bad news. Yet a newspaper which accepted the premise of this Pathetic Fallacy and published nothing but that which can be seen through rose-coloured spectacles would speedily find its readers deserting in their numbers to rivals unafraid of pointing out that life is not altogether a bowl of cherries, and the only reason that such a fate will not overtake the Chinese papers under the new dispensation is that the readers have no rival sheets to desert to.

Words are not things, nor things words. If (and the Chinese rulers are just the lads to try it) the entrance to a sewage-farm were to be decorated with a sign forty feet high bearing the message '4711 Made Here', I can assure those whom it might concern that the surrounding air would still not be fragrant with the scent of eau-de-cologne, or even roast chicken. Portraying the Chinese people as free of all blemish, and the life they lead as no less untroubled by mischance, will not make them so; if it has any effect at all, it will serve only to alienate the people from their leaders, for whatever else the Chinese may be, they are plainly not daft, and they will speedily take the measure of the difference between what their rulers tell them and what they can see with their own epicanthus-laden eyes.

The problem can be summed up in a dozen words: we do not wish to be told that which we already know. We know that most husbands do not murder their wives, that few bank managers abscond with the funds, that although some aeroplanes crash, far more arrive safely, that not every dog will bite. And we know these things for a reason far deeper and more important than that provided by the statistics which bear out our convictions. We are instinctively possessed of the truth that the universe runs on the principle that the bad is the exception to the good; they are not equals, and the Manichee is wrong. We know that every day many people are injured in road accidents, many robbed or assaulted by villains, many struck by an infinite variety of the slings and arrows of outrageous fortune. Yet we do not go about the streets thinking that our next moment is going to be our last one, or even our last trouble-free one, because although we may not believe that there's a divinity doth shape our ends, rough-hew them how we may, we do believe, rightly, that normality is normal.

And it follows from this that what attracts our attention and awakens our interest is the exception, which means, broadly speaking, the bad news. A headline reading 'Nearly 55,000,000 people not struck by lightning in Britain last year' will not sell newspapers, nor will it deserve to. And I cannot believe that things are any different in China, where a news item in the *People's Daily* recording the fact that practically all the wheat sown the previous spring had grown upwards rather than downwards is unlikely to have the readers spilling their breakfast coffee into their laps in their excitement.

I do not believe it is true that people like to read about the misfortunes of others out of *Schadenfreude*. I think it much more likely that we seek, and find, reassurance in bad news – the reassurance that not only has it not happened to us but that it has all along been most unlikely to.

Many years ago I read, or perhaps dreamed, an account of a couple who, convinced that death was only a conditioned reflex, determined to bring up their son in complete ignorance of its very existence, so that if their theory were right he would be immortal, as by the time he discovered death he would be conditioned to remain unaffected by it. His children's books were scrutinized for references to the forbidden topic; plausible explanations were devised for the puzzling fact that he no longer had his puppy and was not visited any more by his grandmother; certainly, he was allowed no newspapers. And the rulers in China seem to be attempting something as absurd as the experiment of these two lunatics, not much less macabre, and equally certain to fail.

The suicide rate in the Soviet Union is among the highest in the world, though all the organs of the state combine to pretend that it simply does not exist. The lesson appears not to have been learned by China's rulers, so they will now have to learn it the hard way; crime in that country will not diminish merely because the newspapers are forbidden to mention it, nor will the incidence of corruption among Chinese officials or politicians be less because there is a general pretence that there isn't any.

Naturam expellas furca, tamen usque recurret. In Paradise, no doubt, nothing unpleasant ever happens. Here below, other standards obtain. When mosques or synagogues are built, a patch or a corner of the building is always left unfinished; perfection belongs only to Allah or Jehovah, and it is not for man to pretend to it. In China, however, though they do not believe they are already perfect, they believe that by telling each other that they are they will presently come to be. I never thought I would live to tell the Chinese, of all practical people, what Kipling told some of his contemporaries:

> Here we sit in a branchy row,
> Thinking of beautiful things we know;
> Dreaming of deeds that we mean to do,
> All complete, in a minute or two –
> Something noble and grand and good,
> Won by merely wishing we could.
> Now we're going to – never mind,
> *Brother, thy tail hangs down behind!*

The Times March 25th, 1981

The secretary-bird has flown

HUNG BE THE heavens with black, yield day to night! Comets, importing change of times and states, brandish your crystal tresses in the sky, and with them scourge the bad revolting stars!

These Shakespearian accents of woe are truly appropriate this morning, for I am, to put it mildly, bereft; after five and a half years of keeping me sane, sober and successful, and out of jail, bankruptcy and injudicious marriage, Claudia is leaving me, for a new life in the world of the film, working for a celebrated director.

For a man as morose, bad-tempered and abominably behaved as I am, I have been quite exceptionally and undeservedly lucky in my secretaries, for a dozen years or more. Indeed, in a dozen years or more I have had only three, and what is most astonishing is that the only thing they have had in common has been their ability to put up with me; a comparison of their methods may be illuminating, though I dare not guess what it will illuminate.

First of the three graces was Carole, a gentle, self-effacing girl whose quiet manner concealed a firm character; with it, she had taken the measure of me about twenty minutes after her arrival, and worked out a technique, for coping with the horrors and lunacies to come, about half an hour after that. She realized that she was not cut out for the hand-to-hand fighting that was necessary, and decided instead to follow Peer Gynt when, faced with the Great Boyg, he was told: 'You must go round'. After, for instance, asking me half a dozen times for

instructions on some pressing matter, and getting either no
instructions at all or six sets, none compatible with any of the
others, she would decide what I ought to do and arrange it
without further consultation; I never complained, partly because she invariably arranged matters for the best, and partly
because, in the circumstances I have outlined, I was hardly in a
position to do so.

Carole never got flustered, she never lost her temper, and as
far as I knew she never wept. Nor did she ever fail me, in great
things or small. She left to travel, and was succeeded by Sonia,
a Cockney with spirit for twenty and no intention whatever of
putting up with my nonsense for even a moment. If Carole got
her way with grace, Sonia did it by simply slugging it out
('bleedin' twit' was one of her favourite epithets for me), and
with an awful literalness, too, for twice, speechless with rage
at some more than usually appalling conduct on my part, she
resorted to missiles. The first was a harmless volume of the
telephone directory (E to K, as I recall) but the second was a
very heavy glass ashtray which, if it had connected, would
have deprived the nation of much subsequent instruction and
entertainment. (No jury, however, would have convicted her;
indeed, they would almost certainly have stopped the case and
recommended a substantial payment out of public funds as
soon as they had heard her story.) Sonia typed the first draft of
my first book, all 200,000 words of it, in her spare time; she
had an exceptionally wise head on her young shoulders, and
made a wonderful confidante; she had a lovely sense of
humour; she left to get married and to live happily ever after.

When I came to *The Times*, at the beginning of 1971,
Claudia was already here, lending a temporary hand in the
office in which I parked myself. It did not take me long to
realize that she had the makings of an outstanding life-saver of
a secretary; the trouble was that others around the place had
had the same thought, and some deft footwork, not to say
knifework, was required on my part before the prize was
landed. (It was some two years, however, before she could

bring herself to confess that she had been under the impression, when she accepted the job, that I was Bernard Braden.)

Since then, I have not had a day's worry, though she, I fear, has had many. A soldier's daughter, she doesn't weep, either, or throw things at me; her technique for coping with the monster has been to deploy her dazzling, absolutely flawless efficiency like a net, in which I flounder, grumbling, and eventually subside into complete satisfaction. And I do not exaggerate her efficiency; she even has that invaluable gift, anticipation, and has used it on countless occasions to save me from disaster. (Once, when I was on a train travelling back to London, utterly unaware that a whole series of catastrophes had been detonated under my programme, she worked out a complete rescue plan, had me met at the station by a taxi-driver bearing the revised instructions, with all times, places and bookings organized and accounted for, *and* rang me late that night to check that everything had gone off as it should.) The picture of the businessman, organizing mighty mergers and brilliant new developments, who is helpless as a baby without his secretary, is a cliché; I can only say that, though I am no businessman, I lead a life as complicated as many a captain of industry, and I live the cliché every waking hour. (Incidentally, if you are thinking that if she typed this without blushing she must be uncommonly brazen, I should explain that she didn't; I gave her an entirely spurious column to do, and had this one done behind her back. So she's reading it for the first time along with you.)

Claudia – she is known as Claude to all *The Times*, though I alone know her middle name, and brandish its disclosure like a weapon when I want my own way – has a zany streak that has issued in such episodes as what happened once when I had gone padding about the office all day in my stockinged feet, only to find when it was time to leave that one of my shoes was missing. With a straight face, she helped me search for it, getting more and more concerned as I got nearer to tears; she kept it up for something like three-quarters of an hour, before bidding me open a large, bulky envelope on my desk. On the other hand, she can be brutally direct; when *The Times* moved from Blackfriars to Gray's Inn Road, she simply forbade me to come into the office at all for a full week, while the chaos was sorted out, saying, 'It's going to be bad enough without you moaning and complaining and getting lost all the time.'

Carole was a very present help in trouble; Sonia a stimulus and a sparring-partner; Claudia is a dear friend, and will remain one, whatever becomes of both of us, to the end of my days. I shall remember her curious habit of suddenly declaiming, in sepulchral tones, a childhood incantation that runs: 'I am a mole and I live in a hole'; I shall remember her almost (though not quite) infinite capacity for being teased; I shall remember her brown eyes and her upright bearing; I shall remember her silver laugh; I shall remember how entirely I have come to rely upon her, and how entirely I have been able to do so. We shall all miss her, around the office; and I shall miss her as I would miss music itself. Angels and ministers of grace defend her.

The Times April 30th, 1976

Prawn cocktail, with capers

THE MYSTERIOUS CASE of the Captive Prawn ('These are deep waters, Watson') clearly deserves more attention than it has so far had. Before I go on to examine its implications, an outline of what has happened hitherto may be helpful, or not, as the case might be.

In the Sheriff Court at Duns, in Berwickshire, a young lady has been accused, under the Protection of Animals (Scotland) Act 1912, of being cruel to a prawn, if not indeed to several prawns. She has pleaded not guilty to this offence, and one of the arguments adduced on her behalf is that a prawn is not a fish – if it were, cruelty to it would be an offence under Section 13, sub-section c, of the Statute – but an insect. The Sheriff, Mr James Paterson – clearly a man who can see trouble coming before he is actually hit on the head with a sockful of wet sand – has adjourned the case until he can hear expert evidence from a zoologist, which is his first mistake, because for one thing a zoologist will be quite unable to express any opinion on the matter in dispute, the question of whether a prawn is a fish or an insect being wholly outwith a zoologist's competence; what is needed here is either an ichthyologist or an entomologist, and preferably both, though as a matter of fact the Sheriff would be well advised to shoot himself before the trial resumes, as statistics show that 87 per cent of those in charge of judicial proceedings in which expert evidence is called suffer irreparable brain damage, and very few of the rest altogether escape some deterioration of the personality. This may be a good point – no worse than any other, at all events – to mention that the Prawn Case is not the first, but the third, occasion on which Duns has found itself treading a wider stage than usual. It is, of course, the venue of a celebrated limerick:

> There was an old fellow of Duns,
> Who swore he'd eat ninety-nine buns;
> At the seventy-first,
> He unhappily burst,
> And the rest were consumed by his sons.

But it is also the birthplace of John Duns Scotus, hight Doctor Subtilis for the ingenuity of his theological disputation, of whom the legend says that he died of apoplexy, which ought to be further warning for Sheriff Paterson. I cannot now remember whether it is true, or *ben trovato*, or whether indeed I invented it myself, that he once had to debate before the Sorbonne the syllogism 'Those who eat oatmeal are barbarians; the Scots eat oatmeal: therefore . . . ' In any case, this is taking us far from prawns.

The Act under which the prosecution was brought amply repays careful study. Its very title is a melody ('An Act to consolidate and amend enactments relating to Animals and Knackers'), and there is a passage in the definitions section which could have come straight out of the Authorized Version, and is worth quoting in full:

The expression 'horse' includes any mare, gelding, pony, foal, colt, filly or stallion; and the expression 'ox' includes any cow, bullock, heifer, calf, steer, or bull; and the expression 'sheep' includes any lamb, ewe, or ram; and the expression 'pig' includes any boar, hog or sow; and the expression 'goat' includes any kid; and the expression 'dog' includes any bitch, sapling, or puppy; and the expression 'cat' includes any kitten; and the expression 'fowl' includes any cock, hen, chicken, capon, turkey, goose, gander, duck, drake, guinea-fowl, peacock, peahen, swan, or pigeon.

On the other hand, Section 1, sub-section 1(a) of the Act not only makes it an offence for any person to cruelly beat, kick, ill-treat, over-ride, over-drive, over-load, torture or terrify any animal – and I think I can truly say that I have never done any of those things to any creature – but also forbids anyone to 'infuriate' any animal either, and I have to confess that I spent a considerable part of last weekend attempting to infuriate a fat and handsome tabby called Dazzicle, on the ground that I thought the beast was far too complacent for its own good, and badly in need of infuriation; I thus laid myself open, on summary conviction, to a fine not exceeding £25 or alternatively or in addition thereto a term of imprisonment not exceeding six months, though as the Act only forbids me to *infuriate* animals, not to *attempt* to do so, and as I was entirely unable to effect my object, Dazzicle remaining contemptuously even-tempered throughout, I claim to have a complete answer to the charge. However, this also takes us far from prawns.

Though I cannot eat any kind of shellfish, I am inordinately fond of every one of the crustacea, from the smallest shrimp to the largest lobster, via the Berwickshire prawn, and am profoundly glad that Section 1, sub-section 3(a) expressly excludes from the Act's prohibition against cruelty anything done in the course of preparation of any animal 'as food for mankind', though to judge from the abusive letters I got when, a year or two ago, I happened to mention that the previous Wednesday I had eaten three lobsters for lunch, the very existence of this part of the Act is clearly unsuspected by many of my readers.

Chez Barrier, in Tours, they serve *écrevisses à la nage*, among other things, and anybody ordering them is instantly advanced upon by a waiter who courteously envelops the diner in a gigantic bath-towel, shaped like a monster bib; last time I was there, only the fact that I could not for the life of me remember the French for a loofah prevented me from asking for one. On another occasion, staying with my kid sister in

Massachusetts, I ate a Cape Cod lobster which not only *was* fresh, but which I very well *knew* was fresh, as not three hours before dinner it had been crawling around me where I sat in a deck-chair on the lawn, and had indeed attempted to bite my big toe.

On the terrible occasion when I couldn't have lunch at the Auberge du Père Bise because the old man had died and the place was closed for the day of his funeral, we went next door to the Cottage instead, where their amazing lobster bisque did much to console me for my disappointment, and to reconcile me to anything else that fate might have in store for me in the way of unpleasantness; I cannot remember what followed, but I know that whatever it was it was accompanied by a Richebourg of such indescribable splendour that I swear I could hear angelic choirs as I drank it. Of the salmon soufflé at Illhauesern I have written too recently to raise the subject again, and in any case salmon soufflé would also take me far from prawns. I look forward to the resumed case in Duns, and meanwhile, wishing only to be helpful, offer all concerned my recollection of an ancient *Punch* cartoon, in which a homely body is standing on a station platform surrounded by her vast variety of pets; a harassed porter has clearly just returned from taking higher instructions, and is reporting: 'Stationmaster says dogs is dogs, and cats is dogs, and so's parrots, but this 'ere tortoise is a hinseck, so it will 'ave to go in the van.'

The Times January 15th, 1974

The end of term

WHEN A MAN, at a cost of a good many thousands of pounds, voluntarily closes down a thriving business which he started twenty years ago on £100 borrowed from his grandfather and built up by hard work into a concern pre-eminent in its field, it is worth asking him why, in case the answer should provide some general comment on our times. And since I think it does, I give it today.

The St Giles School of Languages was founded by Mr Paul Lindsay, partly because his natural bent was towards a career in education and partly because the existing private teaching of foreign languages and of English as a foreign language seemed to him plainly inadequate. (Some three-quarters of such schools even today are not 'recognized' – that is, have not satisfied the Government inspectorate that they meet the required standards.) For nearly two decades he and his wife, and their staff, worked to make it a successful, reputable and valuable contribution to education in an important area. So well did they do in realizing these aims that the St Giles School was one of the first to be 'recognized'; a separate but similar establishment was opened at Brighton; and when Mr Lindsay founded a (non-profit) teacher-training unit at the School, it was not long before a St Giles Teachers' Certificate was being included among the desired qualifications in advertisements for teachers all over the country.

Yet at Easter the School was abruptly closed. Mr Lindsay explains the abruptness by saying that he feared that, if he announced his decision in advance, there might have been a 'sit-in' at the premises by a group of the teachers; he explains the closure itself by saying that a group among the staff, some of whom, he believes, held far-left political views, had been engaged for about a year on a campaign of pressure on him and the School which was inevitably destroying it, and which had already had the effect of leaving him virtually powerless to affect, much less control, the destinies of his own establishment. (The spokesman for some of the teachers denies that there would have been a sit-in, and says that only one teacher was a member of an extremist organization – the Communist Party.)

It began in May last year, when teachers in the department of English as a Foreign Language joined the Managerial, Administrative and Technical Staff Association; a branch of MATSA was formed from language teachers. Mr Lindsay (a lifelong Labour voter) was sympathetic to the wish of members of his staff to be represented by a union, and agreed with the professed aim, which was to improve standards and conditions, especially in the *un*recognized schools; he was told that the union members' efforts were not directed at schools like St Giles, where (as they agreed) pay and conditions were reasonable. He raised no objection to their wish to join MATSA (affiliated to the G.M.W.U.), though he was surprised that they had not chosen to join the N.U.T. or one of the other teachers' organizations; he was one of the first principals of such schools to sign an agreement with the union; and he has from the start afforded the union members the facilities for union work. But he tells me that techniques of industrial harassment were introduced at St Giles at once. Indeed, while he was actually on the telephone arranging a meeting to discuss recognition of the union he was threatened with a strike – 'I'll call my members out and close your school down' were the words used – when he was doing no more than suggest a change in the time of the meeting. (The spokesman insists that the union wanted only normal negotiations, and says that Mr Lindsay was 'anti-union', indeed that he was 'obsessed' on the subject.)

Before this, however, Mr Lindsay had come to the conclusion that the teacher-training unit would have to be closed; it was making a loss, and that, combined with the effects of the worsening economic climate and the problems such schools always have in the irregular, and therefore uneconomic, pattern of their intake (their busiest time is the summer, for instance, and they have many more morning students than afternoon), made it necessary to reduce the size of the School and let off part of the buildings. He communicated the decision to the head of the teacher-training department (in June 1974) who insisted that an assistant being newly taken on must be told that her appointment was a strictly limited one and would end in November 1974, when the department closed. In September, Mr Lindsay gave formal notice to the head of teacher-training; there is a conflict of evidence between them, Mr Lindsay saying that he had given no promise of continued employment unless there was a vacancy on the teaching staff, and the teacher-trainer insisting that he had been given an *unconditional* guarantee. But in any case this was lost sight of in the cry of 'victimization' (the man was a union official) that was instantly raised. And I do mean instantly; Mr Lindsay's offer to discuss the dispute with the union, in accordance with agreed procedure, was ignored, as was his wish to meet the whole teaching staff, *and the next thing he knew about the situation was that a broadcasting company was on the phone asking him for a comment about the strike.* (When he asked the organizers why they had not even told him that they were going on strike they replied that they had not had time – but they had had time to print leaflets and make banners, which were immediately on show outside the building; the strike had clearly been prepared in advance. The spokesman, who was the shop steward – that is what he asked me to call him in writing about the business, but surely it is still an odd term to find in a *school*? – of the union at the School, says that not telling Mr Lindsay was 'indefensible' and that they now deeply regret it.)

There was the usual scene at the premises, with Mr and Mrs Lindsay and the non-striking staff having to run a gauntlet of shouts and accusations; the organizers refused to suspend their action to enable officials of the union's head office to discuss the situation with Mr Lindsay; the strikers made it clear that they would accept no compromise; and every detail of the agreement, which amounted to a complete acceptance of the strikers' demands, had to be settled before the School could reopen.

When it did, Mr Lindsay went to the staff-room, shook hands with all the strikers, and expressed his willingness to forget their differences and to accept the result. But from then on, he says that the School deteriorated under the 'salami tactics' of a group clearly determined to impose their will on the School; and this is no metaphor, for Mr Lindsay says he has been told to his face, during the struggle, that he is 'only' the 'legal owner' of St Giles. (He is, and always has been, also a practising teacher.)

No issue was too small, or too manifestly groundless, to be used. For instance, the School's union members declared that the assistant in the teacher-training department, who had been taken on for a specified, limited time, the length of her appointment being made clear to her in advance in writing (and all this at the very proper insistence of the head of teacher-training, who became the focus of the strike), ought to be kept on. Other teachers, appointed in accordance with the School's long-standing custom (because of the need for extra, temporary, staff during the summer rush) for even shorter periods, and having understood and agreed to such appointments, began, with the backing of the union, to demand to be kept on indefinitely when their appointments ended. The kind of threatening language met with in other militant industrial action was used: in one issue of the union news-letter, for instance, there was an announcement that the Branch Secretary had had a meeting with the secretary of the Association of Recognized English Language Schools, and the statement went on:

> The meeting was arranged to find out if the AREL Schools will be acting as a united body in negotiations with MATSA or are they prepared for MATSA to pick them off one-by-one. We find that the procrastinations we are experiencing at the moment leads [sic] us to think that there is a need for us to adopt a more militant approach as it would appear that a 'gentlemanlike' approach is not appreciated . . . If nothing positive has happened by . . . 15th July, then THE GLOVES ARE OFF.

It is worth emphasizing that, before May of last year when the campaign began, there had been no industrial trouble of any kind at St Giles in all its twenty years, and the School's rates of pay and hours of work were among the best in the field. Yet when Mr Lindsay offered a new and higher salary scale, and was told by teachers he had approached with it that they considered it generous, he was told that a negotiating committee had been formed (it was largely composed of the militants), and they rejected the new scale unless it included a 'threshold' agreement for an extra 1½ per cent for every 1 per cent increase in the cost of living. This was even beyond what MATSA was demanding, and it was MATSA officials who eventually, called in by Mr Lindsay, had to persuade the School's union to accept a compromise figure.

Things got steadily worse. Mr Lindsay, and the Head of the Foreign Languages Department, found it impossible to dismiss staff, no matter how full the notice or generous the terms given, or how unsuitable their work, as the union would not allow it. After one dispute involving a part-time teacher who had been told (well in advance) that she could no longer be guaranteed twenty hours of teaching a week, such pressure was brought to bear on the Head of Foreign Languages that she could not stand any more of it, and submitted her resignation. The standard contract of employment for all staff was rejected virtually *in toto*, even including such clauses as 'The teacher undertakes to be bound by the regulations from time to time in force at the school and will well and faithfully and to the best of his/her ability carry out the duties assigned to him/her'. Even the management's right to have some say (in consultation with the staff, of course) in the dates of holidays – particularly important in so 'seasonal' a profession – was declared unacceptable.

An interesting example of the kind of demands being made is provided by a draft submitted as the basis of a code of procedure for 'employees who become liable to disciplinary action because of failure to meet the standards prescribed by the school rules with regard to conduct, attendance and job attendance'. It laid down a series of procedures so elaborate and prolonged that it would have been virtually impossible under them for any employee to be dismissed for any cause, however outrageous the behaviour. As:

> . . . the normal action in the first instance of a failure to meet agreed standards is an informal verbal warning . . . a similar failure to meet agreed standards will justify a first formal written warning from the head of department, who shall record in writing a brief account of the incident and of the action to which the employee will be liable for a subsequent failure to achieve agreed standards . . . the staff representative will, if the employee wishes, be present when a first formal written warning is given . . . a further occurrence of a similar failure to meet agreed standards will justify a second formal written warning from the head of department who shall record in writing a detailed account of the incident and inform the employee concerned that recurrence may lead to dismissal with notice . . . the staff representative will, if the employee wishes, be present when a second formal written warning is given . . . a further occurrence of a similar failure to meet agreed standards will not lead to instant dismissal – the employee concerned will be sus-

pended without prejudice pending a joint inquiry . . . the inquiry may recommend (a) case not proven, (b) suspension (1–5 days without pay) or (c) a final formal written warning . . .

And the draft blandly concludes: 'Nothing in this agreement prejudices the right of an employee to take a case of "unfair dismissal" to the Industrial Tribunal'.

The breaking-point came when Mr Lindsay finally announced the decision he had first raised with the staff eight months before – the reduction in the size of the School, and the letting of part of the premises. This meant that five temporary (or 'supply') teachers, all on specified short-term contracts, would leave the School at Easter. At this, Mr Lindsay says he was told that he would not be 'allowed' to reduce the School in size. (This, too, is denied.) He then finally decided that he had no alternative but to close the School down, or to see it turned into something that was nothing to do with the ideals with which he had founded it and for which he had laboured for twenty years.

Mr Lindsay has taken pains to see that as many students as possible are accommodated in similar schools, and will, of course, be ready to give references and recommendations, as appropriate, for the staff. There being a number of reputable schools seeking further students and qualified and acceptable staff, it is unlikely that there will be any serious hardship resulting from the closure. But it represents the destruction (I may add that I have known Mr Lindsay – normally a most equable man – for most of my life, and was appalled at the haggard appearance he presented when I met him towards the end of the story) of something that was valuable to the community and rightly cherished by those who had created it and built it up. I do not suppose, and do not think that Mr Lindsay does, that anybody set out to destroy the St Giles School deliberately or for the sake of destruction; no doubt there was a genuine belief that Mr Lindsay was 'only the legal owner'. He thinks it possible, too, that some may have had the idea of turning it into a 'workers' co-operative'; they now plan to use their experience at it to start a school of their own elsewhere (opening, they say, next week!). No doubt some people believe that the kind of tactics employed were justified, that employers should have no rights against employees, but the latter should have total rights against the former, that the militant teachers have nothing to reproach themselves for.

The loss of the St Giles School of Languages will not cause the nation to collapse in economic ruin or lead to an outbreak of cannibalism in Oxford Street. Mr and Mrs Lindsay and their children will not starve, and soon the entire episode will be forgotten. And yet perhaps it would be a good idea if it were *not* forgotten, but recognized as a microcosm, and a portent, of something far larger than any of the issues directly involved. At any rate, that is how I cannot help regarding it, and I think that others might do well to ponder on its implications.

The Times April 9th, 1975

Beware of the gun-dog

'DOG SHOOTS ITS OWNER', said the headline. Oh God, I thought, it's started. Nor was I much reassured by reading the story underneath, in which it was alleged that the beast was not animated by *mens rea*, but had merely jumped up playfully and knocked the gun to the ground, thus setting it off. That, no doubt, is what the dog said. But how do they know it was telling the truth?

I don't like dogs, armed or unarmed, and I have no intention, merely because they are apparently taking over, of pretending otherwise. When they come for me, I shall fight to the last with every weapon I can lay my hands on, and when I am finally overpowered I shall refuse the blindfold and die with a cry of 'Long live cats!'

I was bitten by a dog when I was seven years old; a loathsome spaniel (not that there is any other kind of spaniel). The scene was Hampstead Heath, by the pond, on a very hot day, and the idiotic woman it owned had tied its lead to her deckchair, beneath which it lay and panted, within sight of the cool water. I was playing with a ball, which rolled under the deckchair; I reached for it, and the beast promptly sank its teeth into the right forearm of the infant Levin, just above the wrist. I was promptly transformed into a passable replica of 'Pompey's statua, which all the while ran blood'; family legend has it that I hopped about screaming, 'Has he killed me? Will I die?' My readers will be delighted to learn that I did not die; but I bear the scar to this day, and a grudge against dogs to go with it.

Certain dogs, when I come to power (I am now assuming, no doubt over-optimistically, that I shall beat them to it), will be excluded from the general order for the extirpation of the entire species that I shall sign immediately; these are the dogs that will be officially designated honorary cats, and issued with a certificate to that effect, which they will be wise to carry with them at all times. Some of them will be dogs with which I have struck up as much friendship as it is possible to have with a dog, though a few breeds may be considered honorary cats in general, notable among them being the dachshund, especially the long-haired variety; the Pekinese, too, will be collectively safe, though I have never found it particularly attractive, for it actually is, to all intents and purposes, a cat, though of a distinctly inferior kind, of course. (I am not the first person to make this observation, for John Nieuhoff, a seventeenth-century Dutch visitor to Cathay, included in his account of the marvels he had seen a description of 'Cats with long hair, milk-white, having large ears like a spaniel; the gentlewoman keep them for their pleasure, for they will not hunt after or catch mice, it may be for being too high fed.')

Other breeds will be exempt, provided they keep out of my way, not as honorary cats but as creatures even more repulsive than dogs; chief among these is the chihuahua, which is not a dog but a spider, and a singularly nasty kind of spider, at that. If the Pomeranian still exists (I haven't seen one for years, though its unique yap, once heard, can never be forgotten) it, too, will be safe, ranking as a rat. Alsatians, chows, great Danes, poodles, Scotch terriers, foxhounds, bulldogs and of course spaniels will be *hostis humani generis*, and a bounty will be paid to anyone dispatching one of them, on production of its tail, as is the case with the grey squirrel today. (Squirrels of all colours, for their part, will be designated honorary cats of a particularly high order, and anyone found hurting the bushy-tailed little fellows will be fed to the dogs.)

Almost all metaphorical uses of the dog are pejorative or

derogatory; we call a low fellow a dirty dog, a raffish one a dog *tout court*, a mean one a dog in the manger; we deteriorate by going to the dogs, we ostracize those who have offended us by putting them in the doghouse, and if we die like a dog we die badly indeed. But who ever heard anyone calling anyone else a dirty cat (cats are a very symbol of cleanliness), or urged anyone to let sleeping cats lie, or complained that he led a cat's life?

'Cats make no angles to the wind,' sang that admirable but inexplicably under-rated poet A. S. J. Tessimond, and it would never have occurred to him to pay dogs such a compliment. Moreover, it is noticeable that those who pay dogs compliments do so in terms that a cat would reject as insults; 'dog-like devotion', 'doggedly', 'lying doggo'. There was a cat wandering about *The Times* office last week, a black one, full of character, with glowing eyes and a white patch on its chest. I picked it up and stroked it; it purred, licked its chops and bit my hand, simultaneously trying to scratch my left eye out. I tickled it under the chin to show that I bore it no ill-feeling; had it been a dog I would have been tempted to tickle it behind the ear with a mallet. But the dog would have attacked me from meanness, resentment or fear; the cat merely wanted to show me which one of us was in charge.

I do not like dogs. I do not like them when they are ingratiating and obedient, and I do not like them when they are aggressive and uncontrollable. I do not like their dubious loyalty, and I do not like their frequent treachery. (Cats are neither loyal nor treacherous, and would laugh at being called either; they are uniquely and self-reliantly themselves, and will answer to their names when they feel like it and not otherwise.) Some dogs are more intelligent than others; but the cleverest dog is more stupid than the least clever cat. Cats are never bores; dogs are rarely anything else. I dislike the look of many of them, the sound of most of them and the smell of all of them. And now that they are reported to be turning on mankind and shooting their owners, I thought it was time I made my attitude plain. I have accordingly done so. Long live cats.

The Times November 4th, 1975

African elegies

A Bend in the River by V. S. Naipaul*

Mr naipaul's new novel begins with a sentence as clangorous and haunting as the first words of *The Social Contract*: 'The world is what it is; men who are nothing, who allow themselves to become nothing, have no place in it.' And the book is full of characters who live, because they have no choice, by that pitiless rubric, and fall beneath it like heads beneath the guillotine blade. In the brilliant darkness of this human jungle the tigers bite, and the bogymen – well, the bogymen will get you if you don't watch out:

> At first they were going to have people's courts and shoot people in the squares. Now they say they have to do a lot more killing, and everybody will have to dip their hands in the blood. They're going to kill everybody who can read and write, everybody who ever put on a jacket and tie . . . They're going to kill all the masters and all the servants. When they're finished nobody will know there was a place like this here.

The place is truly anonymous, a city 'where the future had come and gone'; the country, though, must be the former Belgian Congo (not that it matters, any more than does the resemblance of 'the Big Man' who runs it to Mobutu). There the narrator, Salim, struggles not to be nothing, not to become

* André Deutsch, 1979.

nothing. Above him are his two exemplars, the Western-educated, worldly Indar and the business-like, luck-protected Nazruddin, both fated to become nothing, having been everything; below him is Metty, his family's former servant, whose nothingness is to become even more complete. In one way or another, every character in the book has to step on to these scales, and Salim, who travels light, is forever borrowing weight from others; from his two heroes, from his white mistress, from her hollowed-out husband, from the bush-woman's son whom he tutors and who rises to be the most precarious of political somethings. All these, and more, struggle vainly in the quicksand of their identities, while Salim's self-definition is his salvation; he literally travels light, just in time, away from the bogymen who have already begun 'behaving as though knives didn't cut, as though people weren't made of flesh'.

Superficially, then, a black tale, even a horror story. But there is nothing superficial about Mr Naipaul, an artist-archaeologist engaged on a dig through layer after layer of meaning, each with its own characteristic utensils, coinage, hieroglyphs and household gods. There is the past, which has left stranded upon Africa's shores so many who belong neither there nor where they come from, let alone where they will go to; there is the tenacity of man's survival instinct, in the form of the trading that springs up in the sacked town as soon as the destroyers have gone, like weeds seeding themselves on a London bomb-site; there is the gradual crumbling of the restraints – artificial, rootless and doomed – that keep disintegration so briefly at bay; there is the corruption that accompanies, as inevitably as syphilis the *conquistadores*, the attempt to make Africa something she is not; there is a massive, generous irony; there is the author's extraordinary dual use of time, which in the foreground speeds by faster and faster, like a carousel out of control, while in the background it flows unhurried, serene and impartial, like the river upon which the unnamed city stands, and which symbolizes history's indifference to an individual who comes from nothing and is fated to return to nothing, and an entire continent that must apparently work out the same destiny.

A Bend in the River is a threnody for a lost vision, the vision which in 1960 I saw encapsulated in the headline of a Nigerian pidgin-English newspaper the day that the country officially became independent: 'Yaplika wake for sileep no mo'. But Africa's past has proved stronger than her present:

> The polytechnic was still there, but the Domain had lost its modern 'show-place' character. It was scruffier; every week it was becoming more of an African housing settlement. Maize, which in that climate and soil sprouted in three days, grew in many places; and the purple-green leaves of the cassava . . . created the effect of garden shrubs. This piece of earth – how many changes had come to it! Forest at a bend in the river, a meeting place, an Arab settlement, a European outpost, a European suburb, a ruin like the ruin of a dead civilisation, the glittering Domain of new Africa, and now this.

Mr Naipaul, however, has not written a political novel, but a study in humanity struggling to put down roots in soil that will not take them. All his people are racing against time – his foreground time – whether they are hurrying to establish their identity and value in their own eyes and others', or to make themselves economically secure, or simply to get out of danger while they can. Self-made men, all of them, with self-made hearts, and self-made failures that they cannot blame on Africa, though they do.

Semper aliquid novi; the motto of the town's *lycée*, it provides a final layer of irony, as we watch Africa's ancient past, working on the scale of Mr Naipaul's river-slow background time, reaching out to engulf the hurriers. Some of them are engulfed, as it turns out, in the local prison, over which there is a different, but no less ironic, motto: *Discipline avant tout*.

There are not many writers today who see so steadily and so

far, and add so penetrating a quality of observation, so evocative a power of description, and so echoing a combination of themes. Mr Naipaul is our greatest war reporter from the front line of the modern world's *Kulturkampf*, and in *A Bend in the River* he brings that war inescapably before us.

Sunday Times December 9th, 1979

Cooking the books

I READ THE OTHER day of a library whose servants, going through its shelves and its basement, found a large quantity of books – damaged, duplicates, unreadable – that they had no use for, and that they concluded (rightly, I should judge) would be equally unwanted by any other institution or indeed individual. Deciding, therefore, that the books were so much waste paper, they decided also to burn them.

Leave out the emotion and the associations (but, as I hope to make clear in a moment, you *cannot* leave out the emotion or the associations) and the decision seems a perfectly unexceptionable one. If they cannot be read, cannot be sold and cannot even be given away – and if, incidentally, their retention means that the space available for keeping and displaying books which *are* of interest to the library's patrons is thereby reduced – what else is there to do with them but destroy them? But the logic, though inescapable, was not enough; I felt as if I had been stabbed. For it seems to me that there are few sins more shocking than the ill-treatment of a book, an action so intrinsically barbaric that all the instincts of civilization recoil before it in horror.

Book-burners rightly have a bad name; those who accidentally set light to the library at Alexandria, the Nazis who burned books to celebrate their accession to power, the smut-hounds of the present day – they all offend against the canon, but they do so in more ways than one. Their totalitarian conviction that they not only know what is good for other people better than the other people themselves do, but are in addition entitled to impose their view of the matter, is made worse by a crime which is, so to speak, self-contained; the destruction of any book, be it never so rubbishy, is unforgivable, even if it is done (and by such people it *never* is) with good intentions. For any book contains, even in the absence of any conscious desire on the part of the author that it should, the essence of some aspect of humanity. Any book's death diminishes me, because I am involved in mankind, and because a book is, in this sense, a surrogate human being. 'Books', said Milton,

> are not absolutely dead things, but do contain a potency of life in them to be as active as that soul was whose progeny they are; nay they do preserve as in a vial the purest efficacy and extraction of that living intellect that bred them.

That is exactly what I mean, and it is worth noting that it was in *Areopagitica* that Milton said it, thus making that work not only a defence of free speech, but of speech itself.

It follows that one who ill-treats a book is to be condemned, even though in a lesser *degree* than one who ill-treats a human being, for the same *kind* of fault. I knew a man who was once visiting Lord Beaverbrook when the latter, to support or illustrate some point he was making, took down a book from a shelf and, opening it, cracked it violently back upon its spine. 'I never trusted Beaverbrook afterwards,' said this witness, and I instantly understood why. And I remember a production of *The Mastersingers* many years ago in which the Sachs, discovered at the beginning of Act III deep in a book, swept it irritably to the floor as he began the *Wahnmonolog*. The gesture fitted the sentiments of the verse, of course, but the producer cannot have understood the first thing about the opera if he was unable to see that for Wagner's Hans Sachs such behaviour was simply impossible; indeed, if you wanted to define Sachs in a phrase, you would call him a man who could never mistreat a book.

There is a scene in Peter Shaffer's *The Royal Hunt of the Sun* in which the priest accompanying the *conquistadores* presents Atahuallpa with a copy of the Bible, assuring him that it is God's word; the Inca chief can only understand this literally (the Incas had no written language), and holds it to his ear to hear the word speak, flinging it contemptuously to the ground when he hears nothing, and thus incidentally precipitating the massacre of his people by the Spaniards, who are enraged at his sacrilege, or at any rate find it convenient to behave as though they are.

'Come not, Lucifer,' cries Faustus at the last; 'I'll burn my books.' I sometimes think that it is the unforgivable promise which finally damns him, though on the other hand Prospero – Shakespeare's Hans Sachs, now I come to think of it – signifies his own abjuration of magic by a promise to drown his book deeper than did ever plummet sound.

Has anybody ever calculated how many books have been written in all the eras of mankind, and all mankind's languages, put together? It must be hundreds of millions, and of course all but a tiny proportion have come and gone without leaving any mark on the world. And yet 'of making many books there is no end' (and what would Ecclesiastes have said if he could have seen today's flood – 30,000 a year in this country alone?), which surely testifies to the strength of mankind's yearning to immortalize itself in the printed word. The yearning is understandable; less obviously, it is also justified, for humanity *does* tangibly immortalize itself in this fashion, and in no other, or at any rate in no other to a comparable extent; it was the statue of Ozymandias which incurred Shelley's irony, not the tyrant's autobiography.

An ugly book is a sinful object, because it offends from the other end against the canon I have been discussing; if a book enshrines immortality, the shrine should be fittingly handsome. And this instinct must go deep, for really ugly books (I am not now discussing jackets – nor paperbacks, which are not books at all, since they do not even make an attempt at permanence – but the binding, the print and the paper) are far more rare, and beautiful ones far more plentiful, than you would expect of an object made in such teeming profusion.

I am myself pleasurably afflicted with that strange sub-disorder of bibliomania, book-sniffing; I open and sniff a new book before I even glance at the typeface, let alone begin to read it, and here, too, some deep instinct must be at work at the other end of the process, for although I do not suppose that publishers actually scent their books,* the fresh paper very frequently does give off a most attractive odour.

And yet a book must never become a mere object, let alone a chattel; collecting first editions has always seemed to me to be one of the oddest of all human aberrations, and collecting books for their bindings even more so. Though I have, I am glad to say, a good many beautiful books in my library, and no doubt a good number of first editions, I have never bought a book for any reason other than the words it consists of, and I cannot imagine myself ever doing so.

That, of course, brings me back to my point, for a book's sacredness lies in its words (many religions – most, perhaps – have worshipped the texts of their sacred writings, but I have never heard of a sect of real bibliolaters, bowing down before the volume itself, irrespective of the contents), and the man who ill-treats one, as I say, puts in peril the immortality the book reflects, and thus puts in peril his own soul. I sympathize with the library that started me on all this, but I still wish they hadn't done it.

The Times July 24th, 1980

---

* But see p.112.

The Princess of London

SANCHO, SADDLE ROSINANTE; my lady Dulcinea hath need of us. The forthcoming contested election for the Chancellorship of London University would be up my street no matter where I had taken my degree; but as a graduate of that very establishment, and a paid-up member of Convocation to boot, I have a vote in addition to a right to speak. Besides, if a man will not break a lance on behalf of a pretty Princess, he might as well beat his lances into ploughshares. Windmills, are they? We'll see about that.

There are three candidates: Princess Anne, Mr Nelson Mandela and Mr Jack Jones. (The election is caused by the retirement from the post, after many years in it, of the Queen Mother.) We can dispose of the candidature of Mr Mandela quite simply. In the first place, there is no reason to suppose that he knows or cares anything at all about it; his supporters, from most of whom I would be unwilling to buy a second-hand *Panorama* programme, have been talking about 'reports' that Mr Mandela's lawyer has 'indicated' his client's willingness to stand. It is clear enough that the promoters of Mr Mandela thought up their wheeze first and began to seek ways of justifying it later.

None of which, of course, is to be taken as reflecting on Mr Mandela himself. This very remarkable man, imprisoned for life (which in South Africa means literally until death) in the hell of Robben Island for no crime other than believing that the black people of South Africa should be set free of the tyranny imposed by the murderous and mendacious scoundrels who rule that beautiful and tragic land, deserves the esteem of anyone who values humanity, let alone freedom.

But that is precisely why I believe that the stunt mounted by those who have put his name in nomination is inappropriate to the point of disgusting. Has Nelson Mandela trodden every step of his stony and cheerless road with courage undismayed, only to be used by a gaggle of modish London lightweights who want to demonstrate their lack of admiration for the Royal Family? It would not be quite so bad, though it would be bad enough, if the post were anything more than ceremonial; but the whole point of it, however assiduous and dedicated the Queen Mother and her predecessors have been in carrying out their duties, is that it gives the holder no power or even authority, and the Chancellor is never called on to perform any function that could not in practice, even if not under the terms of the University's Charter, be undertaken by a wholly unknown official. (Of course, purely titular though the post is, filling it with royalty can undoubtedly be a help to the University, as a word in a useful ear can often be conveyed more easily and effectively by such a voice than by that of a mere Mr. But that is an additional reason for ruling Mr Mandela out, not for putting him forward.)

Nelson Mandela's character needs no bush; his life of service and suffering on behalf of his people speaks for itself, and he wants no official baubles to pin on a chest already well covered with the decorations for valour that his dignity and manhood have won him. I hope his supporters will withdraw his name, for they can only tarnish it by their action.

Which brings me to Mr Jack Jones, who has been put forward by the same kind of people; indeed, I would hardly be surprised to learn that some of them had absentmindedly signed their names to both sets of nominations. But if Mr Mandela's supporters demonstrate, by their action, their incapacity to see how unfitting that action is, what can be said of Mr Jones's other than that it demonstrates an intellectual and

psychological bankruptcy which is even sadder, in its implications, than the case of their rivals? This aged perk-collector
(the Great White Quango-Hunter, Mr Philip Holland, M.P.,
in 1978 managed to extract from a Labour Government deeply
and understandably reluctant to allow their masters to be
embarrassed in this manner a complete list of Mr Jones's
quango appointments, which at that time amounted to a dozen
or so, and although he must have shed some on his retirement
from office in the T.G.W.U., his increased leisure may for all I
know have led by now to his acquisition of a replacement set)
is, it seems, the best they can do in seeking a challenger for
Princess Anne; in seeking to blow her a raspberry, they have
succeeded only in blacking their own eyes.

Of course, Mr Jones is not to be ruled out, let alone jeered at,
for his lack of scholastically earned academic qualifications,
and not merely because Princess Anne has none either. It is no
shame to him that he left school at fourteen to earn his living
(though he earned it for only twelve years in the productive
sector, the remaining forty years of his working life having
been spent behind a trade union bureaucrat's desk); I can think
of many a man or woman of no educational attainments who
would be an adornment to the post he seeks.

But if we are not to have royalty as the nominal head of our
University, do we really have to put up instead with this
knackered old wheel-horse, dragged from his pasture at the
age of sixty-eight to demonstrate all over again in a new
capacity why he for so long represented, in his lack of any
scrap of imagination or vision, any quiver of flexibility, any
hint of largeness of understanding, what is wrong with
Britain's trade union movement and what harm it does to us
all, including its members?

Let us say for Mr Jones what *can* be said for him. He worked
hard and loyally in his union job for little material reward; he
lived decently and without ostentation; it is obvious that
power did not corrupt him, and that he did not use it for mean
or malicious ends; he made it clear that he did not want the

peerage he could undoubtedly have had, and would not have taken it if it had been offered to him; instead of just waiting for his old age and talking about it, he fought in the Spanish Civil War.

But what did he actually *do* as General Secretary of the Transport and General Workers' Union? He was one of the chief architects of the infamous Social Contract, the terms of which amounted only, in the notable words of a Labour M.P. contemplating the then Employment Secretary, now Leader of the Opposition, to an industrial policy in which 'Michael Foot goes and finds out what the unions want and gives it to them'. He was largely responsible for the dockers' jobs-for-life law (supported, one of the ministers concerned at the time told me, by only three members of the Cabinet, and opposed by the other twenty, but nevertheless enacted because Mr Jones demanded it for his members as part of the price for restraining them from demanding even more). In the General Council of the T.U.C., and at its Congress, he will be remembered for his staunch, unyielding, years-long and almost wholly successful resistance to any criticism of the Soviet Union by the British trade union movement. In general, he was a ball and chain round the ankle of industrial progress, a pack of stones on the back of the economy, a dam across the river of prosperity for all. In the vernacular, he was a bloody disaster, and we have not recovered from him yet.

And these clowns want to make him Chancellor of London University, and he, asked what he would do if he were elected, said that he would make the position 'relevant' – as if the chief characteristic of him from first to last were not his complete irrelevance to anything at all that mattered!

Come, let us reach for our ballot-papers and be counted. The argument for electing Princess Anne is the same as the argument for having a monarchy at all; the post is ceremonial but as far as ceremonial goes important, and she will fill it with dignity, courtesy and charm, and will work hard at the duties it entails, as her grandmother did. Is our world, and our academic world in particular, so rife with colour and glitter and majesty that we must needs go out of our way to make it drabber, smaller and more boring? I think it is not; I think it will do London University no harm at all, and possibly quite a lot of good, to elect Princess Anne its Chancellor, and I hope that the members of Convocation will act accordingly.* Sancho, let go of the stirrup.

The Times January 8th, 1981

* They did.

The false dawn

'CANST THOU DRAW out Leviathan with an hook?' asked God of Job, 'or his tongue with a cord which thou lettest down?' To these questions Job made no intelligible reply: Robert Bolt, however, having evidently pondered long upon them, has come to the startling conclusion that the answer might just possibly be 'Yes', and with *State of Revolution* he sets out to discover whether he is right.

The play seeks to do two mighty things, either of which alone would, in the contemplation, make falter the boldest spirit: to explain the course of the Russian Revolution and the thrice-heated hell that its promises of heaven produced, and to put credibly upon the stage the characters of that stupendous drama. In both of these extraordinary endeavours Mr Bolt has succeeded beyond the dearest hopes of those who wish him well and who regard the seven years that have elapsed since his last play as seven lean years indeed.

Mr Bolt never forgets (most of our younger playwrights have not yet discovered) that monsters are only human. Many a writer might have known that, but done no more with Lenin, Trotsky, Stalin and the rest than to equip them with a selection of their own words and a mannerism or two and propel them on to the stage in the hope that they would there somehow come alive. But Mr Bolt builds them, layer by layer, from the inside out; at the interval I realized, with a shock of delight as I also realized what it must mean, that I had not thought about the acting for a moment, so completely, so convincingly had the author made real the dark legends that these names have become for us in the sixty years since they shook the world. 'I hear that he's a stupid brute,' says Gorky about Stalin; 'What do you hear?' 'That he does what needs doing,' replies Lenin, 'and doesn't make a hobby of his soul.' The play is – has to be – full of such things, yet Mr Bolt fashions them with such passionate understanding and audacity that they never sound as though he is tipping his hat to history or sharing with his audience knowledge that his characters do not have.

At the same time, he unfolds (nothing extenuate, nor set down aught in malice) his terrible truth. It is not just the superficial conclusion that Stalin reaped where Lenin sowed. It is not even the more significant one that revolutions devour their own ideals, and that those who once accede to Bassanio's plea – 'To do a great right, do a little wrong' – must end by doing a great wrong and no right at all. Mr Bolt is saying – and if he isn't, he is saying nothing much worth hearing – that a house built upon sand cannot stand. Right at the end Stalin, now moving towards absolute power, makes a speech to a party congress; 'Marx', he says, 'believed in a material reality', and goes on to draw the appropriate conclusion for his argument. Then he adds, with heavy irony and to dutiful laughter, 'unless of course, Marx was mistaken.' But, of course, Marx *was* mistaken, and so are all those who believe that there is nothing but material reality to rejoice or dismay the heart of man, and that man is its only measure.

Thus believing, this crew of all too human devils move towards the hideous and inevitable apotheosis of power. We see the dashing, eloquent Trotsky become the man who crushed the Kronstadt garrison's rising for freedom; we watch as Dzerzhinsky first announces the new dawn with the words 'Police interrogation is abolished' and later, declaring that 'The slightest sign of opposition must be crushed by mass executions', takes his place as the dehumanized chief of the secret police; we sit helpless as the idealistic Lunarcharsky turns into a living corpse as a Stalinist hack. We mark how

Lenin realizes when it is too late how well Stalin has learned the lesson that he taught him. And each time we are brought up before the pitiless judgment seat of Mr Bolt's imagination, and forced to confess that in all these beginnings was their end.

All this is couched in language with the strength of carved oak and fashioned into scenes of haunting dramatic power (some of the most famous photographs of the Revolution are made flesh). Again and again Mr Bolt uses declamation without declaiming, offers sermons without preaching, tells the truth and shames the devil; 'The average peasant cannot read,' snarls Lenin, 'and we pay him with a pamphlet when we take away his pig.'

State of Revolution is a play to be stirred and enthralled by, to talk about far into the night, to savour and ponder and see again. It tells of true things, and says that those true things are only the outward signs of the more important truth within. It shows how men can believe themselves the hammer of history when they are only the anvil of illusion, and can lay waste whole continents in the name of that apocalyptic misunderstanding. Robert Bolt has come back to the theatre, which is his true home as an artist, after far too long away. But he has made up for his absence by bringing his own fatted calf with him, and we should be glad and proud that our National Theatre has invited us to the feast.

Sunday Times May 29th, 1977

Hard cheese

THERE IS A character in the Bible who complains that 'mine own familiar friend, in whom I trusted, which did eat of my bread, hath lifted up his heel against me', and I know just how he felt. The familiar friend which hath lifted up his heel against me is *Which?*, the magazine of the Consumers' Association, which did, and indeed doth, eat of my bread to the tune of £6.75 a year, and hath hitherto, with the exception of an unfortunate occasion when it jeered at my typewriter for not having a capital comma, fully justified my trust. I would never dream of buying a new yacht, a Rolls-Royce or even a packet of detergent (whatever that might be) without taking into account the appropriate report among the comparison-tests that *Which?* makes upon these and hundreds more varieties of goods and services, and although I may not necessarily come down on the item listed as Best Buy, I would certainly never get any of the items listed as unsafe, unsatisfactory or obviously poor value for money.

Until now, then, the word of *Which?* has been to me as Holy Writ; until, that is, the February issue, in which there is just such a study of Cheese. (A capital letter, if you please, Mr Compositor; one of the noblest works of God and man deserves no less.) The report, as *Which?* readers would expect, is written in English that is a model of lucidity and simplicity. And yet, when I read it, I ordered some Waters of Babylon (the brand recommended by *Which?*, of course), in order to have somewhere to sit down and weep by.

The four-minute warning was sounded in these words:

> Two-thirds of the cheese eaten in Britain is just one var-
> iety – Cheddar. This report tells you about *all* the various
> types of cheese you can buy . . .

And the bomb went off, precisely on time, in the heading,
which read 'Cheese – a guide to 68 varieties'. Ladies and
Gentlemen, and fellow cheese-lovers, *Which?* really does believe that a list of sixty-eight cheeses – *sixty-eight* – comprises
'*all* the various types you can buy'.

Now look here. When I read those words, which I may as
well say now as later are among the most extravagantly idiotic
I have ever set eyes on in my life, I went and took a sheet of
paper and wrote down, with only the most cursory consultation of reference books, the names of *ninety-one* varieties of
cheese I have actually eaten myself. The total number I have
tried in my time is certainly at least double that, and I regard
myself even now as having taken only a few faltering steps
along the great Highway of Cheese; two dozen lifetimes would
not suffice to sample every milestone along that road. And
Which? has the cheek, the folly or the innocence to claim that
all the cheese you can buy will go into a list only sixty-eight
cheeses long. Come, come, *Which?*, are you in a position to
gild refined gold, to paint the lily, to throw a perfume on the
violet? No? Well, nor can you list all the cheese that money can
buy in a list stretching from Belle de Champs to White Stilton,
and with only another sixty-six names in between.

Which?, dear *Which?* listen to me. I am not angry with you;
only sad. And if you promise to sit down and listen while I
speak, and then promise to be a good little *Which?* from now
on, we shall say no more about this matter.

Pierre Androuët's *Guide du Fromage*, which does not claim
to be exhaustive (how could it be?) lists roughly 600 cheeses in
its main section, confining itself almost entirely to French
ones, with only an abbreviated summary in an appendix for
cheese from other lands (though that list puts the total up to
well over 700). T.A. Layton's *Guide to Cheese*, which is not

just a dictionary but a comprehensive encyclopaedia of cheese and cheese cookery, includes at least 400 varieties. On the *Chariot des fromages* at Pic's I have counted forty-eight, and *chez* Bise I once tried *nine* at a go from a selection much the same size.

That *Which?* does not list such masterpieces of the cheese-maker's art as the one-bite Rigotte, the majestic Vacherin d'Abondance or the stately Tomme de Savoie is hardly to be wondered at; a guide to cheese which tells you that the holes in Emmental are larger than those in Gruyère, but does *not* tell you that if the holes in a Swiss Emmental are oval instead of spherical the fermentation has gone wrong and it is not fit to eat, *and* says without wincing that Parmesan is 'usually sold grated', is not likely to know much about such glories. But can you believe that it does not even list the humble but admirable Reblochon, the nice little Carré de l'Est, the smelly Livarot, Olmützer or Limbourg?

I suppose *Which?* is right to omit Blue Vinny, if only because it is so rarely obtainable; indeed, there is a school of thought which claims that it does not exist at all. Certainly, I have never knowingly tasted it myself, though I *have* tried that stuff called Gjetost, which I insist is not cheese at all, but soap, and is liked, as far as I can see, by no one in the world except Katharine Whitehorn's father,[*] this taste being the only flaw (and a slight one, you must admit) in the character of that otherwise wholly admirable man. The only other cheese I have tried and do not like is Roquefort, apart from Danish Blue, of course.

Androuët declares that there are 2,000 brands of Camembert, 500 of them in Normandy alone, though I rather suspect he had been at the *Weinkäse* when he said it. I do not understand how the Germans, who own half the cows in Europe, produce so little cheese; I *do* understand why de Gaulle once said despairingly, 'How can you govern a country which has

[*] Now, alas, by no one at all.

544 varieties of cheese?' *Which?*, incidentally, though it includes Mozzarella, has the nerve to list the Danish variety
before the Italian, and doesn't point out that you have to keep
it in water, or it will dry out in a horrid manner.

Cheese has existed as long as husbandry, and is one of the
greatest of all the attributes that puts mankind above the
beasts. Its range is comparable to that of wine (another of the
attributes aforesaid), and it provides one of the most profoundly satisfying taste experiences in all gastronomy.

When They take over, Woodrow and I have a plan. He
immediately drives down to his house in the country and
strengthens the fortifications. Meanwhile, I commandeer a
lorry, drive it to Jermyn Street, and back it (this is no time to
stand on ceremony) straight through the front window of
Paxton and Whitfield. There I fill it with cheese, and drive
hell-for-leather for Woodrow's. Once I am inside, we raise the
drawbridge, and what with his noble cellar and my cheese, we
live merry as grigs (for who needs more than cheese and
wine?) until They come for us.

At the Relais de l'Armagnac, at Luppé-Violles, they serve a
dessert which consists of nothing but unfermented goat's
cheese from the nearby farm, with white Armagnac beaten
into it. If *Which?* will promise not to tell such horrid fibs ever
again, I will bring it back some next time I am there, to show
that All Is Forgiven.

The Times February 19th, 1980

Stripping for action

Jane at War by Norman Pett and Don Freeman*

I SUPPOSE I HAD better begin by pointing out that nobody under forty or thereabouts will have any real idea of what this review is about, and they will not have a much clearer notion even if they read the book.

An inauspicious start, no doubt; but what is a reviewer *d'un certain âge* to do when dropped into such a bath of nostalgia as is provided by this republication from the *Daily Mirror* of six years of the most famous strip-cartoon any British newspaper has ever carried? For Jane, when I was a schoolboy, was the very last word in naughtiness, the ultimate refinement of illicit thrills, the 1940s' equivalent of the 1970s' unexpurgated editions of de Sade. And yet, as this book makes no less clear than astounding, she was a lady of such decorum, high-mindedness and virtue that she would have slapped the face of St Athanasius if he had wished her good morning.

Then how did the strip get its reputation? This is where I part company from my younger readers, for it is impossible to convey to them the effect, in those days, of a realistically drawn cartoon character who spent her time taking her clothes off *for every reason other than sexual fulfilment*.

Her clothes came off because she was going to her maiden bed, or rising from her no less solitary rest; because she was taking, or emerging from, a bath; because she wanted a swim; because she had to change, in pursuit of her adventures or her duty, into or out of disguise; because she had become en-

* Wolfe, 1976.

tangled in the ropes of a barrage-balloon (oh God, they don't know what a barrage-balloon is, either), because she was fleeing from a fire, a bomb or a burglar, because she was getting ready for an evening out, because she had caught her dress, her slip, her knickers or her bra on a hedge, a wall, a tree, barbed wire or a garden fork, because her clothing had been blown off while she was descending from a burning aeroplane by parachute, because she was putting out to sea in a rubber dinghy, because she had fallen into a pond, out of a car, or overboard, and because she had fetched up on a South Sea Island where the customary attire consisted only of a garland or two of flowers.

And yet, despite this, the extraordinary truth about Jane was that she was not only rigorously celibate (she was engaged for the best part of twenty years to a quite exceptionally long-standing boyfriend she called Georgie-Porgie); she was clearly a virgin. (They certainly don't know what *that* is.) The strip had none of the folk-wisdom of, say, 'Peanuts' or the meticulous class delineation of 'The Cloggies' or the directly contemporary comment of 'Flook', but as a reflection of a certain form of *mores* Jane has a certain social and historical value, though it must be remembered that the *Daily Mirror* has always been an exceptionally prissy newspaper: even at her nudest Jane almost invariably had a well-placed towel or arm to spare the editor's blushes, and she was practically never allowed nipples. (After Jane's few exhibitions of these, the nipple disappeared altogether from the *Mirror*, like Aristotle's manuscripts during the Dark Ages, and was rediscovered only a few years ago, long after the *Sun* had made it safe.)

The bosoms to which the usually invisible nipples were attached fluctuated, interestingly, in size, though from the evidence of this book it seems that this was due to vagaries of the drawing rather than either fashion or a glandular imbalance in the lady. Her panties were invariably frilly and her slip transparent; she also frequently wore what I believe is known technically as a cami-knicker; her hair was worn shoulder-length throughout, and curled at the ends; most remarkable of all, she never aged, which is just as well, because the strip ran from 1932 to 1959 without a break, and if nature had taken its course, she and Georgie-Porgie would have gone from their honeymoon straight to the Darby and Joan Club.

Jane was, of course, intensely patriotic and singlemindedly devoted to winning the war, though I suspect that this may have been partly a defensive response to the embarrassing fact that she was the owner of a dachshund called Fritz (or, in full, Count Fritz von Pumpernickel); he had been a present to her in the very first strip, and she so doted upon him that the *Mirror* could hardly have had him killed off (unless, perhaps in an air-raid). She seemed to have a kind of roving commission as a one-woman private army, and was forever turning up in remote places on the other side of the world, foiling Nazi Plots, bringing neutrals over to the Allies, unmasking spies, yet never forgetting, even in the most desperate and dangerous situations, to drop her knickers.

The continuity of Jane and her knickers was hardly more remarkable than that of her creators. Norman Pett drew the strip single-handed from 1932 to 1949, and also wrote the words until 1938; Don Freeman took over the script and Mike Hubbard the pictures, and both these continued to the end. After 1940 her appearance did not significantly change, though it became a little more sophisticated in the 1950s, and the picture on the cover of the book (which I think must have been specially drawn, for the hair is shorter than Jane wore it in the paper, and the pose is far more overtly sexy than any she ever adopted) has a faint hint of Marilyn Monroe (instead of, as I recall, Vera Lynn), though I must be one of the few people able to reveal the true identity of the original model: the late Richard Church told me that Jane was based (in appearance, that is, not in her knicker-losing capacity) on his secretary. Ideally, I suppose, she ought to have been Miss Joan Hunter Dunn.

Observer October 3rd, 1976

The ghost of witch-hunts past

IT IS WELL known that, in Santayana's words, 'Those who do not remember the past are condemned to repeat it'. What is less well known is that there are some people who remember the past perfectly well and *enjoy* repeating it. And anyone who heard the self-righteous, humbug-flavoured, mean-souled drone of Mr James Wellbeloved, M.P., on the radio at the weekend, talking about the *affaire* of Young Winston, will know what I mean. You do not have to be more than about thirty-five to have first-hand adult recollections of the *affaire* of 1963, and even if you are a good deal younger you can read one of the many accounts still available of those heady days. I wrote one such myself in my book *The Pendulum Years*, from which I am going to take the liberty of quoting today, because from some of the comments passed so far in the matter of Mr Churchill it is easy to believe that we have learned nothing whatever from the shoddy witch-hunt which pursued the central figure of that earlier disgrace.

For some of the lines in the present drama are taken word-for-word from the earlier one; I would not have believed, without the sensible and true avouch of mine own ears, that there could be people today maintaining that they are concerned about the security aspects of the Churchill affair, just as their predecessors did.

What vile cant it was, what viler cant it is! Mr Churchill had an affair with the wife of a man who, among other things, dealt in armaments on a considerable scale. Mr Churchill, for part of the time during which the liaison continued, was a junior defence spokesman for the then Conservative Opposition. Therefore . . .

But therefore what? Would Mr Wellbeloved, or anybody else chasing this gamy and flea-ridden hare, care to describe the presumed train of events by which Mr Churchill's role as an assistant to the Tories' front-bench defence expert connects in a sinister manner with his role as the lover of the ex-wife of an armaments trader?

In case Mr Wellbeloved and company are reluctant to accede to my request, let me show them how it might be done. Let us envisage Mr Churchill and Mrs Khashoggi relaxing together. She smooths his brow, he basks. He sips a drink, she nibbles a stuffed olive. Then she speaks.

'Darling.'

'Mmmm?'

'It must be so interesting, the work you do – I mean, having to see all those generals and admirals, and discuss the defences of your country.'

'Oh, well, you know – it's really just another job, and besides, I'm not exactly a general myself, or even a minister.'

'No, but you must know a lot that you can never reveal.'

'Well, not really – I mean I don't know how the H-bomb works, or anything like that.'

'Darling, I'm sure you're being too modest. I bet you know lots about whether the Belgian-made C23 rifle is going to become standard issue in NATO forward areas despite the rival claims on resources of the American-patented recoilless fast-loading anti-tank projectile-launcher, and how far cross-standardization of weapons-systems has gone and particularly whether Saceur has expressed himself satisfied with the rate of progress lately, and when the long-promised – nay, impatiently awaited – redeployment of "tac-nukes" for BAOR is to take place.'

'Well, funny you should ask that, because it so happens that I *do* know a bit about it. For instance . . . '

Yes? Something like that, was it? Or not? And if not, what? Just *how* is this a matter which concerns security? How did Mr Churchill give away military secrets he didn't have to a woman who wouldn't have understood them acting on behalf of a man who could have made no use of them? If it didn't take place as I have suggested, how did it take place? And if it didn't take place, and couldn't have taken place, and *obviously* couldn't and didn't take place, what is left of Mr Wellbeloved and his 'case'?

An odour by no means of sanctity. And some smell even worse. Mr Denis Canavan, M.P., for instance, affects to believe that Mr Churchill should 'do the honourable thing and resign his seat', apparently on the ground that he has committed adultery. My own researches into the sex lives of M.P.s, the fruits of which are to be published in a six-volume, copiously illustrated study by the Oxford University Press, are still incomplete; still, they already show that if every Member of Parliament who had committed adultery were to resign his or her seat, there would be so much green leather vacated by the resigning ones that inexperienced visitors to the public gallery might assume that they had come to the wrong place and were at Wembley Football Stadium. (And this, I may say, does not include those like the former Chairman of Mr Canavan's party who was in the habit, while a member, of buggering the occasional House of Commons waiter on the premises – *and* he wasn't even a member of the Kitchen Committee.)

O hypocrisy, what crimes are committed in thy name! And not committed just once, but again and again, down the years and the decades. 'With a roar of unholy joy', I wrote in *The Pendulum Years*, 'the deprived flung themselves on the sated', and I went on to quote Swift's 'Censure is the Tax a man pays to the Public for being eminent'. And here we go again.

True, a few members of the former cast will not be treading the boards this time. Sir Harold Wilson is unlikely to declare that the revelation of Mr Churchill's affair has 'shocked the moral conscience of the nation', if only because so many of Sir Harold's friends have since found themselves escaping criminal prosecution only through timely death, suicide or precipitate flight from the country, and Mr John Cordle will hardly insist this time that the business is 'an affront to the Christian conscience of the nation at a time when standards in public life need to be maintained at the highest level', his own claim to be a good judge of the standards of public life having been brought rather sharply into question when he was obliged to resign from the House of Commons after the disclosure that he had been in the pay of Mr Poulson.

But that will leave plenty more. I called the 1963 affair 'the most staining episode of the entire decade'. And I went on to say something that Mr Churchill may now perhaps draw some comfort from:

> When, perhaps tomorrow and perhaps next year, another public man is found to have private standards that do not accord with the nation's unspoken assumptions about public life, he may well admit to the House of Commons that his sexual relations are not what the House of Commons would like them to be, and trust successfully to public opinion, purged of guilt by its excess of righteousness in the Sixties, to defend him against the House's reaction.

And later in the book I summed up the whole business in words which do not seem to me to need the slightest amendment to describe the events of the past few days. Of the man in the eye of the artificial storm, I wrote that he

> was not as good as the impossible and imaginary figure of the 'public man' who had for so long been invested with qualities no man could possess or at least maintain for long, and who had then been put under half-fearful, half-gleeful watch by a public which was waiting for him to fall. Nor was he as bad as, once he fell, he was made out to be . . . when the boil burst, the truth about the public men

(which is only, after all, that they are the same men as private ones) became known, and with it the recognition that the whole argument was spurious, a screen thrown up to hide the real argument behind.

But if the present argument is 'spurious, a screen thrown up to hide the real argument behind', what real content is there in the affair of Mr Churchill? Well, whatever it is, it is not a public matter. The only people concerned are Mr Churchill, Mrs Churchill and Mrs Khashoggi, and the first two – the third having bowed out of the business – will settle, or have already settled, matters between them in a manner which *they* find fitting, and which *we* have no *locus standi* to find anything at all.

The House of Commons behaved disgracefully in 1963. It then had some shadow of a miserable and unworthy excuse in the claim to be representing public opinion. I do not believe it has any such excuse today. The people are usually wiser than their masters, and in these matters almost invariably so. Faced with a proposal that it should discuss Mr Churchill's behaviour, the House of Commons will be wise to turn to Next Business, and at once.

The Times December 18th, 1979

Wrong notes

I HAVE SAID this before, and I have no doubt that I shall say it again. Meanwhile, I am saying it today. I went to the Festival Hall to hear Abbado and the L.S.O. do the Mahler Fifth, preceded by Pollini playing the Schoenberg Piano Concerto, a work which put me powerfully in mind, and with rather more objective justification, too, of Rossini's celebrated remark to the effect that the overture to *Tannhäuser* would sound just as well played backwards. (The concerto is supposed to be in four movements, but it ended – or more precisely left off – after twenty minutes or so without my having noticed any particular alteration in the nature or quality of the sounds.) The Mahler was very exciting, though it left me, as Mahler almost invariably does, quite unmoved, whereas Bruckner's almost equally spacious symphonic wrestlings find me deeply involved in his struggle. Bruckner universalizes; Mahler doesn't.

But that is not what I am about this morning. What I am about is the programme notes for the concert, by Ates Orga, who sounds like an anagram, possibly, of O, EAT RAGS, which is what Marie Antoinette *really* said, or AARG! TOES!, which is what the startled policeman said when he found a horrid clue in the case of the gentleman who had dismembered his wife, or A RAT GOES, which will be the headline on my obituary of a certain politician, or simply GOAT-ARSE, a term of abuse common among Cypriots, I believe.

Anyway, Mr Orga, in his guide to the evening's music,

amply bore out the truth enshrined in the definition of such writing that I first put forward many years ago: those who can understand it don't need it, and those who need it can't understand it. As witness:

> this Adagietto functions to some extent as an introduction –
> in the present case to a predominantly linear, stratified
> Rondo-Finale of immense scope in which the structural
> parameters of sonata-rondo and variation are combined
> with a masterful display of fugal and imitative texturing
> worthy of late Beethoven, not to say the Mozart of the
> *Prague* or the *Jupiter*, in the toughness and cohesion of its
> procedure.

Now a man who can write drivel like that about Mahler will obviously be inspired to even greater efforts when it comes to Schoenberg, and so he is, with this result:

> In the 40s, Schoenberg reinterpreted this trait in harmonic
> rather than textural terms, contrasting instead the anti-
> gravitational equality of serialism with the gravitational
> inequality of diatonicism. With the Piano Concerto such
> tendency gives rise to several passages of seemingly re-
> trogressive nature. In the long term, however, these prove
> paradoxically to be not so much backward-looking as anti-
> cipant of the future. At this mature moment of his develop-
> ment (as we have suggested) Schoenberg's art had reached
> that point when many of those rigid features typical of his
> technique in its formative stages could now actually be
> discarded without the overall serial logic of the whole
> suffering. Thus ['Thus' is a fine word in the circumstances, I
> must say] the Piano Concerto freely encourages the appear-
> ance of diatonically/tonally implicit or [sic] combinations,
> the often frequent application of the *Grundgestalt* in vertical
> (chordal) rather than horizontal (melodic) form, the use of

pedal points, a relative simplification and elucidation of rhythmic structure, and so on.

In the name of Saint Cecilia and all her harp-playing angels, what use is that to any human being alive? Note that I do not ask what it *means*; it doesn't mean anything, but even if it did, and there were someone who understood every word of it, in what way would it add to the total of such a paragon's happiness or knowledge?

It is true that Mr Orga is attempting one of the most difficult tasks that language can set its users. He is trying to convey the essence of music in words, whereas the essence of music does not lie in words, and if it were possible to catch the musical essence verbally composers would all be novelists, or at the very least poets. But the solution to this insoluble problem is not to write gibberish; it is to accept that the programme-note writer's function is a humbler one: to guide the listener who needs guidance through a piece of music in a way which enables him to hear more clearly how the composer is reaching his effects. How he is reaching them, mind; what the effects *are* is something that altogether bypasses such ratiocination, and they stir us in ways which are not dependent upon reason at all, and could not stir us at all if they were, or even if they tried to be. (Have you ever shed a tear at a concert of the music of Satie or Webern – unless, perhaps, from the thought that you could have been having dinner instead? Come to think of it, though, where does that leave *The Art of Fugue*?)

Such a guide will not waste time on pseudo-erudite twad-dlings about the *Grundgestalt* or parameters; he will point out the way in which the main themes are introduced and de-veloped, draw attention to contrasts of melody or tempo that the composer stressed, touch upon the quality of the scoring, indicate which instruments are prominent at which significant points, refer to useful parallels or analogies which may be presumed to lie within the listener's experience, and then shut up and let art do the rest. For in the end, as we all know, art is magic, and magic in its purest form, too, which must not yield to one of woman born.

Now at this point, Mr Orga, or his lawyers, may ask me whether I can provide any evidence that what I demand can be done, let alone that it has been. As it happens, that's easy; there are half a dozen regular writers of concert-notes today who do exactly what I have demanded above, our own Mr Mann, I am happy to say, prominent among them. But a study of what is at present available in London's concert halls may be thought invidious; let me then offer an example of what I mean from a somewhat earlier day. Perhaps some of my older readers will recognize the style – by its simplicity, its honesty, its straightforward, practical helpfulness – from their own first steps on the journey into music, and certainly they, and many others who do not know who the writer is, may also recognize what music is here being written about, which is a good deal more than anybody could do with Mr Orga:

> The long slow movement (*Larghetto*) is happily designed to contrast with the virile energy of the *Allegro*. The strings start with a melody of eight bars, reechoed by the woodwind. The character of the theme is melancholy, but tender rather than poignant. The second subject (also eight bars) is treated in the same way as the first by the strings and woodwind. A syncopated melody for the first violins seems to be leading us away from the restrained sadness of the opening theme, and presently the second violins and cellos bring in a new figure, distinctly cheerful in character. The first subject is repeated in the minor, developed with fanciful ingenuity, and passed to and fro among the various groups of instruments. There is a modification of the lighter figure alluded to above. The movement ends with a restatement by the full orchestra of the opening strain.

That is an account of the slow movement of Beethoven's Second Symphony, by the great Rosa Newmarch, and I do not believe that the job has ever been done better, or indeed that it can be. Certainly it provides true nourishment for the concert-goer, in a way that the work of Mr Ates Orga does not. A matter, you might say, of TEA OR GAS.

The Times February 13th, 1980

No fiddles for the taxman

Here's a lamentable business. At Newark, in Nottinghamshire, staff of the Inland Revenue have found that musicians, approached to play at their social functions, refuse to do so when it is revealed that those who at night are suiting their action to Milton's words

> Come, and trip it as ye go
> On the light fantastic toe

are engaged by day in the far more controversial task of extracting money from the citizenry (musicians and non-musicians alike) by virtue of the powers invested in them by Section 5, sub-section 2 of the Income Tax Act 1952.

Reporting his and his fellows' distress at this unfriendly response, a spokesman for the tax-gatherers said, 'We are human beings', a statement which should go far towards allaying the suspicions of those who believe that the collection of taxes in this country is entrusted to an entirely different order of creature, closely resembling Humpty Dumpty's description of toves – 'They're something like badgers, they're something like lizards, and they're something like corkscrews.'

All the same, I think that the musicians of Newark should be beaten about the head with their own fiddles. Speaking for myself, I must say that I have long had the happiest relations with the officials of the Inland Revenue. Whenever I absent-mindedly claim £2,000 for a year's supply of carbon paper, it is with the utmost diffidence that they wonder whether such an item of expenditure has really been incurred wholly, necessarily and exclusively in the pursuit of my profession, and with the greatest courtesy that they reduce the claim to eighteen pence. For my part, whenever the Government writes to say that it wants a new aircraft carrier or educational system, I willingly provide the funds. And on this basis of what might be called give and take we remain the best of friends.

But even if I were constantly at loggerheads with the satchel-men, it is the iniquity of the laws which compel me to part with too much of my income that would provoke my wrath, not the conduct of the officials charged with collecting the money. There is, after all, no suggestion on the part of the musicians that the Newark taxmen have carried out their duties with offensive words or unseemly gestures, or that they have demanded more than is due, or that they have failed to send the money collected to the Government, but have instead spent it on blondes or boxes of chocolates.

In the United States, there is an official whose job, whose sole job, is to remain close to the President at all times, carrying a bag with a combination lock, in which are, among other things, the codes with which a nuclear attack can be launched, together with estimates of the megadeaths to be expected from each of the various possible strengths of retaliation. The interesting, and sad, thing about this man is that he is shunned as a pariah by the rest of the President's entourage: there is a revealing passage in Mr William Manchester's *Death of a President*, in which he says of the officer that 'No one called him by his Christian name, his surname, or even by his code name'. He was simply called 'the bagman'. Yet everybody knew that not only was he essential, but that it was essential that he should stay within instant reach of the President.

Some deep, irrational spring had been touched there; the bagman's fellows found it necessary to forget the very existence of the man whose job was to carry around the tangible substance of the unspeakable and unthinkable, in the hope that by ignoring him and his bag he would never have to open it.

Such primitive magic appears to be at work in Newark. If the taxmen can be kept from mind, they can also be kept from pocket; if they cannot dance, they will not demand; if they must stay at home in the evenings, they will go to the office in the mornings full of generosity and forgiveness.

I doubt it. And even if I did not doubt it, I would feel that there is something repulsive in one man's refusing to supply the goods or services of his trade to another merely because the other does a necessary and honourable job that occasions grumbles. And anyway, how far do Newark's musicians take their attitude? Do they refuse to play for traffic-wardens who sometimes put tickets on their cars? Do they shun policemen who may have to arrest them if they transgress the law? Do they bar surgeons who may stick knives in them, publicans who may ask them to leave at closing-time, landlords who may ask for the rent? Is the capacity of these people for dancing less than that of butchers, bakers or candlestick-makers?

Come, come, you musicians of Newark. Just reflect what sacred day this is,* what box of goodies is to be opened for us all at 3.30 this afternoon, what rebates, what refunds, what repeals are due to pour from the offices of the Inland Revenue as soon as Mr Barber gives the word. Is this a time, while all other folk are dancing in the street, to prevent the officials of the Inland Revenue from dancing in the Town Hall or the Banqueting Rooms? Surely not; surely it is a time to agree with St Augustine that we should hate the sin but love the sinner. And after all,

> When a felon's not engaged in his employment
> Or maturing his felonious little plans,
> His capacity for innocent enjoyment
> Is just as great as any honest man's,

---

* It was Budget Day.

and if that is true of a felon, only think how much more true it is of an income-tax inspector. Besides, if the officials of the Inland Revenue are felons, the musicians of Newark may rest assured that fate will find them out. Indeed, we have the Book of Daniel to tell us as much: 'Then shall stand up in his estate a raiser of taxes in the glory of the Kingdom; but within a few days he shall be destroyed, neither in anger, nor in battle.' Though I suppose it is possible that Daniel was the Secretary of the Holy Land branch of the Musicians' Union.

The Times March 21st, 1972

Mind over matter

IT MAY NOT be universally known, but journalists, and indeed their secretaries, are among the most modest and unassuming of people, always reluctant to draw public attention to their gifts or achievements. My own readers will, of course, have noticed such qualities in me, and may well have wondered whether I am as exceptional in this respect as in so many others; I can assure them that I am not, and that it is the custom throughout my profession to do good by stealth, and blush to find it fame.

I begin thus because today's column is directed not only to you, gentle reader, but to one of my *Times* colleagues, whom I now invite to step forward and claim, with demurely downcast eyes, the credit for a discovery which ranks with those of Archimedes, of Newton, nay, of Galileo himself. I have to do it this way, because I do not know, and cannot otherwise find out, which of my fellows has thus enriched mankind and made so notable a contribution to Western civilization; I do not even know whether a lady or a gentleman is responsible, whether a veteran of many years in the writing trade or the youngest and most recently joined secretary. All I know is that we have a genius amongst us. Now mark my words.

There are, on the editorial floors of *The Times*, a number of machines which dispense food (if that is the right word, and in the case of the pork pies it may well not be) for cash down – down the slot in the side of the contraption, that is. Naturally, the machines go wrong, thus demonstrating yet again the validity of Hutber's Law (named for its originator, the financial journalist Patrick Hutber, whose recent tragic death in a road accident leaves us all the poorer), which states that 'Progress Means Deterioration'; when we were in the old building at Blackfriars we had tea-ladies, who dispensed their wares with much welcome cheerfulness and never went wrong at all, but in the move to Château Seifert those good souls were permanently mislaid, and now we have only these soulless constructions.

In addition to their habit of mechanical failure, the food-dispensers have one crippling drawback, which has frequently brought me close to pushing their glass faces down their aluminium throats. They will only accept the exact sum specified on each of the displayed containers for the particular item inside. Since the prices are almost never in round figures of five, ten, fifteen or twenty pence, it follows that an appallingly unproductive number of man-hours is spent by those who, famished in the arduous labours of journalism, wish to sustain themselves till the next square meal with a sandwich, a biscuit, a bun or a humble packet of crisps, in scurrying about the office trying to find someone with a supply of copper, so that something costing 9p or 13p may be obtained from the otherwise unyielding bowels of Robot the Rotter.

Now before I get to the point, I must explain – for otherwise you will not understand it when I do get to it – that the machine, repulsive and unhelpful though it is, can count. When a coin is inserted, the machine emits a series of audible clicks, as many clicks as there are pence in the coin, from, naturally, one to ten. When the exact number of clicks in the number of pence demanded has been registered, pressing the button opposite the container of the food the customer seeks results in the mechanism moving round until the item may be extracted from the delivery-slot. (I know it's difficult without a diagram, but put a wet towel round your head and carry on trying.) But the most infuriating aspect of the machine is that its insistence on the exact sum required extends not only to a refusal to release the food for less than the stipulated charge (which is reasonable), and to a further refusal to give change (which is not), but to an almost incredible refusal *to let the customer over-pay it.*

Thus, if I want a sevenpenny bun and, with that indifference to the cost of satisfying my wishes that has led me to be known as Lavish Jack Levin, Last of the Big-Time Spenders, I am willing to give the thing a 10p piece with a cry of 'Keep the change, my good machine', it thumbs its mechanical nose at me, obliging me to join the copper-hunt I have mentioned.

Enter Prometheus, or possibly his sister. In one brilliant, instantaneous flash of inspiration someone in this office has solved the problem, and solved it, moreover, in a peculiarly satisfying way, because the discovery demonstrates that the machine is stupid as well as unpleasant. Take the telephone off the hook and attend *very* carefully; a concrete illustration should make all clear. Suppose that you want something priced 8p, and you have only a 10p coin. You *first* press the delivery-button, *and keep it pressed.* You then put the 10p in the slot, and you hear the click-counter go into action. When the count reaches eight, the machine automatically releases the food, because it is too thick to have foreseen that the money inserted is more than the sum it wants. And what makes it all the more delightful is the look on the beastly thing's face as the clicker continues for two more clicks, and it realizes, too late, that it has been had.

When I heard of this discovery, I naturally went in search of its author, so that I might lay my humble tribute at the feet of one of the world's great innovators and benefactors. The news was communicated to me by Mr Marcel Berlins, the paper's Legal Correspondent, but he – a man exceptionally modest even by the normal standards of journalists – at once disclaimed all credit, and referred me to Mr Rodney Cowton, the Home News Editor, from whom Marcel had had the information. Mr Cowton, however, was just as quick to deny authorship, and sent me on to Miss Annabel Ferriman. Closing in on my quarry, I taxed Annabel with having thus erected an enduring monument to the power of human reason; she blushed, and denied it in turn, adding, in response to my next, obvious question, that she could not remember who had told her.

I am therefore obliged to make this appeal *coram populo*, so that when an appropriate plaque is put up in *The Times* office to commemorate the great discovery (my proposal is that it should be affixed to the wall of the corridor immediately opposite the food-dispenser itself, so that the creature may be tormented by this ever-present reminder of Man's superiority to the Machine), it may bear the name of the man or woman to whom the credit is due, and thus ensure that he or she is honoured and remembered, as is only fitting.

The very first job I ever had in journalism was with the B.B.C., in radio. The building in which I worked was the Langham (formerly the Langham Hotel), opposite Broadcasting House. In those days, the B.B.C. owned only half of the building, the other half being occupied by the Metal Box Company, and the division was vertical; each floor was divided into two by a glass door, separating the exploited wage-slaves of the ruthless capitalist enterprise from the proud freemen of the harmoniously run public corporation. It was, however, noticeable that, even as we went back and forth to the B.B.C. canteen, sipped our horribly stewed tea from chipped cups half an inch thick, and swallowed with difficulty rock-cakes which would have been more correctly named cake-rocks, on the other side of the partition the Metal Box tea-ladies, dressed in tasteful uniforms, could be seen trundling trolleys laden with fine china and gleaming silver, and groaning under the weight of an array of most tempting and delicious-looking comestibles. If it turned out that the now defeated food-dispensers at *The Times* were made by the Metal Box Company (and they are certainly Metal Boxes, so I don't see why they shouldn't be), it would constitute the sweetest revenge that has ever come my way after nearly thirty years of hungering for it. I shall nip along the corridor immediately and check, taking with me a 10p coin for a 6p item, and, having humiliated the machine by effecting the transaction in the manner described above, I shall give it a good kick in the side as I go, just to emphasize the point.

The Times February 5th, 1980

Lost and found

REVISITING HAROLD PINTER'S *The Caretaker* after many years was an extraordinary experience. I sat in amazement at the prodigality of the author's talent, his masterly technical skill, his impeccable ear and faultless deployment of varying speech patterns and rhythms, his literally incomparable ability to suggest unlocatable fear – and the emptiness, weightlessness and triviality of his entire play. This contrast between artifice and art struck me like a blow in the face; I went home dazed with the implications of what I had seen, and I have not fully recovered yet.

Of course, it is too late to say all this; the received belief of the world is that Mr Pinter is a great playwright whose works have a profound inner meaning, and although I suppose that fully nine-tenths of his audiences sit there convinced that they are wasting their time, more than nine-tenths of the nine-tenths guiltily blame their failure to feel any emotion that matters, or think any thought worth remembering, on their own imperfections rather than his. Shelvesful of books discuss which of his characters represent the Id, and which the Mother-Archetype; teachestsful of doctoral theses demonstrate his revelation of hidden significances in the universe; airwavesful of experts discuss his version of the Heracles-myth and his attitude to the alienation of industrial man; and the truth remains that Mr Pinter has nothing whatever to say, and that a drum makes a noise when you hit it because it is empty.

I must not be thought to be calling Mr Pinter a charlatan; *he* has never told us that his works express a consistent vision of life. It is true that when, many years ago, I suggested in a public discussion that his plays should be thought of as entirely abstract, he denied it, and insisted that they had meaning; but it was notable that he did not venture to suggest what that meaning was. And ever since, he has kept his own counsel.

Yet there is *The Caretaker*, with its famous silences, its famous pauses, its famous hints of menace, and its terrible but complete absence of any subject-matter or any philosophical point. There is no sense of a view, however oblique, of these characters, no disclosure of a general truth based on particular conclusions, no comment, wise or otherwise, on anything. We come out exactly the same people as we were when we entered; we have been entertained, we have admired the author's ability, we have not been bored. But we have advanced our understanding and our humanity not a whit, and every experience we have had has been of an entirely superficial nature. The needle is sharp, the thread fine, the material sumptuous, the seamstresses the best. But the Emperor's clothes do not exist.

No greater contrast with Olwen Wymark's heartfelt play *Find Me* could be imagined. Her play is a rich lode of meaning, feeling and thought, and very considerable dramatic skill into the bargain. It is based on a true story, though how closely the play sticks to it I cannot say; nor does it matter, because Mrs Wymark does the very thing Mr Pinter does not – she presents truths about all mankind in the form of the things that happen to individuals.

The chief individual is a profoundly, and it seems incurably, disturbed girl, Verity. (Not her real name, but I can hardly believe Mrs Wymark chose the pseudonym at random.) Uncontrollable from early childhood, her behaviour – hideous and clearly pathological tantrums, wanton destruction, appalling public scenes – grows worse as her despairing parents follow her from social worker to psychiatrist and from special school to court of law, seeking the help that is not to be found. She ends in Broadmoor.

The inevitable demeaning rubbish in *Time Out* ('. . . miscarriage of psychiatric justice . . . in the top-security prison hospital for the crime of having caused £6 worth of damage to a hospital chair . . . victim of a society which . . . ') suggests that *Find Me* is mere agitprop, a denunciation of the unfeeling citizens of a capitalist state and inadequate funding for the National Health Service. It is nothing of the kind. Almost everyone, starting with the parents and going on with the doctors and teachers and even the uncomprehending neighbours, is seen to be truly concerned and involved in the tragedy, yearning to bridge the unbridgeable gap with skill, love or simply patience. Society is shown as being unable to cope with her; there is anger at her fate, but Mrs Wymark faces without flinching the fact that the warp in the girl's personality is not to be explained in terms of the surrounding world. The result is a burning truth, the heat of which fuses the brute facts into a memorably dramatic achievement.

She uses a dangerous, but entirely successful, theatrical device; all the characters, from Verity and her parents to the people they meet on their *via crucis*, are shared out among the cast, so that, for instance, each of the actresses at some time plays the girl and each of the actors her father. This may symbolize the fragmented nature of the girl's personality and of the society through which she wanders; but it has the vital effect of preventing us from identifying with anybody or anything, and thus keeps the play from being either sentimental or didactic.

There are some almost unbearably affecting moments (Sam Walters, who directs, denies us any slackening of the tension in which to take refuge), most powerful of which is the one scene in which Verity is entirely happy; she is seen swimming, the chthonic psychological significance of water being here unmistakable, and the connection with the amniotic fluid, to which Verity's tormented spirit longs to return, no less so.

There is no cause of Verity's disorder, and that which has no cause can have no cure. The author shirks nothing of this bitter truth, and lays no easy blame on anyone, not even God. I was reminded of the haunting last lines of Robert Massie's *Nicholas and Alexandra*, and I offer the passage to Mrs Wymark as a tiny gift in return for her wonderful and searching play:

Why Lenin triumphed, why Nicholas failed, why Alexandra placed the fate of her son, her husband and his empire in the hands of a wandering holy man, why Alexis suffered from haemophilia – these are the true riddles of this historical tale. All of them have answers, except, perhaps, the last.

Sunday Times October 30th, 1977

The governors and the governed

The History of a Town by M. E. Saltykov-Shchedrin,
translated by I. P. Foote*

MY LONG-HELD conviction that practically all publishers
are mad has received powerful reinforcement from the
fact that this extraordinary masterpiece of nineteenth-century
Russian comic writing has had to be put forth more or less
privately by a man with a name like a cat being trodden on.

Its neglect – this is also the first time it has been translated –
is astonishing. To call it Gogolian, which is the obvious
comparison, would actually be to diminish it; the satire is
more precise and deadly, and the author's imagination much
freer, the fantasy of his invention being comparable to that of
Rabelais and its explosive effect to the havoc wrought by *The
Good Soldier Schweik*. Yet Saltykov-Shchedrin stands squarely
within the Russian tradition, among the landed or aristocratic
radicals of the mid-century (he was born in 1826, the year after
the December rising and the accession of Nicholas I, his work
began to appear in 1856, the year before Alexander II pledged
himself to the emancipation of the serfs, and *The History of a
Town* was published in 1870, a decade after Alexander made
good his promise before he was assassinated), and in it, the
author achieved a remarkable synthesis of the views of the
Westernizers and the Slavophils.

Now what is the town, and what is its history? Glupov

---

* Meeuws, 1980.

(meaning 'Stupidtown') is, of course, Russia, and its history consists entirely of a succession of twenty-one governors, of widely different degrees of intelligence and brutality, all of whom, by design or accident, cause the Glupovites misery, pain and bewilderment, variously repressing them, flogging them, debauching them or ignoring them. An early chapter takes the form of a *catalogue raisonné* of the whole succession of town governors, from which we learn that one of them had a head with a music-box inside it and another a head stuffed with forcemeat (his secret is revealed when the Marshal of Nobility notices that he smells of truffles), that a third was seven feet seven inches tall, boasted of his descent from a Moscow bell-tower and 'broke in half in the great gale of 1761', that a fourth 'led the campaign against tax-defaulters and burnt down thirty-three villages, by these measures exacting two and a half roubles in tax arrears', that a fifth was a fugitive Greek 'captured in the market at Nezhin' (where, incidentally, my maternal grandparents came from) who 'traded in soap, sponges and nuts, was in favour of classical education and in 1756 was bitten to death by bed bugs', and that a sixth 'wrote a book called *A Description of the Lives of the Most Notable Monkeys*'.

Something of the spirit of the book may perhaps be sensed from those brief excerpts; the full force of the satire only becomes apparent in the course of the narrative. This is deliberately episodic, one of the author's purposes being to demonstrate the unpredictability of the rulers, whose wretched subjects are never sure what is required of them even within one governor's period of office, let alone from one such period to the next.

It is also apparently random, and the reader will expect the book simply to stop when the last governor's mismanagement has been recorded. But this expectation is falsified, a true culmination achieved, and the full didactic purpose of the book revealed, in the description of the governorship of Ugryum-Burcheev which brings Glupov's history to an end.

As a portrait of totalitarian monomania I know of nothing to touch it; Saltykov-Shchedrin depicts with merciless completeness the cumulatively lunatic precision of Ugryum-Burcheev's arrangements for the town and its citizens:

> In each house there would be two elderly people, two adults, two adolescents, and two infants . . . People equal in age would also be equal in size . . . There would be no schools and no provision for literacy; mathematics would be taught on the fingers. There would be no past and no future, and the calendar would be abolished . . . Work would be done to words of command. The inhabitants would bend and straighten in time together; scythe-blades would flash, hay-forks toss, picks tap and ploughs turn the earth – all by orders . . . there would be no passions, enthusiasms or attachments . . . The whole world appeared covered with black dots, in each of which people moved in straight lines to the beat of a drum . . .

In this portrait of hell lies the most extraordinary of all the book's qualities; its prophetic vision. Ugryum-Burcheev himself says, 'There cometh one after me who will be more terrible than I'; it is not clear who is meant, but it could hardly have been Stalin, yet the reader will be ineluctably forced to think of the monster and his terror:

> For him there is no lesson to be learned from the futility or patent harmfulness of these misdeeds. He is not concerned with the results of his actions, since they affect not him (he is too lost to feeling to be affected by anything), but some other object, with which he has no organic connection. If through the concentrated efforts of his idiocy the whole world were turned into a desert, even that would not daunt the idiot. Who knows, perhaps a desert is what he regards as the ideal setting for the communal life of man?

And yet that is not the end: the all-powerful idiot is defeated at last by something as simple and symbolic as a river, which will not fit neatly into his rewriting of geography, and which he can neither stop in its course nor divert. In his final pages Saltykov-Shchedrin thus tells us that even the Glupovites will not for ever be controlled, and that no governor can tear out the river of unpredictability and freedom from their hearts. A mighty work with a fitting end, *The History of a Town* is a classic of its time, of our time, of any time.

Sunday Times April 13th, 1980

Are you sitting comfortably?

IT IS REPORTED by the Associated Press that a burglar in Milan, fleeing from the scene of his crime pursued by the police, took refuge in a shop window, where he remained undetected for an hour by standing perfectly still and posing as a dummy.

Beyond remarking that when the gentleman in question, a Signor Giovanni Montedi, comes out of the *galera* he has a promising career ahead of him as a member of the right wing of the Parliamentary Labour Party, I have no philosophical conclusions to draw from the episode. Nevertheless, Signor Montedi is most cordially invited to dine at Bagutta at his earliest convenience (some months hence, I take it) and send the bill, wine and *coperto* included, to me. My offer is not prompted by my admiration for his audacity, though I do indeed admire it, nor as compensation for the fact that his ruse was, in the end, penetrated (Milanese burglars, incidentally, must be snappy dressers, or else Milanese men's outfitters must be singularly short of the latest modes). No; Signor Montedi, though he could not have known it, has set the wells of memory gushing for me, as you shall hear.

Long, long ago, when I was a student (it was so long ago that we were known as undergraduates), I was, as students have been since Erasmus was a lad and possibly a good deal longer, somewhat short of the ready, a condition in which three of my friends equally and simultaneously found themselves. We sat for some hours over our *haricots blancs au four avec sauce de tomates sur pain grillé*, accompanied by a fine *thé Brooke Bond étuvé, sans soucoupe*, trying to devise a means of raising the wind, and in the end conceived an audacious plan.

We would, we decided, offer ourselves (as a job lot, you understand, our pledge being 'All for one and one for all') to furniture shops, and in particular to the furniture sections of the large department stores, where we would, in return for a suitable fee, spend the day sitting on their sofas or in their armchairs, *looking comfortable*. Potential customers passing the windows of the shops in which we were plying this recondite trade, or wandering round inside (where we were equally willing to take up position) would see us draped elegantly over the furniture, obviously luxuriating in the softness of the upholstery, the ergonomic perfection of the design and the general pleasure of sitting in such obviously superior furniture. (I rather think that the idea had come to us from seeing the Marx Brothers in *The Big Store*, in which a good deal of amok is run in just such a place as we had in mind; and there was, if I remember rightly, a play in the West End at the time in which Robertson Hare was either a window-dummy which came to life or a shop assistant who turned into a dummy, or possibly both.)

As my regular readers will, alas, expect, my own variation on the general plan was of greater audacity. Why not, I asked my comrades and fellow-workers, extend the basis of our operation to the bed and mattress department? What could be more clearly demonstrative of the suitability of bedroom furniture for the purpose of providing a good night's sleep than the sight of four healthy young men curled up and audibly snoring in four of the emporium's beds? My bold and imaginative plan was vetoed, over my bitter insistence that if Napoleon had been surrounded by such small-minded colleagues he would never have won the Battle of Waterloo; having given a pledge to democracy early in the proceedings, however, I agreed to go along with the original, more limited, idea.

You will scarcely believe what I am going to tell you, but from one end of Oxford Street to the other, we could find not a single shop willing to entertain our proposal, and in several of those we tried we were obliged to make a hasty tactical withdrawal after the manager had indicated that if we didn't stop pestering him he would send for the police) notwithstanding the fact that, as we went further and further without success, we reduced our price more and more. (I forgot to mention that another example of the infant Levin's precocious tendency to think big was my suggestion that we should be provided by the shops engaging our services with ample supplies of fine wines and a variety of exotic *canapés*, to lend even greater verisimilitude to our pose as four exceptionally comfortable members of the *jeunesse chromé*. The other musketeers nervously reduced that to mugs of beer even before we set out.)

Our total lack of success was naturally discouraging. We pointed out to the obdurate and short-sighted people with whom we were dealing that they were missing the opportunity of a lifetime; we told S★★fr★★★es that J★★n L★★is would be bound to bid a huge sum the moment we walked in at the door, and implied at B★★ne and H★ll★★★★worth that the only reason we had not already signed up with M★★sh★ll and Sn★★gr★ve was that the latter had wanted to take us on a contract with a minimum duration of a year, to which we felt unable to commit ourselves.

In vain; though we begged the stony-hearted merchants to remember that England had once been a nation of shopkeepers, and even appealed to the customers to proclaim the obvious truth that they would be much more likely to buy a three-piece suite if it had us in it (provided, of course, that we were removed from it before it was delivered), we could make no headway, and finally called off the whole project, confident that within a few months Oxford Street would be little better than a desert, so precipitous would be the decline in trade among the furniture shops.

We did, as I recall, discuss an alternative strategy, which was indeed to take a leaf out of the good Signor Montedi's book and pose as dummies in the windows of clothes shops, but we soon spotted the flaw in it; the clothes would not look any better on us than on the dummies (we were a modest lot in those days), so that there would be no gain to the shopkeepers in hiring us for this purpose. On the other hand, the shopkeepers could see no gain in hiring us for the purpose we eventually settled upon, and the furniture would certainly have looked better, or at any rate more comfortable, with us sitting all over it looking pleased. I cannot say that I realized from this early episode that I was not destined to earn money as any kind of entrepreneur, for that conviction dawned on me only slowly. Nor shall I maintain that I foresaw the whole of Britain's industrial decline in the shocking lack of enterprise displayed by the merchants of Oxford Street. But at least the memory gave me a warm feeling towards Signor Montedi when I read of his own enterprise, whence my invitation to him to refresh himself at my charge. *Corriere della Sera*, please copy.

The Times December 17th, 1980

Inquire, not too closely, within

THERE LIES BEFORE me a book, bound in a most tasteful shade of purple, which bids fair, as we writer-johnnies say, to become – and to deserve to become – one of the greatest best-sellers in history, notwithstanding the price charged for its mere seventy limp-covered pages, which is £10. Indeed, it is not easy to see, tenner or no tenner, how any household with even the smallest pretensions to literacy, cultural awareness, an involvement in the real world or respect for learning can possibly be without it, so persistent and clamorous would be the jeers of their neighbours at the barbarism, sloth and indifference to their intellectual duty that failure to acquire a copy would imply. In announcing the appearance of a book that is to modern politics and international affairs what the *Summa Theologica* was to Catholicism, *Das Kapital* to Marxism, *Bradshaw* to railway travel and *Wisden* to cricket, I take particular pride in the fact that the publishers, Newspaper Archive Developments Limited, are a subsidiary of Times Newspapers. The paper that gave this country the first news of the Battle of Waterloo, and whose correspondent got his dispatches out of besieged Paris in 1871 by carrier pigeon, has done it again. Compiled with the unstinted co-operation of the B.B.C. Monitoring Service and Reference Library, the book* is a list of every member of both houses of the Parliament of the Soviet Union, with the constituency of every member listed, together with his or her profession; it is

* *Composition of the USSR Supreme Soviet* (Newspaper Archive Developments, £10).

based on the results of the General Election of March, 1979 (which was won by the Communist Party). There are a couple of pages at the beginning which provide such essential information as the names of the Chairmen of the various Parliamentary Committees (Legislative Proposals, M. S. Gorbachev), and a couple more at the end, listing such even more significant details as membership of the Cabinet and Government (Minister of Geology, Yevgeniy Kozlovskiy); but the rest consists entirely of an alphabetical list of Soviet M.P.s.

No home, you will agree, should lack a copy – better still, to avoid the danger of matrimonial disharmony, two copies. It is true that *Composition of the USSR Supreme Soviet* lacks a good deal of the information that is included in *The Times Guide to the House of Commons*; there is, for instance, no analysis of the overall share of the poll received by each party, no lists (even in an Appendix) of defeated candidates or of those who lost their deposits, no discussion of the various party manifestos, and – most surprising omission of all – not even the detailed results, with winners' majorities, for each constituency. (It follows, of course, that there is no way of telling what the general 'swing' was from the previous election, let alone what it was in any particular seat.) Nevertheless, despite these limitations the book is indispensable for anyone who wants to familiarize himself – and who does not? – with the *Who's Who* of the Soviet Parliament. As a leaflet inserted in the book by the publishers points out:

> These are, after all, the people who will decide the destiny of the Soviet Union and possibly the world, until the next elections, which are due in 1984.

With which reflection I turn to the contents of the book itself, of which it would not be going too far to say that there is much of interest on every page. There is, for instance, something oddly comforting in the knowledge that Andropov, the head of the K.G.B., sits for Stupinsky, and that the member for Kishinev-Oktyabrsk is a Mr Buga. (Brezhnev sits for

Baumansk, by the way, which is not believed by Soviet psephologists to be a marginal constituency.) And G. V. Romanov, who sits for Moskovsk, must have to put up with a good deal of teasing in the Division Lobby, not to mention back home in Moskovsk.

But it is when we get down to detailed examination of the backbenchers here listed that the book begins to provide an excitement almost comparable to that generated by Beachcomber's *List of Huntingdonshire Cabmen*. There are three M.P.s called Orlov, for instance, who sit respectively for Kishinev-Oktyabrsk, Chapayevsk and Zaporozhsky-Leninsk, but I do not believe that any of them is related to Professor Yuri Orlov, the dissident, any more than I can persuade myself that D. F. Ustinov, who sits for Kuntsevsky, is as funny as his cousin Peter. On the other hand a pop singer appears to have got into the Soviet Parliament, a kind of Russian Screaming Lord Sutch, called Ya Ya Vagris. (He may, on the *other* hand, be a nursery-rhyme: Ya Ya Vagris, have you any wool?)

Trapeznikov is a Member aptly named for following the swings of Soviet policy without falling into deviationism; I hope Reprintsev gets his full syndication fee; Mrs Myshkina is presumably not the wife of Dostoievsky's Prince Myshkin; Taratuta presumably has the right to an official fanfare of trumpets on entering the Chamber; R. F. Dementyeva is presumably barmy; L. A. Peips presumably keeps a diary; A. P. Pork is presumably a swine.

There are some real swine in the list, as a matter of fact. Tikon Khrennikov, for instance, the hatchet-man of Soviet music; he is here listed as a Composer, but he is no more a composer than his fellow-thug Surkov, the Secretary of the Writers' Union, also an M.P., is a writer. (There is worse than these to be seen gracing the green leather – more probably red leather, I suppose – of the Soviet Parliament; Mikhail Sholokhov, chief denouncer of dissident Soviet writers, sits for Rostov. *He* actually got the Nobel Prize for Literature; but then Brezhnev recently awarded himself the Lenin Prize for the same discipline.)

. Each M.P. has his or her profession noted, and some sound very odd. L. I. Fokina, for instance, is described simply as a Worker; well, I should damned well hope so. Another's trade is given as Garments, which would present an opportunity to a Soviet Benny Hill, if there is one. ('What do you do?' 'I'm in garments.' 'Yes, I can see you are, but what do you *do*?') Another's occupation is listed simply as Oil, which provides an even more obvious, and indeed traditional, opening. ('My husband's in oil.' 'Why, what is he – a sardine?') And Mrs Mika is in knitwear; what Soviet Willie Hamilton, what Russian Andrew Faulds, will be the first to declare that the Hon. Member for Liepaja should stick to her knitting? (Hon. Members: 'Ha-ha.')

The Member for Polotsk is a Poet; the Member for Razdan is in Cement; the Member for Klaipeda is a Fishing Captain. ('To your mother you're a Fishing Captain, and to your father you're a Fishing Captain, but to a Fishing Captain are you a Fishing Captain?') There is at least one Doctor in the House, and the Member for Kolyma (the site of the very worst of Stalin's extermination camps) is listed as a Hunter, though I doubt if he would be instantly recognizable as such by your average Leicestershire M.F.H.

As you can see, *Composition of the USSR Supreme Soviet* is indeed an indispensable work. True, it will be instantly outdated if the present Soviet Government is defeated at the next General Election, but for my part I would count the £10 it costs well worth it. V. V. Shimkus, incidentally, who sits for Taurage, is in 'Land improvement'. Over here, we call it reclamation.

The Times, July 2nd, 1980

Dickens complete, in nine hours

'I THINK IT HAS a happy ending,' said the lady to her friend in the last interval; 'some of it, anyway.' All of it, dear lady; for we were at the Aldwych Theatre, where the Royal Shakespeare Company is playing an adaptation of *Nicholas Nickleby*. It is in two parts; if you see the two halves in succession on a Saturday, as I did, it spans nine and a half hours in all, with three short intervals and a gap of exactly an hour between Parts One and Two. And it does indeed have a happy ending, because the book does, and the adaptation follows Dickens with an extraordinary degree of fidelity and fullness. (The adaptation is by David Edgar, so I spent some hours apprehensively waiting for the scene in which the National Front, assisted by the Conservative Government, the Labour Opposition, the Army, the Church, the educational system, the newspapers and Big Business, tries to take over the country, resisted only by a tiny group of class-heroes led by Mr Anthony Wedgwood Benn and defeated in the end by an expeditionary force of volunteers from the gallant anti-colonialist liberation forces of democratic Cuba. To my amazement and relief, no such scene is included; there is hardly a hint – truly only a few words – of the frightful rhubarb-juice that on a windless day can be heard sloshing about in poor Mr Edgar's head from three miles away, and Dickens is allowed to speak for himself, and provided with ample space in which to do so.)

Some of the critical comment that has greeted the production makes one despair not just of criticism but of the human race. (Two notable exceptions, I am happy to say, have been the critics of *The Times* and the *Sunday Times*.) The response has exhibited that most dreadful of all the *vices anglais*, the terror of being thought enthusiastic; most of the reviewers have spent their time carefully balancing praise for one detail against regret for another until they were clear of the danger of having to admit either that they were swept along in the flood of Dickens's stupendous genius, which would be what the Russian language so handily calls *ni-kulturny* (indeed, Dickens himself is *ni-kulturny*, never mind being carried away by him), or that the fact that they were *not* swept away is a criticism of them, not of Dickens or the adapter.

A murrain on all such niminy-piminy folk. There is only one way to behave at the Aldwych; to surrender completely to the truth, which is that not for many years has London's theatre seen anything so richly joyous, so immoderately rife with pleasure, drama, colour and entertainment, so life-enhancing, yea-saying and fecund, so – in the one word which encompasses all these and more – so Dickensian.

Dickens is as good a test of a real understanding of literature as Haydn is of a real feeling for music. If a man says that Haydn wrote a lot of pretty tunes, but that his music is of no real significance, you may confidently dismiss the speaker as one who knows not whereof he speaks. And if another man (though it is all too likely to be the same one) declares that Dickens is nothing but a sentimentalist with a talent for thinking up characters and sub-plots, you need not fear that if you cudgel him soundly I shall report you to the police.

The proof that he deserves cudgelling will be found at the Aldwych. The production is by Trevor Nunn, assisted by John Caird, and anyone who saw and remembers (and no one who saw will have forgotten) Mr Nunn's production of *The Comedy of Errors* will know what I mean when I say that, just as that reading captured the spirit of Shakespearian comedy by divining that the spirit of Shakespearian comedy is in fact the spirit of universal comic harmony, so this one captures the spirit of Dickensian morality by divining that Dickensian morality is no less the spirit of universal moral truth.

One of the reviewers pointed out, for all the world as if he thought he had just discovered it and it was his duty to reveal it to a nation that would otherwise remain in ignorance of the matter, that Dickens's characters tend to be either wholly good or wholly bad, whereas few human beings fall so exclusively on one side or the other of the line. But that is, after all, the point; Dickens, in addition to all the other things he is doing in his novels, is rooting all those things in a foundation built from a clear distinction between right and wrong, a distinction that has since been abolished by acclamation and will shortly be officially prohibited by Act of Parliament. But the Cheeryble Brothers, Newman Noggs, Nicholas himself and Smike (we shall come to Smike in a moment) contrast with Ralph Nickleby, Hawk and Squeers (particularly Ralph, whose evil is conscious in a way foreign to the other scoundrels, so that he is therefore damned as well as doomed) to show that there is good and bad and a choice between them for all of us.

The huge and glorious pageant Mr Nunn and Mr Edgar have made of *Nicholas Nickleby* never loses sight of this central truth, which is why it succeeds; as a pageant alone it could not sustain the immense length at which it is presented, magnificent though the individual scenes of the pageant are. (All visitors will, when they emerge, have their favourites among these; for me the Crummles story ranks highest. I have always supposed that Dickens based the character on Mr Harold Macmillan, and the performance of Graham Crowden, though it clearly does not go along with this interpretation, is not to be missed or forgotten.)

The casting is virtually flawless all round, but it is not for me to go into detail, though I must salute the very remarkable double brought off by Suzanne Bertish as the hoydenish and horrible Fanny Squeers and a sensationally attractive Snevellici, and the scarcely less remarkable right-and-left of

Julie Peasgood as Tilda Price and The Infant Phenomenon.
But, given the loving strength of the adaptation, it is the
production that makes the evening so gigantic a triumph. The
feel of Dickensian London is easy to catch superficially, hell-
ishly difficult to portray deeply and solidly; but Mr Nun has
managed it, and the result is an experience that grips as the
book itself grips anyone with imagination, as a real world in
which real deeds, bad and good, are done.

There remains Smike, portrayed by David Threlfall as what
would today be called a spastic, but presented with a tact and
care that rob it of any danger of a false note. And Smike is, in a
sense, the hinge of the book and the play.

For Smike is love: love given and love received. If you miss
out love from Dickens you cut out his heart, and only if you
understand the part it plays with him will you understand him
truly. Mr Edgar, Mr Nunn and Mr Threlfall have all understood, whether they have worked it out consciously or not,
and the result is that the pageant and the morality-play alike are
grappled to our souls with hoops of steel. This production of
Nicholas Nickleby is ceaselessly entertaining, dramatic, funny,
touching, beautiful and right; it is a tribute to England's
greatest writer of prose and of the teeming world he conjured
up; it is an evocation of England herself; but it is something
more than all of these. It is a celebration of love and justice that
is true to the spirit of Dickens's belief that those are the ful-
crums on which the universe is moved, and the consequence
is that we come out not merely delighted but strengthened,
not just entertained but uplifted, not only affected but changed.

If you book for both parts at once, the R.S.C. give you a
discount. The fools! They should charge double!

The Times July 8th, 1980

Black mischief

THERE IS AN extraordinary work at Her Majesty's; *Paul Robeson* by Philip Hayes Dean, presents, to one trying to form a judgment upon it, a problem that has nothing to do with its theatrical or literary qualities. But it is the problem that makes it extraordinary. The play, which in form is almost entirely a single monologue, consists of a biographical chronicle of the life and work of the American Negro singer and actor whose name it bears; for those to whom Robeson is *only* a name, if that, I may perhaps summarize his life by saying that he was one of the first American Negroes to achieve public position, success and respect at a time (he was born in 1898) when the doors to advancement and acceptance were largely closed to them, when the lynch mobs of the South were still active, and when there had been no effective emancipatory legislation passed since the Constitutional amendments that followed the Civil War.

Robeson fought prejudice, brutality and fanaticism to carve his way into American society, conscious all the time that he had a further and more important duty; the last line of Act One of this play is 'We owe a place to those who come after us.' It must be added that, by all accounts, he was in his person a most lovable, and undoubtedly much loved, man.

Then where does the problem come in? Not in Act One, which takes him through his early struggles and up to his eventual breakthrough (signalled by his being chosen for the first London production of Jerome Kern's *Show Boat* and by his immense success in it); until the interval it is sentimental but decently so, amiably and gently written, full of light American humour ('My father didn't just come from North Carolina – he escaped from it').

Then where does the problem come in? In Act Two, when the play faces (or rather does not face) one more, and very terrible, fact about Paul Robeson, which is that he was a fellow-travelling hack of the Soviet Union, one of those who, in Rebecca West's deadly phrase, spent his life 'pimping for Stalin'. The Terror, the Nazi–Soviet Pact, the seizure of an Empire in Eastern Europe, the 'secret speech', the Hungarian Revolution – none of these shook his political allegiance to unspeakable evil. (It has been said in his defence that he found in the Soviet Union a land where people of his colour were not discriminated against. Apart from the fact that his adulation of the Soviet Union was at its worst when Stalin's anti-semitism was at *its* worst, the argument was crushingly answered by Roy Wilkins of the N.A.A.C.P., who said, 'The American Negro wants to be equally free, not equally unfree.')

It is Robeson's political activities (these, incidentally, led to suffering, penury and danger for him in his own country, a price which he paid with courage and dignity) that form the substance of the second half of *Paul Robeson*, and that lead me, at last, to my point.

The point lies in the author's attitude to his hero. It is one of unquestioning identification with Robeson's position, of ignominious flight from the responsibility of setting it in its moral context, of craven avoidance of anything that might risk having to touch upon the truth. This is carried to lengths that are almost incredible; Robeson speaks movingly, for instance, of the murder of Lorca by Franco's troops during the Spanish Civil War, and almost in the same breath he speaks of meeting Meyerhold in Moscow, without so much as a mention of the fact that Meyerhold was beaten to death on Stalin's orders. And Mr Dean cannot get out of it by saying that he is only presenting Robeson's own words. The play is full of invisible characters, all listed in the programme, with whom he is understood to be talking or arguing; yet the only ones who oppose ʰis vile and slavish politics are hounds like the members of the Un-American Activities Committee.

Now, I trust, you can see what I am talking about. As it happens, the second half of the play is dramatically bad as well as morally, a welter of grey and lifeless jargon. But long before it is over, the author has made clear that he is not simply presenting an entertainment, to be judged on artistic grounds, but a case and a conclusion, that must also be judged on moral and political ones. Well, let him have such judgments; here is mine. Robeson might have been naïve, ignorant and unable to resist the heady wine of adulation. History and hindsight combine to deprive Mr Dean of any such defence. His play is one of the most ignoble I have ever seen.

Sunday Times July 30th, 1978

Mr Valiant-for-Truth

LAST WEEK, IN Arlington, Virginia, there died a man. He was forty-seven years old, and a Colonel in the United States Air Force; he died, however, not in an aeroplane, nor on any military exercise, but of a heart attack in the course of a game of tennis. I am not surprised; I think that Death must long since have given up hope of killing Robert Craner in the course of his professional duties.

I first made his acquaintance when his English-born wife, Audrey, came to see me many years ago; within an exceptionally diffident character (on that first occasion she stopped every ten minutes to apologize for bothering me) there was, I later discovered, the fortitude of a Roman matron and the faithfulness and hope of Penelope. Her story, by then, was a familiar one; her husband's aeroplane had not returned from a mission over North Vietnam, and she had no idea whether he was dead, or alive and a prisoner. She had come to see me, she explained, because she had heard, that I was more sympathetic than most commentators to the American action in Vietnam, and might be able to do something to help her learn whether Robert was still alive, and if he was, to make it possible for her to communicate with him. She was right about my views (though it must be said that Mr Anthony Lewis of the *New York Times*, laboured tirelessly on her behalf despite the fact that he was entirely opposed to America's involvement in the Vietnam war), but wrong about my influence; I explained that my espousal of her cause, if it led to anything at all, would be more likely to result in an implacable refusal, on the part of the

North Vietnamese, to give any information whatever to one who was not only married to an enemy officer but championed by a notorious enemy of communism.

She took the point, but insisted that she wanted also to take the risk. She also hinted, at that first meeting, at something that she was later to make explicit; in her efforts to discover the nature of her husband's fate, she had been in touch with the 'peace' movements both in the United States and Great Britain, and it had been made clear to her that they would help her only if she were to make statements attacking American involvement in Vietnam. (They did this again when, having been told with a fair degree of certainty that Robert *was* alive, she was trying to get letters to and from him. I often wonder whether the honourable men and women who supported those movements because they truly wanted peace in Vietnam would have done so if they had known that the movements were run by people who were less interested in peace than in communist victory, and were willing to employ that kind of blackmail to further their aim.)

Well, in the end Audrey Craner discovered that Robert was indeed alive and in a prison camp. She never learned anything else for a long time, which was perhaps just as well, because while she was trying to discover how he was, Colonel Craner was being repeatedly tortured to try to persuade him to make a statement denouncing his country's determination to resist the communist aggression in Vietnam. When the Vietnam war ended, and the surviving prisoners returned, some of them told their stories, and in a volume of such accounts there was a striking and memorable remark by one of Robert Craner's brother officers. This was a man whose arm had been broken, and who had then been suspended by it from a rope, and jerked up and down, by those heroic fighters for peace and liberation, the North Vietnamese communists. He refused what was demanded of him; how, he was asked, had he been able to endure such treatment and still say No? He answered not only for himself but on behalf of his fellow-sufferers: I guess, he said, that we couldn't have gone back and faced Bob Craner if we'd given in.

From time to time, I wrote about the man who had thus set a standard of courage for his fellows; Audrey, meanwhile, travelled the world trying to get the ear of anyone who might be able to help her; to help her, that is, send letters and parcels to her husband, and to know that they had been delivered. The blackmail became more insistent; she, in turn, became more adamant. 'My husband', she would say, 'has not denounced his country, and I shall not do so either.' So she never did know, until the war was over and Robert returned, whether her missives ever reached him. (A few did.)

Audrey Craner and her two children, Lorne and Charys, became my dear friends; indeed, I watched the children grow up, and felt how proud Robert Craner would be, if he ever came home, of the young man and woman whom he had left as infants. Audrey, of course, was in no doubt that he would come home, and when, at the end of the war, the first authenticated list of surviving prisoners had his name on it, I took her and the children out to dinner to celebrate. They came to my flat first for a drink, and as they were coming up the stairs the telephone rang; it was a call from Wake Island (the trans-shipment post for the returning prisoners). I shouted the news down the stairs, and they came up the last flight at a gallop; I went into the bedroom and put my hands over my ears.

I met Robert, of course, both here and in the United States; I remember that we all went to see the Tall Ships at Boston during the Bicentennial celebrations. He was what I expected him to be, not only because I had already seen him through the eyes of his family, but from the fact of his career and conduct. He was, as I said when I started this column, a man.

In the best sense, he was an old-fashioned one. The code of honour, truth and loyalty by which he lived, and which inspired his wife and children has been thoroughly besmirched these last few decades, even in the United States itself, let alone

Britain. Robert Craner's virtues, and what he did with his life, would today mystify millions who have been taught that the first duty of a citizen in a free country is to hate it, and that the second is to work towards the destruction of its freedom. Robert Craner fought for freedom, and very nearly died for it, because he believed in it. He believed that the open society is better than the closed one, that totalitarianism is evil and must be resisted, that the state exists to enhance the life of the individual, not the other way round. He was extraordinarily free of personal rancour or bitterness for what communism had done to him, but granite in his hatred of the thing itself. He stayed in the Air Force, but became – somewhat to his own surprise, I dare say – a military attaché, posted to the military missions of his country's diplomatic service; he had just finished a period *en poste* in Budapest.

He did his duty, as millions did before him; he would have gone again, without flinching, through his experiences in the Vietnamese camp if that duty had called him to do so; he did not regard himself as a hero. If it is the fashion to sneer at such men, I know a family which will remain out of fashion for the rest of their lives, and be glad to do so. The cause for which he suffered is in disarray today, and his enemies, who are our enemies too, have since achieved bloodless victories far greater than those they won from the conflict in which he fought. But I doubt if he died discouraged; the word was not in his vocabulary, nor the thought in his mind. His work remains to do, as it always will; he was one who knew better than most what the price of liberty is.

When I heard the news of his death, I had a strange fantasy; of him addressing last week's Labour Party conference. I think that the fanatic rabble of the far left would have been too stunned even to boo; it would have been as though a Martian had emerged from a spaceship and made sounds beyond interpretation. But the language Robert Craner spoke is the oldest in the world, and the best, for it is the language of freedom, and it is spoken, from generation to generation, by the brave. Throughout his short life, he spoke it, not mumbling, but in ringing tones, and what he said in it will go on echoing down the years. I salute the memory of a valiant man.

The Times October 7th, 1980

The ladies' man

THERE WAS A remarkable incident the day before yesterday at a creditors' meeting. (*A* creditors' meeting, damn your impudence, not *my* creditors' meeting.) The firm which was up the spout was yet another travel agency, and my attention was caught to begin with by the fact that the boss of it was called John de L'Ouest, which, you might say, is what he seems to have gone. A good many allegations were bandied about in the course of the proceedings, and at one point Mr de L'Ouest was punched smartly in the face. (None of this, I had better say at once, has anything to do with me, and I have – or shall shortly acquire – an affidavit to that effect sworn by both Goodman *and* Derrick.) But the item that caused me to walk hurriedly up and down in a state of considerable excitement was quite incidental to the main narrative. It seems that the man who did the punching (Goodman says I ought to sprinkle a few 'allegeds' over that bit, but Derrick thinks it is unnecessary) announced his intention in advance, with the memorable words, 'When the women leave I'm going to crack your teeth.'

There, as far as I can see, goes the very last gentleman in England, and I, who have always thought that that title belonged to me, am now content to accept that I am only the last but one. Here is a man, in an age which can scarcely *spell* chivalry, never mind practise it, who is possessed of so perfect an instinctive understanding of the respect due to the fair sex that even in the grip of otherwise uncontrollable rage, he remembers to wait until its representatives have left the room before taking action unfit for their delicate eyes.

I know, of course, what the cynics will say: that our hero's scruples were unnecessary and absurd and that if he had really wanted to serve the interests of the womenfolk he would have invited them to take a ringside seat before he gave Mr de L'Ouest the old one-two. It is true that many women today are not what women were when I was a boy; certainly it cannot be denied that the women's page of the *Guardian* exists, pleasant though it would be to believe that it does not, and if the page exists so, presumably, do the women who write it, though at some point, as Dr Johnson said, credulity must make a stand. But the Roland of Carey Street, who is a publican, incidentally, will plainly have no truck with such developments; as far as he is concerned, ladies are what they always were – innocent and tender-hearted creatures who scream at the sight of a mouse, and swoon at that of blood.

I hope you fully understand by now the extent of the *délicatesse* displayed by the Oliver of the Four-Ale Bar. Even in these degenerate days, a few men will still hesitate before using language that might cause a blush to mantle the cheek of a lady; but there is no suggestion that he was planning to swear at Mr de L'Ouest, let alone that he actually did so. He thought only that the sight of one man punching another was something that no lady should see, and on that assumption he acted.

Now the trouble with the times we live in is that many will assume that a *preux chevalier* of the kind we have here thinks *less* highly of women than he should, that his compliment to the opposite sex is in truth an insult, that he is opposed to equal pay, the abolition of domestic science as a subject in girls' schools, unisex hairdressers and even A Woman's Right to Choose. I do not think this follows at all, and indeed my own observations strongly support the view that a man who holds a door open for a lady, or offers her his seat in a bus, is more likely to believe her his equal, not less, and the horrible Things who fill the correspondence columns of the *Daily*

Telegraph regularly once a fortnight with the suggestion that Manchester should be renamed Personchester are the ones who believe, or at any rate behave as though they believe, that a woman is only a woman, but a good cigar is a smoke.

What our gallant friend has divined is something rather more subtle. We shall in time have true equality between men and women, and quite right too. But there is a terrible urge on the lunatic fringe of the women's movement, where it is indistinguishable from the political lunatic fringe, to insist not that men and women are *equal*, but that they are *identical*.

Vive to be sure, *la différence*; but there is something more important to be said. At the heart of the modern totalitarian left in countries like Britain – that is, the *groupuscules* generally called Trotskyite – is a hunger, largely but not entirely unconscious, to get rid of, by submerging in the mass, the individual human personality, which they cannot forgive for reminding them that their political 'philosophy', dependent as it is on the pathetic belief that human beings can be fully predicted and scientifically controlled, is nonsense. It was surely no accident that the tutelary deity of this movement was Mao Tse-tung, who really did seem to have achieved the reduction to complete uniformity of about seven hundred million people; that always was untrue, of course, and some of us did not need the events in China which have followed the death of Mao to tell us so, but for a time it looked plausible to those who needed to believe it.

Nor, surely is it an accident that the more extreme militants of the women's movement are politically part of this totalitarian drift. Some have dismissed these women as unconscious Lesbians, women-haters in women's clothing, but that has never seemed to me to be an adequate or convincing explanation; it is in their political, not their sexual, orientation that the clue lies. (Those who believe that there is no difference between any two human beings that cannot be explained in terms of society will inevitably tend to believe that there is no difference between men and women other than a physical one.) There are in this country people, not in madhouses nor in any danger of being put there, who believe that everyone could play the violin like Yehudi Menuhin if it were not for the constraints imposed from birth by society – in full, by *capitalist* society.

Those are happily few; but there are already very many who believe, less luridly but no less ludicrously, that no one is born more intelligent than anyone else. *Facilis descensus Averni*; from there, it is only a short step to believing that no one is born more feminine than anyone else, *whatever sex one may be*.

But he of the ready fists and readier manners does not believe such sad rubbish, any more than I do; whence his conduct, and my encomium. No doubt there were some women present when he made his stand who wished he had not, and would have liked nothing better than to see the fur, and even the teeth, fly; nor need we condemn these as unwomanly. But his statement of intent was normative, and sought to show, what as a matter of fact all sensible people of both sexes have always believed and still do, that there are certain things owed by men to women because they *are* women, and for that reason alone. 'When the women leave, I'm going to crack your teeth.' I cannot, of course, approve of the intention in the second half of the statement, still less of its carrying out. But the implication of the first half seems to me something to cherish and applaud, and the speaker, though he may be a publican, is in my eyes at least no sinner.

The Times September 18th, 1980

A buzzing in my ears

I BET I know more about bumblebees than you do. In fact, I bet I know more about bumblebees than anybody in the world except Dr D. V. Alford, who got his Ph.D. for a thesis on them, and knows so much about them he even runs an outfit called the Bumblebee Distribution Maps Scheme, and has just published the definitive study of the jolly little fellows, under the title – the only title he could have chosen, really – *Bumblebees*; it is published by Davis-Poynter, and will set you back no less than twenty-five quid. (They sent me a free copy merely because I was overheard saying I would like to know more about bumblebees.) But it will tell you absolutely everything there is to be known about bumblebees, as I can swear from personal experience, for I have just read it, which is how I come to be such an expert on the subject all of a sudden.

I can assure you that there is more to the bumblebee, or *Bombus*, to give him his Latin name, than meets the eye, or the ear for that matter. (I suppose Macbeth's 'shard-borne beetle with his drowsy hums' must have been a bumblebee.) To start with, there is an almost unbelievable number of species of bumblebee (I say 'almost' unbelievable, because Dr Alford is a very plausible fellow, and besides he lists the lot of them), and they go by names of such variegated magnificence, such evocatively poetic beauty, that I must introduce you to a selection.

There is *Bombus agrorum*, for instance, who is obviously a rustic bumblebee, forever sucking straws and leaning over gates; there is *Bombus americanorum*, who, no doubt, chews gum; *Bombus appositus*, known for producing the *mot juste*; *Bombus confusus*, a rather daft bumblebee who is always blundering into things; *Bombus distinguendus*, who comes of a very old family of bumblebees, and *Bombus elegans*, who only goes to the best tailors; *Bombus fragrans*, who sprinkles himself night and morning with attar of roses, and between you and me is as queer as a coot, though why a coot should be considered the very essence of queerness I am unable to say; *Bombus frigidus*, a very reserved bumblebee; *Bombus hortorum hortorum*, who stammers; *Bombus humilis*, a very Uriah Heep among bumblebees; *Bombus ignitus*, much in demand among bumblebees on Guy Fawkes night; *Bombus impatiens*, a restless bumblebee; *Bombus inexpectatus*, who is apt to pop out from behind lamp-posts and cry 'Boo!'; *Bombus mendax*, a teller of tall bumblebee tales; *Bombus polaris*, said to have nuclear mandibles; *Bombus ruderatus*, who sticks his tongue out at lady bumblebees; *Bombus senilis*, poor old thing; *Bombus subterraneus*, who has read more Karl Marx than is good for him; and *Bombus virginalis*, or so she says.

Many a lesson can be learnt by the human race from its furry friend *Bombus*; for instance, Dr Alford reveals that 'the mouthparts are controlled by the suboesophageal ganglion', which at last explains Mr Peter Shore, and in the majority of species 'any co-operation between individuals is limited to brief and temporary associations for the purpose of reproduction', which as Lady Bracknell might have said, savours of the worst excesses of the permissive society. Sometimes, it is true, Dr Alford seems somewhat too easily impressed with the achievements of his little playmates, as when he says that 'bumblebees are remarkably proficient at remembering the precise location of their nest'; dammit, I can find my way home, too, and nobody writes books calling me remarkably proficient. On the other hand, the learned author sometimes makes very questionable claims, such as that 'inhalation also occurs through the abdominal spiracles, while exhalation takes place through the propodeal spiracles', which I for one am unable to accept, and that the hind tibia of a bumblebee is 'convex, dull and hairy all over', which is a wicked libel. (A much worse error is Dr Alford's claim that 'Wagner assumed that bumblebees of the various species entered hibernation at about the same time of year, in response to the onset of autumn weather'. Wagner made no such assumption – on the contrary, he used to insist that no two bumblebees entered hibernation, or even a pub, at the same time if they could help it; indeed, the first draft of *Götterdämmerung* contains a long and moving statement by Alberich on this very point.)

Badgers eat bumblebees – some do, anyway – which is the only thing I know about badgers that I don't like; skunks, less surprisingly, are also numbered among their enemies, and 'in Ireland, brown trout have been reported to take bumblebees which inadvertently land on the water' – though that last statement suggests that Dr Alford can't tell when he is having his leg pulled. Bumblebees are deaf, it seems.

Some species 'possess rather pugnacious workers', who are no doubt enrolled into the National Union of Public Employees, though the habit they have of 'flying one after another along established routes, each bee pausing at intervals to hover momentarily at a series of predetermined visiting places', rather suggests that if so they have missed their vocation, and ought to be driving the No. 11 bus.

I have to confess – you will see how little I knew of the subject on which I am now such an authority before I read Dr Alford's monograph – that I used to be of the opinion that the difference between a bumblebee and honey-bee was that bumblebees have no sting. But they do; the bumblebee's sting, however, is not equipped with the barb that the honey-bee's has. This means, of course, that a bumblebee, unlike its better organized cousin, can wound its enemy, withdraw its sting, and live to strike again – a fact which has caused me to revise my intention of inviting any passing bumblebee to visit my window boxes; *Bombus hypnorum*, for instance (he presumably has a glittering eye), 'shows a particularly strong preference for areas inhabited by man', and I would have loved to see him browsing among the undergrowth if it had not been for the feeling that he might slip into the room, sting me, and slip out again. Incidentally, one of the bumblebee's insect enemies is a species of wasp called *Philathus triangulum*. I presume that all a bumblebee attacked by one of them has to do is to knock the square off its hypotenuse.

The Times July 9th, 1975

Pass it on

I THINK I AM about to attempt the impossible by trying to describe in print something which did not take place in print and which cannot be conveyed without visible demonstration. But I must try; for the game I am talking about, and to which I was introduced the other night by Robin Ray, is too good to keep to myself. (Robin is one of the few men I have ever met with a mind even more uselessly ingenious than my own; he once devised the idea of a restaurant that would serve nothing but the left-overs from other restaurants, the point being that the left-overs would be from the finest and most famous places in London, conveyed by a fleet of motor-cycles equipped with heated containers to keep the food warm, and sold at prices a tenth of those charged in the restaurants from which the fragments had originated. He had even thought of a name for his establishment: Swill's.)

Anyway, four of us had been to see the show that Robin is at present in: *Tomfoolery*, at the Criterion Theatre. It is an evening of songs of Tom Lehrer, that 1950s' master of the macabre, the bad taste and the cynical, and I must say that they have survived extraordinarily well, in addition to being most stylishly put over by Robin and his fellow performers. A good time was had by all, and afterwards, joined by Robin's wife, Susan, we all went out to dinner. (Not at Swill's, but most certainly at a restaurant from which Robin's place will derive some of its most delicious items.)

The merriment-level was high throughout dinner; little did

we know that it was, before we parted, to climb all the way to hysteria. But when the coffee was reached, I saw in Robin's eye the cherubically innocent look that he adopts when he is about to do something exceptionally wicked, and a moment later we were off.

'Can you', he asked us, 'repeat exactly a few simple words and a simple action?' Of course we can, we replied; what did he take us for? What he took us for were his victims, as he was about to demonstrate; but we did not know that yet. 'Very well,' he said briskly, and took his cigarette-lighter from his pocket. Turning to the lady on his immediate left (it was, I should point out, a round table, though the trick would work – albeit a little less elegantly – with an oblong one), he offered it to her with the words 'This is a lighter', instructing her that she was not to take it at once, but was to reply, 'A what?' She did as she was bid, and he replied, 'A lighter', at which point she was to take it from him and turn to the gentleman on her left, who happened to be me. Following instructions from Robin the Devil, she offered me the object with the same words: 'This is a lighter', to which I, too, was ordered to reply 'A what?' Now, however, there was a development, for instead of replying to me immediately she had to turn back to Robin and repeat, 'A what?', whereupon he replied, 'A lighter', and she was to turn back to me and repeat the explanation, 'A lighter', when I was permitted to take it and turn to *my* left, where was seated Susan.

'This', I was to say to her, 'is a lighter.' 'A what?' says Susan (who had played the game before, incidentally). I swivelled to my right and inquired, similarly, 'A what?' My right-hand neighbour swivelled back to Robin and asked 'A what?' 'A lighter' says he to her; 'A lighter,' says she to me; 'A lighter,' say I to Susan, who takes it. Susan turns to her left; 'This is a lighter,' 'A what?' 'A what?' 'A what?' 'A what?' – 'A lighter.' 'A lighter.' 'A lighter.' 'A lighter.'

And so we went round the table until it got back to Robin. Well, it is true that that is what happened eventually, but it did not happen at once. For, while he jeered at us for our confident assumption that we could easily repeat a few simple words and a couple of simple actions, we got it wrong again and again and again, and had to hand it back to Robin to start the cycle all over. We forgot the formula; we gave the lighter over before the verbal ritual was completed; we answered 'A lighter' without turning right to send the question back to the Lord of Misrule and to await the answer as it came round to us. I cannot tell you how many times the chain broke before it was completed; but what I can tell you is that, confronted by our own lack of finesse in the matter, we began to laugh more and more immoderately, until we could scarcely go on with the game.

Still we tried; still we failed; still he jeered. Eventually, however, and by now in pain from laughing, we learned how to do it without a mistake, and the object went right round the table without ('A what? A what? A what? A what? A what?' – 'A lighter; a lighter; a lighter . . . ') a single hitch. But we weren't finished with Robin's wickedness. The lighter made a complete circuit without error and was returned into Robin's hand. He immediately turned to his left and, without varying the formula, sent it on again; it began to progress, still clockwise, round the table once more, for we had at last got the hang of it. When it had gone a couple of places, *he turned the other way*, and said to his right-hand neighbour, 'This is a fork', as indeed it was. 'A what?' 'A fork.'

The full extent of Robin's tortuous ingenuity was now apparent; two different objects were circulating in opposite directions, accompanied by the same formula but with different keywords. What is more, those engaged in the fork-transaction could, naturally, hear the exchanges of those involved in the lighter-ritual, and those who had but a moment before been turning right to receive and left to convey were now obliged to turn left to get and right to give, in addition to which the daisy-chain of 'A what?' was going round the table in both directions simultaneously, and the two daisy-chains of 'A lighter' and 'A fork' were doing likewise. Chaos was come again.

At some point, of course, one of the party was going to be dealing – or trying to deal – with both objects at once, and I began to wonder whether the restaurant was sufficiently equipped with doctors skilled in the art of uncrossing eyes and psychiatrists qualified to treat schizophrenia. I need not have worried; before the irresistible force met the immovable object we had all, Robin included, collapsed completely, helpless in the grip of the inexplicable joy that is expressed in laughter which sweeps away every last scrap of resistance. We had eaten of the insane root that takes the reason prisoner, and we finally reeled out into the street as men and women who have seen wonders and lived (though only just) to tell the tale.

I don't know if you have understood my account; certainly you will by now realize why I thought it could not be done without demonstration. But you will also realize why I tell the tale on this day rather than on another; tomorrow, most of us will be sitting round a table in company, and a festive mood will, I trust, be the order of the day. I offer you Robin's Game to play, and the Compliments of the Season to go with it. Don't try it with the turkey.

The Times December 24th, 1980

Comrades, come rally

A FEW YEARS AGO, there was an attempt by a group of Soviet workers to start a trade union for the first time in their country, where of course no moves towards industrial combination, let alone strikes, are permitted to the workers, and any attempt to take any form of action in their own interests is rigorously repressed. But that is not what this column is about.

The first attempt was launched by a group of men and women from various trades; none of them had any association with dissident groups, or indeed any political aims; they merely wanted an organization which, as is the function of trade unions in countries that permit them, would represent Soviet workers in such matters as safety, opportunities for promotion, working conditions and possibly even pay and hours worked. Naturally, all the known members of the group – with tragically complete courage they had given their names when they made their public statement – were arrested, and soon found themselves in jail, concentration camp or psychiatric prison. Among them was a coal-miner, Vladimir Klebanov, who was (and remains) imprisoned in a particularly dreadful psychiatric 'hospital' in the Ukraine, where he has undergone beatings and is now being tortured with massive doses of drugs he does not need (he was examined by a genuine Soviet psychiatrist, Dr Alexander Volosanovich, who disclosed that Klebanov was perfectly sane and was himself immediately subject to the full force of

Soviet persecution for doing so); his condition is deteriorating, and he may not have long to live. But that is not what this column is about either.

A message from Vladimir Klebanov (who has been adopted as a 'prisoner of conscience' by Amnesty International) together with an appeal for Western voices to be raised on behalf of the persecuted workers of the Soviet Union, was smuggled out, directed in particular at British trade unions and more particularly still at the National Union of Mineworkers, who were specifically asked to speak up on behalf of their fellow-miner. And the N.U.M. Executive washed their hands of him and sided with his persecutors and torturers. And that is what this column *is* about.

The precise boundary between men and swine is not always easy to draw; but in this case it presents little difficulty. I am not, as a matter of fact, disposed to become indignant at the conduct of the communists and fellow-travellers on the N.U.M. Executive. Nothing else could be expected of them, and in offering their assistance to those who oppress Soviet working miners rather than to the oppressors' victims, they are only acting according to their political lights; men whose lives have been dedicated to the work of establishing communist totalitarianism in this country cannot be expected to condemn it in the country on whose tyranny their ambitions are modelled. But the Soviet tyrants can count only on a minority of the N.U.M. Executive to support them; this decision – to abandon to his fate a fellow-miner whose only crime was to try to start a trade union in a country where they are prohibited under fearsome penalties – was also taken by men who do *not* simply go by the principle that whatever the Soviet Union does is right. Those voting to side with the torturers against the tortured, with the bosses against the workers, with Caesar against Spartacus, also included – must have included – some crawling things from the non-communist majority on the N.U.M. Executive.

Ay, in the catalogue ye go for men! But the Soviet oppressors knew what manner of men they were dealing with as well as Macbeth did, and to their

> . . . I will put that business in your bosoms
> Whose execution takes your enemy off,
> Grapples you to the heart and love of us,
> Who wears our health but sickly in his life,
> Which in his death were perfect,

the members of the N.U.M. Executive who voted for the abandonment of Mr Klebanov could give the same reply as the dogs with whom Macbeth was dealing:

> . . . We shall, my lord,
> Perform what you command us . . .

It is not to be supposed that the N.U.M.'s decision was taken without reasons being given. The N.U.M. leaders have explained that Mr Yefremenko, who is the head of the Soviet organization charged with preventing Soviet miners following their own interests and ensuring that they are bound only to the State's, told them that Mr Klebanov had hurt his head in a mine accident and thus became deranged. They also told them that he is a Jew (he isn't, incidentally), and for good measure that he had left his wife and gone to live with another woman. This last point much impressed one Sid Vincent of the Lancashire miners. In an excellent radio programme about the Soviet workers' struggle to establish trade unions, in the File on Four series a few weeks ago, Sid was heard making it clear that this helped to persuade him not to cast his vote for interceding. 'There could have been a better case,' he whined. Well, there is now, actually; the case of another miner, Alexei Nikitin, who took part in the movement which sprang up soon after Mr Klebanov's was crushed, and who is also being tortured in a psychiatric prison. But the N.U.M. Executive has now decided to ignore him, too. (Possibly Sid Vincent has been told that Mr Nikitin once kept a goldfish and neglected to feed it.) Another remarkably brave Soviet psychiatrist, Dr

Koriagin, has examined him, too, and revealed that he also is perfectly sane. For doing so, Dr Koriagin was arrested, and is now awaiting 'trial'.

Enough of this tip-toeing about. *All* the members of the N.U.M. Executive, communist and non-communist alike, know perfectly well that Yefremenko's job includes, as a crucial element, telling lies to people like them. And they all knew, and know, perfectly well that Mr Klebanov and Mr Nikitin are suffering because, and only because, they wanted to start an organization that would represent miners in the Soviet Union, as the N.U.M. leaders represent miners in Britain. They prefer to connive at lies as well as persecution, and to leave Soviet miners to rot in the K.G.B.'s dungeons, rather than risk offending the Soviet authorities, and possibly forgo in consequence the junketing and boozing they enjoy from time to time at the hands of those who oppress their fellow-miners in the Soviet Empire.

Mr Klebanov would certainly have been immediately informed of the N.U.M.'s decision to side with his persecutors, and Mr Nikitin would likewise have been told that he could expect no help from the British miners. (Even the French communist miners' organization, incidentally – and you can't get more implacably Stalinist than that – have protested to the Soviet authorities.) Whenever there is a pause in Western publicizing of the fate of Soviet dissidents, it is always used by the authorities there to help weaken the morale of those in the prisons, the concentration camps and the madhouses; see, they are gloatingly told, your friends have abandoned you. And that is the line taken when nothing more serious has happened than a temporary absence of comment: can you imagine how much more intense such pressure becomes when, as in the present instance, the Western body that has been directly appealed to for help has not only refused to give it, but has decided instead to take the part of those against whose persecution the help was sought?

One of the most extraordinary phenomena of our confused

time, to which Alexander Solzhenitsyn in particular has repeatedly drawn attention, is what I may term the seesaw of freedom. In the Soviet Union and the captive nations of her Empire, the struggle for liberty at all levels is pursued by growing numbers of astoundingly brave men and women. Most of them – within the Soviet Union itself there is almost no exception – have never known freedom or had access to its literature or its representatives. But they have found inside themselves the yearning to be free, and have thus incidentally given the lie to those who insist that the slave is comfortable in his chains, and cannot conceive of anything outside his own experience. And the terrible paradox lies in the fact that at the other end of the seesaw the lands of freedom contain growing numbers who yearn no less eagerly to have done with the pain of choice, of self-mastery, of moral and political independence, and to resign themselves to a future in which men and women are at one with the brutes.

In such a climate, the betrayal by the N.U.M.'s leaders of freedom, of brotherhood, class solidarity, the miners' tradition, honour, truth and humanity is understandable. But it is no less disgusting for that. Two Soviet miners, Mr Klebanov and Mr Nikitin, appealed for help, supported by those in the Soviet Union who seek to sustain them in their agony. They appealed directly to the leaders of free British miners for that help, and a majority of those leaders refused to give it. With what contempt must Mr Klebanov and Mr Nikitin and their friends and fellow-sufferers regard such curs! And how richly justified is that contempt!

The Times April 15th, 1981

The libel on the wall

IT SOUNDS LIKE one of A. P. Herbert's *Misleading Cases*, but there are those, I feel, for whom it may be no joke: at last, somebody has been done for libel over a painting. The said libel was contained in a work by a Mr Georges, entitled 'The Mugging of the Muse', which portrays a partly clothed young lady being set upon with knives in a dark alley by two assailants bearing the lineaments of two of the artist's fellow-painters, Messrs Siani and Silberman, who proved, at any rate to the satisfaction of the jury, that the picture implied that they were 'violent criminals or at least artists intent on murdering art'.

Peace, peace, dear lawyers: all this happened in far-off New York, though if it will make you happier I am perfectly content to add that I take no sides in the matter, offer no opinion on the justice of the verdict or the closeness of the alleged likenesses, and for that matter express no view on the appropriateness of the damages ($30,000 a head). All I want to say, really, is that the case does undoubtedly open up new vistas, and jolly ones, at that.

I suppose the oddest vehicle for a libel hitherto known was the open visiting-card left at Oscar Wilde's club by the 'screaming scarlet Marquess'. 'To Oscar Wilde', it read, 'posing as a somdomite'. (That spelling of the fatal word was the Marquess's own; no doubt the state of rage he was in made him careless.) I have always wondered about the phrasing: why '*posing as*'? Could it be that even Queensberry feared to go all the way to the direct accusation? Anyway, the hall porter, as we know, put the card in an envelope and gave it to Wilde when he arrived: the evidence at the trial was that the porter did not understand the words but sensed that they would be better concealed. (A dozen or so years ago, by the way, I mentioned the card and the action of the club servant in something I was writing, and blow me if history didn't tip-toe in with her own visiting-card: I got a letter from the daughter of the hall porter in the case.)

I think that Mr Georges, the unsuccessful defendant in the American case, has improved on the Marquess's notion; libel by painting is a most strikingly original idea, particularly since this one was genuinely pictorial, as opposed, say, to a representation of a brick wall bearing graffitic words such as 'Sir Anthony Grogblossom, Q.C., is a roaring poofdah'. (A. P. Herbert did in fact compose a hardly less ingenious case, in which the words complained of were spoken on a gramophone record, and the lawyers waxed fat on the question – vital in English law – of whether they constituted a libel or a slander. In the House of Lords hearing, Lord Lick cited the case of Silvertop *v*. The Stepney Guardians, in which a man had trained a parrot to say three times after meals, 'Councillor Wart has not washed today', and was held to have libelled the plaintiff. But A. P. Herbert was joking.)

Of course, the American case cannot possibly be the first time an action for libel *might* have been mounted over a painting, though I imagine that most of the earlier possibilities would have concerned portraits that the sitter thought less than flattering, even if the artist did not intend them to be. Sir Winston Churchill, by all accounts was so incensed by Graham Sutherland's portrait of him that he might easily have sued for libel, and I have always thought that *any* portrait by Annigoni should be held to constitute *prima facie* evidence of defamation. (As for Madame Tussaud's, nothing short of criminal libel would suffice, though an action over a waxwork would be even stranger and jollier than one over a painting.)

The point about the New York case, however, is that it was,

or at least was held to be, a consciously adverse *comment* on the plaintiffs, and for that it is not easy to think of a precedent. Géricault's *Raft of the Medusa* pointed the finger of a deadly accusation, and is indeed the pictorial equivalent of Zola's *J'accuse*; but it portrays only the victims, not the criminals, and the spectator was left to supply the names in the indictment. Of course, the history of art is full of pictures of alleged tyrants tyrannizing, alleged murderers murdering and alleged traitors betraying, to say nothing of a substantial assortment of alleged naughty persons a-mollocking when the sukebind is out, but it is noticeable that these are always *past* sinners, artists customarily having been seized with discretion when it came to portraying the villains among their own contemporaries. That is understandable, but a pity; the Royal Academy's Summer Show would surely have been brightened by, say, a huge Ruskin Spear (and he would certainly have been the fellow to do it) entitled 'Lords Brayley, Kagan and Plurenden, Together With Sir Eric Miller, Get Up To An Immense Amount of Financial and Other Mullarkey While Sir Harold Wilson and Lady Falkender Fail, To Their Subsequent Surprise and Sorrow, To Notice Anything Going On.'

Cartoonists and caricaturists, of course, have commented adversely on their adversaries since their art was invented; but these I classify, even the greatest of them, as the pictorial equivalent of journalists, indeed of very columnists, whose job it is to criticize those in public life who demonstrate by their public activities the need for criticism of them. (No, madam, the Raphael Cartoons in the Victoria and Albert Museum are not a series of biting comments on the author of *The Glittering Prizes*.)

I have never believed that Cromwell told Lely to put in all the warts (we have only Horace Walpole's word for it, and that old fribble would much rather have told a false good anecdote than repeated a true bad one), and I am quite sure that he didn't mean it even if he said it. Lely did, of course, put in the warts, at least the big one in the centre of Oliver's forehead; he took care, however, to make it look odd but distinguished, not disgusting. Today, Lady Babablacksheep may tell Mr Terence Cuneo to paint her just as he sees her, but I dare say that what she means is that she will be much obliged if he will endeavour to make her look indistinguishable, at least in a dim light, from the Rokeby Venus, or even Miss Anna Ford, and although milady may be disappointed if the result is closer to the truth than she would wish, she would have genuine ground for a solicitor's letter if he went past the truth in the opposite direction and made her look like – well, well, we don't want to set off the litigation ourselves, do we?

The greatest missed opportunity for a lawsuit over a painting is surely Mrs Giovanni Arnolfini (née Cenami) *v.* Jan van Eyck. She could have taken him to the cleaners (or perhaps the restorers), for scholars agree that the picture is of the couple on their wedding-day, yet the merest glance at it makes clear that the artist has painted the lady to look as though she has been in the pudding-club for about eight and a half months, a fact to which even the little dog in the foregound would testify, and if van Eyck had tried to maintain that the whole thing is an optical illusion caused by the way she is holding her bunched-up skirt it would only have increased the damages.

All in all, I think I prefer the legal risks of the writer's trade to those of the painter's. If I say of a politician that he bears a marked resemblance to a pig, a rat and a weasel, and that in view of what I know about his character I am not in the least surprised, the only question for the jury will be whether my words are fair comment on a matter of public interest. If I *painted* the politician similarly, and they also had to decide what the picture was supposed to convey, it would keep the lawyers in cream buns for a century. The justices of the American Supreme Court would be well advised to lay in a stock of headache powders, as well as pencils, against the day when Siani and Silberman *v.* Georges reaches them.

The Times January 13th, 1981

Farewell, I hope, my lovely

THERE IS A most engaging compilation, conceived and put together by Mr Stephen Pile, called *The Book of Heroic Failures*,* which, as its title suggests, records not the shots which went wide of the bullseye but those which never even came out of the barrel of the gun. The book seems to have been a great success, making it probable that another edition will in time be called for; this is just as well, for in the last few days there has passed into history an achievement in the realms of failure that surely dwarfs not only anything previously recorded by Mr Pile but anything the most extravagant imagination could invent. I refer to the gentleman who was sent to prison for life after a trial in which the court was told of *seven* unsuccessful attempts he had made to murder his wife, without her noticing that anything out of the ordinary was going on.

Now on the whole, I do not usually find murder, or even attempted murder, matter for laughter, though some theatrical farces have used sudden and unnatural death to considerable and hilarious effect, notably Mr Royce Ryton's *The Unvarnished Truth*. But as I read through the prosecution's *catalogue raisonné* of the defendant's vain efforts to do away with the wife of his bosom I was seized with a wild laughter of the kind released by the best surrealist art, and by the end was helplessly hysterical at the breakfast-table.

Having first taken out £250,000 of insurance on his help-

* Routledge 1979.

meet's life, a circumstance which apparently failed to arouse her curiosity, let alone suspicion, our unsuccessful felon got down to work. First he put mercury, a dangerous poison if ingested, into a strawberry flan he had made for her. It fell out, however; it seems that he used too much of it – a case, if ever there was one, of over-egging the pudding.

Nothing daunted, Bluebeard then tried stuffing a mackerel with the same deadly substance (a matter, I suppose, of putting the poison in the *poisson*), but for some unaccountable reason it had no effect on the little lady. Warming to his work, he took her on holiday to Yugoslavia, where he invited her to sit on the edge of a cliff; the court was told that she had declined, prompted by some 'sixth sense'. I am glad it came to her rescue, though I must say that by now I should have thought a sixth sense unnecessary; one or two of the better-known five ought to have been quite sufficient to alert her to the fact that the magic had gone out of her marriage, particularly when, on their return from Yugoslavia, he repeated the cliff suggestion, this time at Beachy Head. (What do you suppose he actually *said*? 'Darling, it would be rather nice if you were to go over there and sit on the edge of the cliff, with your legs dangling over.' 'Why, darling?' 'Oh, I don't know – I just thought you might like to get the weight off your feet.')

Two goes of mercury poisoning and two cliff-hangers having failed, our hero took to arson. While she was in bed, ill, at the matrimonial home, he started a fire outside the bedroom door, but some interfering busybody put it out before the goose (and *what* a goose) was cooked. Clearly a believer in trying anything twice, he waited a bit and again set light to their flat, but this time succeeded only in razing the place to the ground, thus inauspiciously defying the spirit, if not the letter, of that ancient Chinese proverb which says, 'It is not worth burning down your house simply to inconvenience your mother-in-law.'

By now, even if the missus was still unaware that hubby had found new meaning in the bit about having and holding in sickness and in health till death us do part, she must at least have come to the conclusion that her footsteps were being dogged by something quite exceptional in the way of bad luck. (How do you suppose it went when she mentioned the fact to him? 'Nonsense, darling, you're imagining things.' 'Yes, I suppose I am.' 'Of course you are, sweetie – why don't you go and lean out of the window?') Nor was the run of ill-fortune quite over yet; one day, when they were out in their car, he proposed that she should go and stand in the middle of the road, in order, he explained, that he might 'test the car's suspension'. I am not a driver and understand nothing of cars; for all I know, that is the normal and accepted method of testing a car's suspension. But even if it is, I cannot help feeling that our friend's better half might by now have cottoned on to the fact that whenever she had one of her strokes of mischance, her husband was invariably near by, and that a good case could be made out for a plea of *post hoc, propter hoc*.

It seems, however, that she had never heard of Sir Karl Popper's solution to the problem of induction; she did not, as bidden, go and stand in the middle of the road, but neither did she repair with all deliberate speed to the nearest police station. Instead, she stood patiently at the *edge* of the road, while the man of the house drove the car straight at her 'but at the last second veered away'. (*Ah, monsieur, quelle délicatesse!*)

At this point, *he* went and confessed, which is just as well, because having without success exhausted all other means of making away with his dear old Dutch, his next attempt would probably have involved the dropping of a fifty-megaton thermo-nuclear bomb on her, which might have had truly serious consequences – probably not including, though, the arousal of her suspicions.

There is also room for speculation about the details of the dialogue that ensued when the police arrived to break the news that they had just arrested the man of the house on some exceptionally interesting charges. ('Your husband, madam, appears to have made no fewer than seven attempts to murder you.' 'Nonsense – we're perfectly happy, and in any case he wouldn't hurt a fly.' 'Nevertheless, madam, we have his signed confession.' 'I tell you it's impossible; besides – no, hang on a minute, there *was* something rather odd, come to think of it, that happened the other day.')

If it's heroic failures you're after, then you will allow that they don't come in bigger sizes than this one. Mind you, the wife in the case, though she does not qualify for heroic-failure status, certainly has a right to be considered for another, older, work of reference. *The Guinness Book of Records*, in which she would, I suppose, figure under some heading such as *Most Unobservant Victim of Homicidal Husband*. 'It is more honourable to be deceived', said Confucius, 'than to distrust our friends.' No doubt; but as this case shows, it can also be more dangerous. My advice to super-faithful Penelope, should she go to visit her husband in prison, is to treat with the greatest reserve any claim he may make to have left a large sum of money for her, wrapped in waterproof cloth, at the bottom of the crocodile pool in the London Zoo.

The Times March 4th, 1981

£18.50 down and the devil to pay

I HAVE BEEN CARRYING about with me for weeks a letter which appeared in the *Guardian*, and has been haunting me ever since: today, I shall try a little exorcism. Here it is in full:

> As a young, unemployed, first-class honours graduate contemplating the amount of 'freedom' provided by my weekly £18.50 Giro cheque, I would be very happy to have Mr Benn as Prime Minister, or even to become part of the Eastern bloc, if this meant that I could get a job.

Now that, I must admit, chilled the blood a trifle, for more than one reason. Before discussing the reasons, let us agree to leave Mr Wedgwood Benn out of the discussion; it is not Mr Wedgwood Benn I want to argue with on this occasion. Nor, indeed, is it necessary to argue with him, in view of the *Guardian* correspondent's succeeding words. Here is a young man at what I believe is known as the threshold of life, obviously ('first-class honours') clever, who expresses himself as willing to barter the freedoms of this country for a regular wage-packet larger than the £18.50 which he gets, and which presumably represents unemployment or other social security payment.

It is possible, of course, that given a real choice between the two, he would not in practice choose as he suggests: there is a closely analogous precedent in the famous 'King and Country' motion at the Oxford Union. All the same, he did say it, and we have to consider the implications of the fact that a young man in Britain would be willing to accept the helot status of a subject of the Soviet Empire, because, and only because, he is unemployed and thus financially far from well off.

There is a debating point to be made first, and since this is something of a debate I may as well make it; what makes our young friend so sure that he would get a job in the Eastern bloc, or that if he did it would be paid, in real terms, at a rate better than he gets by being unemployed in Britain, or that if it were he would be able to buy anything worth having with it? As, I presume, a regular *Guardian* reader, he no doubt saw the excellent report from Warsaw by John Torode in that paper shortly after his letter appeared, and if so he might have stopped to wonder whether this passage was at all relevant to the dilemma he posed:

> I turned for a reaction, to a middle class Warsaw housewife. She insists that things have been getting steadily worse for the past two or three years. 'If there is meat in the shops there is a queue. It is automatic. If there is no queue there is no meat. You queue for chicken, for pork fat, for hard cheese, for milk, butter and eggs. In the past few days in central Warsaw there has been no bread in the shops until four p.m.'
>
> An Orwellian system of shops . . . has been created quite cynically. 'There are the normal shops which are usually empty or sell rubbish. Then there are "commercial shops" where you can sometimes get good meat, pork loin, sirloin, steak, decent sausages, if you pay twice the official prices. Next there are "super-commercial shops" with even higher prices. Finally there are special subsidized shops restricted to the security police, to government and party officials and senior military men. They get the best of what is going.' My housewife smiled. 'There is the black market, too,' she said. ' . . . We buy. It is illegal but very helpful if you are hungry.'

Esau sold his birthright for a mess of pottage, but at least he got the pottage; our unemployed first-class honours graduate would look fairly blue, I imagine, if he struck his devil's bargain and then found the devil defaulting.

But that is not the most important question at the heart of this matter, and the most important question is a very terrible one indeed. Are there really young people in this country, not themselves possessed by the frenzied fear and hatred of freedom which consumes the far-left *groupuscules* who wish to do away with the liberty of others because they cannot bear the thought of it for themselves, who would nevertheless be willing to sacrifice it to fill their bellies? For I think that the letter I have quoted makes it clear that the writer is not moved by any ideological admiration of the Eastern bloc; he does not *want* to be a Soviet colonial subject, he is merely – merely! – *willing* to be if he could get a job out of it.

It is no use saying that young people today have no first-hand experience of the struggle for freedom, that if the letter-writer is not much turned twenty he would hardly have been born at the time of the Hungarian revolution and would have been only a child during the Czech Spring and the killing frost that engulfed it, while as for the Second World War, his father was probably not born when it broke out, let alone him. (The Korean War he has probably never even heard of.) He does not say in what subject he got his first-class honours, but even if it wasn't history he could hardly be unaware that for centuries men and women have sacrificed jobs and homes and marriages and life itself to preserve or regain even a fragment of freedom. Why does he suppose they did that?

Nor can it be (by which I mean, alas, nor *should* it be) that he knows nothing of the conditions in which the subjects of the Eastern bloc live, of the pervasive fear that runs among them, of the system by which injustice is built into the very foundations and pillars of the state, of the incessant din of lies from official mouth and mouthpiece, of the corruption of power, of the cruelty with which dissent is crushed, of the moral squalor in which millions are compelled to live. Our letter-writer does not have to read me to know about such things; there is a good deal even in the *Guardian*, and presumably his sources of information are anyway not entirely limited to the morning newspapers.

And yet, it seems, he feels that all this is less important, and less painful, than unemployment accompanied by a Giro cheque for only £18.50 a week, and that he would swap freedom itself for the relief from his conditions of financial stringency.

Nemo repente fuit turpissimus. Somebody has taught this young man to think that freedom does not matter, and that material prosperity does, and has added to the lesson the thought that they are alternatives, and has added to *that* the further thought that the latter is preferable to the former if only one of the two is obtainable. He has heard freedom called 'bourgeois' freedom, and tyranny called the real kind; he has heard that everyone has a right to an ample and indefinitely rising standard of living; he has heard Britain's friends called her enemies, and her enemies her friends.

He heard this stuff at school; he heard it at university; he sees it on television; he reads it in magazines; eventually, he comes to believe it. Millions are exposed to the same influences and do no such thing; but believing what we hear is always easier than thinking for ourselves, and there will always be many who wish to avoid even the limited amount of discomfort involved in doing that.

And yet our young friend has surely one question to answer that no amount of accepting other people's answers will silence. What does he imagine material prosperity is *for*? For its own sake? Then a pig is the most fully realized creature on earth, at any rate until it gets its throat cut. Human beings, surely, are not so easily satisfied. They wonder, like Captain Boyle, 'What *is* the stars?' and the more they wonder, the more questions they ask. They ask, like Montaigne, 'What do I know?'; they ask, like Tolstoy, 'What do men live by?'; they ask, like Pilate, 'What is truth?' and frequently stay for an answer.

And however they answer their questions, they must think the questions more important than filling their heads with tripe and their guts with onions, and prefer their eternally unresolved inquiries to the condition of

> . . . the wretched slave,
> Who with a body fill'd and vacant mind,
> Gets him to rest, cramm'd with distressful bread.

Or so I believe. But a young man with a first-class honours degree and no job believes otherwise, and for the sake of letting his belt out a notch is willing to have the handcuffs tightened on his wrists. I do not know how widespread such an attitude is among young people in Britain, but if there are many of them we are in a bad way. As I say, our correspondent gave no clue as to the subject of his degree, so in case it was not German Literature, I will quote Goethe in translation, and beg him to remember the lines:

> Possessions lost, something lost;
> Honour lost, much lost;
> Courage lost, everything lost.

The Times February 24th, 1981

The cats of my life

THIS YEAR'S CHAMPION dog at Cruft's, I see, is called Alansmere Aquarius, and if you think that is sufficient burden for a particularly soppy-looking spaniel to bear, I can only say that it is mild by the usual standards, previous winners having been called things like Le Vicomte de Fichemoy-Lapaix with Mercury in the Ascendant, or Pride of Tralee (née Treppengeländer) the Third. Mind you, if you think that dogs (revolting creatures one and all, which deserve no better) are alone in the business of having names above their station, I must reveal that cats themselves are not immune, as an experience of mine a few years ago showed me with embarrassing clarity.

I was seeking a birthday present for my redheaded goddaughter, and had determined upon a kitten. (I have always followed the principle that you may give a child almost anything, even a musical instrument, without asking the parents, but not a pet, on which the elders have a right to be consulted, and I added toolkits to the rule after an unfortunate experience with a young friend to whom I had presented one on his birthday with a breezy suggestion that he was now perfectly equipped to saw one leg off the dining-room table, only to discover half an hour later that he had entirely missed the note of facetiousness in my voice, and was happily engaged in carrying out my suggestion.)

I went to Harrods pet department, which is really a small zoo, and there had to resist, as I always have to, the temptation to ask for a ring-tailed malagazook (this was an enchanting though mythical furry creature rather like a large squirrel, which figured in a strip cartoon I followed in my childhood, its name being Muriel and its usual companions a bear called Happy and a tortoise named Oswald). Instead, I demanded a kitten, and was shown a group of the most exquisite Russian Blues. I picked the most exquisite of all, and ordered it wrapped in a comfortable carrying-basket. What I had forgotten was the pedigree, at the sight of which the entire enterprise very nearly foundered, for apart from being some nine or ten times the length of the creature it referred to, it disclosed that the name of the kitten was, so help me, Ruchotski Dostoievski, and the contrast between this nonsense and the thing purring in the crook of my arm was so great that I burst on the instant into screams of laughter, heedless of the danger that if Mr John Aspinall had been passing through the store at that moment he would have bought me on the spot as a hyena and added me to his collection.

Anyway, though Mr Aspinall was not present, the Harrods staff were, and were so shocked at this act of lèse-ancestry that I really thought they were going to refuse to sell me the kitten on the grounds that I was not a fit and proper person to buy it. Nor did my appeal to them to envisage my redheaded friend going to the back door and calling 'Ruchotski Dostoievski, Ruchotski Dostoievski, come and have your milk' go down much better.

Well, I made my getaway, and next day the kitten was handed over and duly fallen in love with. When I produced the pedigree, however, there was general agreement that some abbreviation of Ruchotski Dostoievski was clearly called for, and after a brief discussion over tea the kitten was rechristened Smoky, which it remains to this day, having in the meanwhile grown a great deal larger and even more beautiful – which could also, it occurs to me, be said of my redheaded goddaughter.

Later, a puppy was introduced into the family, a present (not from me) for the redhead's brother, and was instantly christened Tolstoy. The introduction of Smoky (who by then had firmly taken over the household) to the newcomer was expected to pose problems. They were brought together in a gingerly fashion, and put down face to face. Smoky first stared at the eager, friendly little dog with a look of stupefaction mingled with contempt. He then walked carefully right round Tolstoy, inspecting him from every angle, then returned to the front end and did something which until then I would have sworn could only happen in a Tom and Jerry cartoon: he raised his right front paw and cracked Tolstoy across the face with it like an old-fashioned girl receiving an improper suggestion. Thereafter they became firm friends, and remained so until Tolstoy's untimely death, but from that moment there was never any doubt on who was in charge.

Smoky, however, is far from the most extraordinary cat that has ever passed through my life, though it would be hard to say which one deserves that particular title. The first, which still, more than a third of a century later, remains the noblest and handsomest cat I have ever known, was called Tim; he was a magnificent Persian, who could hear the cat's-meat man coming down the street long before we could, and who used to sleep in the shop window, thus ensuring that, not less often than once a month, a passer-by would enter to inquire, sometimes having struck a bet on the point with a companion, whether this wonderful creature was real or stuffed, at which my grandfather would call 'Tim!', and Tim (who did not, of course, need the cue, knowing perfectly well what the visitor wanted to know) would leap from the window and rub himself up against the inquirer's legs.

Tim lived to an immense age, surviving countless hazards such as being frozen solid one winter's night when he wouldn't come in, and even being poisoned by a neighbour; his predecessor died badly, after falling into a pot of paint, and so did his successor, a lean, glossy, black one who was hit by a car and had a leg unsplintably broken.

Then, after a few unmemorable ones, and one which was

memorable for the fact that it was afraid of mice, came the one which never had a name at all, being addressed simply as 'Cat'. (Old Possum, of course, pointed out that

> The Naming of Cats is a difficult matter,
> It isn't just one of your holiday games;
> You may think at first I'm as mad as a hatter
> When I tell you, a cat must have
> THREE DIFFERENT NAMES.)

Cat arrived one day on the doorstep, only about four inches long, and his face lopsided from a kick. Since no cat has ever been turned away from any doorstep beyond which any member of my family lives, he was taken in and fed and, knowing a good thing when he saw one, announced that he was going to remain (he did this by crawling under the stove and flatly refusing to come out for three days). Unfortunately, the kick had permanently disfigured him, and his face never grew straight again. This did not seem to worry him at all, though he looked bizarre, as a great length of pink tongue always hung, unretractably, from the corner of his mouth. One day, sleeping in the sun over the porch, he rolled off and fell to the ground, landing on his head and biting off the surplus tongue. To our astonishment, all he did was to unroll a fresh length, which protruded as far as before, though the end of it was now concave in shape.

Cat, incidentally, later on fell from a window-ledge two storeys up, and survived even that, though I think he was never quite right in the head thereafter. Later still, he developed some problem with his jaw, as well he might, and was in great pain; we suggested having him put to sleep, but the vet would not hear of it, briskly saying that all he needed was to have his teeth out. Out they came, and he was as fit as ten immediately, though the fact that the two canine teeth had been left, combined with his by now very irregular-shaped face, made him look like a feline Dracula. He never seemed to have any trouble eating, though he never learnt the trick of doing so with his paw like the one in the television advertisement. Cat died of a fit.

Nowadays I live in a flat too high, and am out of it too much, to keep a cat, for cats, despite all their marvellous self-sufficiency and independence, do not like being alone, especially without being able to come and go at will. Below me there lives a corgi, with which I have established a kind of armed neutrality; a friend of mine dubbed it Baskerville, and it is as Baskerville that I always think of it. It could eat Alansmere Aquarius alive, though it wouldn't have gone three rounds against Cat, let alone Ruchotski Dostoievski. But I shall dream of Tim tonight.

The Times February 13th, 1973

The eternal mystery

WHO WAS MOZART? I do not mean who in the sense of who was Shakespeare; this is not going to be a demonstration that his music was written by Bacon, let alone Count Zinzendorf, who wrote in his diary, after the first performance of *The Marriage of Figaro*: 'The opera bored me.' Perhaps I ought to put the question differently: *what* was Mozart?

I have raised this question in print before, on more than one occasion. Mozart, again and again, wrote masterpieces in fair copy straight out of his head: no sketchbooks, no notes, no drafts, no erasures – out it came and down it went.

That is the first clue: there is no evidence of any musical gestation, even of the briefest, in a huge proportion of his work, including some of the greatest. I have said that Mozart was a conduit, through which music poured into the world's lap. But that inevitably raises the question: who or what was putting it in at the other end? In a sense, of course, all artists are such channels, and their art flows along the arteduct of their life and personality, sometimes (as in the case of Beethoven) with unremitting pain and labour, sometimes (as with Schubert) with apparently effortless ease. In Mozart's case, however, the art didn't even touch the sides; he seemed almost to produce it unconsciously. *Who was he*?

It is to this question that Mr Peter Shaffer has addressed himself in his new play, *Amadeus*, which is to be seen at the National Theatre, and has been widely and grossly undervalued. Mr Shaffer's answer can be deduced from his title, at least by those who know what Mozart's middle name means;

but it is in his facing of the implications, and the dramatic working-out of the question, that there lies the fascination and value of his masterly play.

It is well known that rumour has suggested over the years a sinister explanation of Mozart's early death: that he was deliberately poisoned by Salieri, the court composer in Vienna, to whom there came the worldly and material prosperity that eluded Mozart, but whose music is now utterly forgotten. From the delirium of his last fever, Mozart himself made the accusation, and ever since it has floated just out of reality's reach, though there is nothing in it, and never was.

One of the many things to the credit of *Amadeus* is the way in which Mr Shaffer makes the theory one of the central strands in his story; while never allowing credibility to it, he shows us how it arose, and indeed suggests that Salieri wanted Mozart dead and did nothing to help keep him alive when his penury was hastening him to his grave.

But why would Salieri wish Mozart dead? He was no threat to the favourite's position or income, and it is stretching jealousy too far to suggest that the thought of an artistic rival in his vicinity was so unbearable that he wanted Mozart made away with.

It is at this point that Mr Shaffer makes his great imaginative leap. For Salieri divines (a particularly apt word in the circumstances) that it is not Mozart who is his enemy; the play is a duel not between the two composers, but between the lesser composer and the power that he sees as animating his rival. Mr Shaffer, in short, has allowed Salieri to answer the question: what was Mozart? Mozart, he says firmly, was a musical instrument, played by the hand of God.

To emphasize the point, the author makes Mozart a vessel that, in one sense, is conspicuously unworthy to serve as the Grail of art. Mozart as a man had a silly and childish side, and he also had a pronounced taste for billiards, word-play and scatological conversation, and this is the version of Mozart which we see in the play, and which has scandalized those who can see Mozart only as the beautiful and tastefully dressed prodigy of the Carmontelle portrait, a picture which has probably done more harm to a true understanding of Mozart than anything Salieri could have done if a Wicked Fairy had granted him three wishes and he had used them all to spite his rival.

Hear first how Salieri stumbles upon the truth, during a performance of the Wind Serenade in B flat, K 361. Almost struck dead by the pain of the revelation, he flees:

> . . . the pain cut deeper into my shaking head until suddenly I was running, dashing through the side-door, stumbling downstairs into the street, into the cold night, gasping for life. 'What? What is this? Tell me, Signore! What is this pain? What is this *need* in the sound? . . . Is it Your need? Can it be Yours?' Dimly the stars shone on the empty street. I was suddenly frightened. It seemed to me I had heard a voice of God – and that it came from a creature whose own voice I had also heard – and it was the voice of an obscene child . . . at night I prayed for just one thing: 'Let your voice enter me! Let *me* conduct you! *Let* me!'

His prayer denied, Salieri takes up arms against his adversary:

> I have worked and worked the talent you allowed me . . . Solely that in the end . . . I might hear Your Voice. And now I do hear it – it says only one name: MOZART . . . Him you have chosen to be your sole conduct. And *my* only reward – my sublime privilege – is to be the sole man alive in this time who shall really recognise your Incarnation . . . So be it! From this time forth we are enemies . . . I name thee now *Nemico Eterno*. And this I swear. To my last breath I shall block you on earth, as far as I am able . . .

There, then, is Mr Shaffer's explanation of Salieri's hostility to Mozart, and indeed his explanation of Mozart himself.

God's frightful betrayal of his servant ('You gave me the desire to serve you – which most men do not have – then saw to it the service was shameful in the ears of the server . . . ') demands an opponent of fitting stature to challenge it, and if Mozart is God's Incarnation, then Salieri is Goethe's Mephisto and Job's Satan, forever doomed to be defeated. 'God *needed* Mozart, do you see, to let Himself into the world'; but He was not going to let Salieri deny Him that need.

Mr Shaffer works out his tremendous, his colossal, theme in language of great strength and deceptively obvious subtlety; and there is a performance, as Salieri, by Paul Scofield that alone should pack the Olivier until Count Zinzendorf's view of *Figaro* becomes the generally accepted one. But a playwright like Mr Shaffer is not to be judged by standards applicable to the forgettable *boulevardiers* of our theatre; the angel he has conjured up, and wrestled all night with, is too big to be contained in a mere recital of the entertainment qualities of his play, and those who go to it prepared to understand what it is about will have an experience that far transcends even its considerable value as drama.

'Whatever else shall pass away,' says Salieri after hearing *The Marriage of Figaro*, 'this must remain.' I heard *Figaro* broadcast only a few days ago, in an indifferent performance recorded at this year's Salzburg Festival, in which even Kiri's Countess lacked its full glory, and the Vienna Philharmonic seemed to be playing with boots on their hands. But it didn't matter; whatever else has passed away, this remains, and lovers of Mozart – true lovers, who *do* know what his middle name means – should be profoundly grateful to Peter Shaffer for the courage with which he has faced an eternal mystery, and the humility and grace with which he has offered a tentatively eternal solution to it.

The Times December 6th, 1979

The blinding light of Blake

BLAKE IS A problem – so much of a problem, indeed, that many have tended to solve it by classifying him as little better than mad, which is very convenient, as it means that no further examination of what inspired him is necessary. More to the point, and very much to Blake's own point, too, dismissing him as a self-contained eccentric means that there is no longer any necessity to discover just what it is about him that disturbs us. The same thing is true, of course, of Wagner: if you go about parroting 'Noise . . . no tunes . . . too long . . . fat singers . . .' and the like, you never need to ask why he has such an effect on you. After all, you can dislike the music of any other composer without feeling the need to rationalize *your feelings* by projecting them on to *his attitudes*, and exactly the same is true of Blake. Have you ever heard anybody who doesn't care to look at the pictures of Franz Hals or Renoir or Hockney denouncing them in terms of personal injury, as though these painters only existed to do harm to the complainant? Obviously not; those who do not like their work are content to ignore them, as are those who can hear nothing to their taste in the music of Haydn or Britten.

Yet Blake is virtually accused of creeping into people's bedrooms at night and hitting them on the head with dangerous weapons. Which, of course, is exactly what he does do; whence the hostility, for although Blake hits us on the head for our own good, it is undeniably difficult for us to understand this while we are concentrating on soothing the bruises. And yet if you go to the Blake exhibition at the Tate, where there

are more than 300 of his paintings, drawings, illuminations
and etchings to be seen, the disturbance he causes cannot so
easily be ignored, rationalized, transferred or resolved.

The important thing about Blake was that he really did
mean what he said. A man who could typically begin a poem
with the words (they may well constitute the most arresting
opening line in English literature) 'You must agree that
Rubens was a fool' puts himself immediately into a position in
which he is obliged either to make good his assertions or be
dismissed as a charlatan. Blake has frequently been dismissed
as a charlatan; but only, I feel, by those unable to face the
possibility that he might be speaking the literal truth.

Not, perhaps, about Rubens, for whether Rubens and Cara-
vaggio were as bad as Blake thought them, or Raphael as
good, is not very important. And it is not difficult to nod
patronizingly in agreement at

> Kill not the moth nor butterfly,
> For the Last Judgment draweth nigh

or at

> The strongest poison ever known
> Came from Caesar's laurel crown

or at

> Every harlot was a virgin once

or even at

If the fool would persist in his folly he would become wise.

But when Blake said,

'What', it will be questioned, 'when the sun rises, do you
not see a round disc of fire somewhat like a guinea?' 'O no,
no, I see an innumerable company of the heavenly host
crying "Holy, Holy, Holy, is the Lord God Almighty!"'

it is a little difficult, and indeed uncomfortable, for us to understand that he meant it, especially when we learn that he wrote it in the preface to a catalogue of his works accompanying an exhibition, where today we are more accustomed to encounter tactile values, the influence of a seaside upbringing or the shamefully parsimonious attitude of the Arts Council. (Not, I must add, that anything of the kind is to be found in the excellent catalogue for *this* exhibition.)

It is not enough, though it is certainly true, to say that Blake was God-driven. The question is: where did he think God was driving him, and why? He clearly believed not just that 'everything that lives is holy', but that that was equally true of every grain of sand in the universe; he no less clearly felt the principle of energy that fills everything – if you close your eyes and try to conjure up a typical Blake, you will always see motion, whether in the form of streaming hair or garments or in that of the sun's rays, and at the Tate the walls seem to quiver with the representations of unchained energy.

On those walls we can see Blake arguing that the universe, for all its incessant whirling, its perpetual pouring out of light and heat, its continual vibration to the music of the spheres, is one by nature, and everything in it is part of the force that set it in motion.

Within this truth, there was another concentrically embedded; that although everything in the universe is part of the force at its centre, it cannot be understood or even measured by reason, and indeed does not depend upon reason for its essence. Everything in the universe is there because it has to be there, including Satan and the Great Beast, though the presence of these is not to be explained by Newton's principle that for every action there is an equal and opposite reaction. Newton, indeed, is a limiting force for Blake, who is at the opposite pole from Pope's

> Nature and Nature's laws lay hid in night:
> God said *Let Newton be*! and all was light.

Blake was born almost exactly half-way through the eighteenth century, but the Enlightenment is his great enemy, precisely because it believed that human reason could encompass all understanding. *Encompass*: Blake's allegorical portrait of Newton shows him drawing with a *compass*. The catalogue refers the reader to a parallel drawing three years later, done to accompany the profoundly significant text: 'He who sees the Infinite in all things sees God. He who sees the Ratio only sees himself only.'

It does not seem to be going at all too far to say that for me the Tate exhibition (compiled and catalogued by Mr Martin Butlin) makes coherent and consistent sense of Blake for the first time. If you look at the *Urizen* plates (from the British Museum) or *Elohim Creating Adam* (from the Tate's own collection) in isolation, you could well believe that Blake was a mystic, casting no general light on the ground that ordinary men must walk. Blake *was* a mystic, but he cast on the ground we walk a light so blinding that, if we open our eyes, we can see nothing else, and the value of seeing a really large and really representative selection of his visual achievement (not that he made any distinction between the painted word or the written) is to come face to face with a man through whom the vital current passed, and who understood all things because he was part of all things, as all things were part of him. Ecstasy and light stream from the Tate's exhibition, and not surprisingly: Blake's vision was made up of those two elements, and when he said he saw the heavenly host at sunrise, and heard them singing, he meant what he said.

The Times April 4th, 1978

Nine bullets, one knell

GOD REST YOU, peaceful gentlemen, let nothing you dismay,
But – leave your sports a little while – the dead are borne
  this way!
  Armies dead and Cities dead, past all count or care.
God rest you, merry gentlemen, what portent see you
  there?
    Break ground for a wearied host
    That have no ground to keep
    Give them the rest that they covet most . . .
    And who shall be next to sleep, good sirs,
    In such a trench to sleep?

Thus spake Rudyard Kipling, and not a moment too soon, if
you ask me. For it is hard, and getting harder, to find new
ways in which to say old things; *occidit miseros crambe repetita
magistros*. What is the point of announcing for the hundredth
time that Christmas comes but once a year, that the sun
shines by day and the moon by night, that twice two make
four? Only, I think, this: that the more we fail to remind
ourselves that these true things *are* true, the more we run the
risk that the contrary view will eventually prevail. And
perhaps the most significant and terrible truth about our world
is that there *is* a contrary view; there are people who insist that
Thursday follows Friday, and not the other way about, that in
some right-angled triangles the square on the hypotenuse is by
no means equal to the sum of the squares on the other two
sides, that black, contrary to the hitherto universally accepted
view, is in fact white, and vice versa.

That is why, though I do not enjoy banging my head on a brick wall, I have to have another thump or two today. For a week or so ago there was a report, so irrelevant to the world's concerns that I could find no trace of it in any newspaper other than the *Daily Telegraph*, where it was recounted in exactly fifty words, which tells a story often recounted by me in the past and no doubt even more often to be repeated by me in the future.

A pregnant girl of eighteen – we even have her name, Marinetta Jirkowski – was shot dead by East German border guards while trying to escape to the West with two men. The two men survived, and got to freedom; Fräulein Jirkowski did neither, but fell dead with *nine* bullets in her. (That total seems, even for the *Vopos*, to be over-egging the pudding a bit, but it may be that the careless young thing caught her foot in the wire which sets off the automatic multiple-fire guns that are mounted on posts all along the border and which differ from weapons on other frontiers, as does the entire East German armoury in those parts, in one strange and striking particular; they all point inwards towards their own citizens, not out-wards against a possible aggressor.)

> God rest you, peaceful gentlemen, but give us leave to pass.
> We go to dig a nation's grave as great as England was.
> For this Kingdom and this Glory and this Power
>   and this Pride,
> Three hundred years it flourished – in three hundred days
>   it died.
> Pour oil for a frozen throng,
> That lie about the ways.
> Give them the warmth they have lacked so long . . .
> And what shall be next to blaze, good sirs,
> On such a pyre to blaze?

Just so: you have a powerful feeling of *déjà-vu*, or: old Bernard's banging on again. We have supped full of horrors these past few decades, and the worst result of such a diet is not indigestion but loss of appetite. And yet it seems to me that even if we have to hold our noses and make a face as we swallow, sup we must. For what lies upon our plate is the knowledge that some things are evil – evil *sans phrases* – and that what was done to Marinetta Jirkowski is one of those things. And if we do not force that knowledge into ourselves and keep it down against the rising gorge, but instead listen to those who offer us more palatable but poisoned fare, we shall be doomed first and damned afterwards, and serve us right on both counts, particularly the first.

> God rest you, thoughtful gentlemen, and send your sleep
>   is light!
> Remains of this dominion no shadow, sound or sight,
> Except the sound of weeping and the sight of burning fire,
> And the shadow of a people that is trampled into mire.
> Break bread for a starving folk
> That perish in the field.
> Give them their food as they take the yoke . . .
> And who shall be next to yield, good sirs,
> For such a bribe to yield?

There are plenty all around us who could answer that question, and not a few who have already done so. There are those who tell us (some of these, incidentally, believe it) that unilateral disarmament ought to be undertaken by Britain because the action might bring such moral pressure to bear on the Soviet leaders that they would be compelled to follow suit. Others insist that the standard of living in East Germany is the seventh highest in the industrialized world – or the fourth highest, or the third, or the eighth, for the figures are all imaginary anyway and which is selected at any moment is of little importance – and that that can only mean the people are contented with their lot. Yet others assure us that the 'brain drain' from eastern Germany would be crippling to the country's economy if its citizens were allowed to leave, a state of affairs which any country is entitled to prevent. One, on the letters page only a month or two ago, said that if Soviet troops invaded Poland the West should on no account do anything in return that might displease the Soviet leaders. Why, perhaps Mr Sebastian Coe would see nothing wrong in running – and for glory and medals alone, not for cash – in Leipzig or Potsdam, or for that matter in a Warsaw occupied by the Red Army, and possibly in either case Sir Denis Follows would come trotting and puffing behind, wagging his tail and yapping, 'Let's keep politics out of sport.'

And so I feel it necessary to bang my head against the wall again today, upon the strange death of Marinetta Jirkowski. I do not know how the filthy thing that killed her is to be destroyed, though I know that sooner or later it must be. I do know that there are people in this country who admire that thing, and wish to see it rule us, too, and some of them are in our universities, and some in our press and television, and some in the councils of our trade union movement, and some in Parliament, and many of them hardly bother any longer to pretend that their beliefs are other than they are, which suggests that they think they are near to their goal; and in so thinking they may well be right.

But they are not right in saying that twice two make five, nor that rivers flow uphill, nor that grass is blue. One day, there will be a reckoning for those who fired nine bullets into Marinetta Jirkowski. But every time one of us fails to feel rage at what was done to her, or to recognize our rage as the correct moral response to unmitigated evil, the failure not only postpones the day of judgment on her killers, but brings nearer a very different judgment on ourselves.

God rest you, merry gentlemen, and keep you in your
  mirth!
Was ever Kingdom turned so soon to ashes, blood and
  earth?
'Twixt the summer and the snow – seeding-time and
  frost –

Arms and victual, hope and counsel, name and country
  lost!
  Let down by the foot and the head –
  Shovel and smooth it all!
  So do we bury a Nation dead . . .
  And who shall be next to fall, good sirs,
  With your good help to fall?

The Times January 22nd, 1981

Index

Non-fiction

☐	**The Money Book**	Margaret Allen	£2.95p
☐	**Fall of Fortresses**	Elmer Bendiner	£1.75p
☐	**The British Way of Birth**	Catherine Boyd and Lea Sellers	£1.50p
☐	**100 Great British Weekends**	John Carter	£2.95p
☐	**Last Waltz in Vienna**	George Clare	£1.95p
☐	**Walker's Britain**	Andrew Duncan	£4.95p
☐	**Travellers' Britain**	Arthur Eperon	£2.95p
☐	**The Tropical Traveller**	John Hatt	£2.50p
☐	**The Lord God Made Them All**	James Herriot	£1.95p
☐	**The Neck of the Giraffe**	Francis Hitching	£2.50p
☐	**A Small Town is a World**	David Kossoff	£1.00p
☐	**Prayers and Graces**	Allen Laing illus. by Mervyn Peake	£1.25p
☐	**Kitchen & Bathroom Book**	Jose Manser	£5.95p
☐	**Best of Shrdlu**	Denys Parsons	£1.00p
☐	**Dipped in Vitriol**	Nicholas Parsons	£1.75p
☐	**The Bargain Book**	Barty Phillips	£1.95p
☐	**Thy Neighbour's Wife**	Gay Talese	£1.75p
☐	**Just off for the Weekend**	John Slater	£2.50p
☐	**Dead Funny**	Fritz Spiegl	£1.50p
☐	**The Third Wave**	Alvin Toffler	£2.75p
☐	**The World Atlas of Treasure**	Derek Wilson	£6.50p
☐	**Shyness**	Philip Zimbardo	£1.95p

All these books are available at your local bookshop or newsagent, or can be ordered direct from the publisher. Indicate the number of copies required and fill in the form below

9

....

Name_____
(Block letters please)

Address_____

_____

Send to Pan Books (CS Department), Cavaye Place, London SW10 9PG
Please enclose remittance to the value of the cover price plus:
35p for the first book plus 15p per copy for each additional book ordered
to a maximum charge of £1.25 to cover postage and packing
Applicable only in the UK